ON BOARD

ON BOARD

My Years in BCCI

TEST. TRIAL. TRIUMPH.

RATNAKAR SHETTY

RUPA

First published by
Rupa Publications India Pvt. Ltd 2022
7/16, Ansari Road, Daryaganj
New Delhi 110002

Sales Centres:
Allahabad Bengaluru Chennai
Hyderabad Jaipur Kathmandu
Kolkata Mumbai

Copyright © Ratnakar Shetty 2022
Photo credits: Ashutosh Sharma, Pradeep Mandhani,
Rajesh Shah and author's personal collection

The views and opinions expressed in this book are the author's own and the facts are as reported by him which have been verified to the extent possible, and the publishers are not in any way liable for the same.

All rights reserved.
No part of this publication may be reproduced, transmitted, or stored in a retrieval system, in any form or by any means, electronic, mechanical, photocopying, recording or otherwise, without the prior permission of the publisher.

ISBN: 978-93-5520-287-1

Second impression 2022

10 9 8 7 6 5 4 3 2

The moral right of the author has been asserted.

Printed at Parksons Graphics Pvt. Ltd, Mumbai

This book is sold subject to the condition that it shall not, by way of trade or otherwise, be lent, resold, hired out, or otherwise circulated, without the publisher's prior consent, in any form of binding or cover other than that in which it is published.

To my family and all those who have contributed to making Indian cricket the force it is, on and off the field.

CONTENTS

1. The Pinnacle — 1
2. Formative Years — 22
3. My Cricketing Alma Mater — 36
4. On 'Board' — 50
5. Emerald Island, 1997 — 64
6. Mentors — 75
7. A Fresh Start — 92
8. Across the Border, 2004 — 107
9. AGM Tales — 124
10. A New Look — 140
11. Transition — 155
12. Stability — 167
13. The IPL Story — 185
14. In a 'League' of Its Own — 201
15. Instability — 214
16. MCA Tales — 233
17. The Exit — 251
18. Challenges — 267
19. Ace Administrators — 288

Acknowledgements — 305
Index — 307

Note: The Bombay Cricket Association (BCA) was rechristened Mumbai Cricket Association (MCA) in 1996. The abbreviations 'BCA' and 'MCA' have been used interchangeably to denote the Bombay/Mumbai Cricket Association, so as to not disturb the narrative.

1

THE PINNACLE

Mahendra Singh (M.S.) Dhoni advanced his front foot down the wicket and swung purposefully at the ball delivered by Sri Lankan pacer Nuwan Kulasekara, sending it soaring high into the Vithal Divecha Pavilion. At around quarter past 10 on the night of Saturday, 2 April 2011, there was bedlam at the Wankhede Stadium and everywhere else in the country. India had won the tenth Cricket World Cup!

As tears of joy were shed by the Indian players, spectators and even some officials who had congregated on the playing arena moments after that six, I must confess to having allowed the fan in me to prevail over my official capacity as the host tournament director, for a few moments. A lot of hard work had gone into the execution of the International Cricket Council (ICC) Cricket World Cup (CWC) 2011, as it was known. The final marked the culmination of what had been a roller-coaster ride, replete with twists and turns, highs and lows.

It all began in 2006. There was an understanding between the members of the ICC that every third World Cup would be held in the subcontinent, a region which had become the pivot of the sport by then. Accordingly, the tenth edition of the ICC CWC was earmarked for the subcontinent, but the India-Pakistan-Sri Lanka-Bangladesh combine missed the deadline for the submission of the Participating Nations Agreement (PNA) for the tournament, which was 1 April 2006.

The PNA had to comprise, among other things, a document authorized by the governments of the prospective host nations, guaranteeing income-tax exemption on the earnings of the ICC from the event, apart from security and other support.

The ICC tentatively awarded the hosting rights to Australia and New Zealand as a result of the delay, but smelt an opportunity in the subcontinental combine's request for additional time to submit the PNA.

At that stage, the Board of Control for Cricket in India (BCCI) had made its views on Twenty20 (T20), the game's newest and shortest format, quite clear. The Working Committee of the Board had opposed this format and opined that it would adversely affect the game in the long run, as youngsters who played it would end up lacking in terms of technique, patience and application, and consequently, struggle in the traditional and multi-nuanced multi-day format. The BCCI emphasized this point in meetings of the ICC as well, but it had little support from the rest of the cricketing world. At the ICC meeting where the inaugural T20 World Cup was mooted and confirmed, the BCCI was outvoted 1-9.

The ICC World T20 2007, as the T20 World Cup was christened, was planned to be hosted in South Africa, but the prospect of India, the game's biggest draw, not participating in the tournament, worried the ICC. Hence, the subcontinental combine's request for additional time to submit the PNA for the ICC CWC 2011 was replied to with a rider; the ICC would grant an extension if India confirmed its participation in the ICC World T20 2007.

The BCCI agreed. The PNA for the ICC CWC 2011 was prepared and compiled under the guidance of Mr Inderjit Singh (I.S.) Bindra, the former Board president, and submitted. Sure enough, the ICC then confirmed that the tournament would be played on the subcontinent.

As the chief administrative officer of the BCCI, I was

involved in the ensuing meetings with our co-hosts. We worked backwards, with Mr Sharad Pawar, the then BCCI and Mumbai Cricket Association (MCA) president, proposing in our very first meeting, which was held in Pakistan in mid-2006, that the final be played in Mumbai. It was decided that Pakistan would take the lead in organizational matters, with the Tournament Directorate to be based at the offices of the Pakistan Cricket Board (PCB) in Lahore. The broad framework and the process of allotment of matches to each co-host were also discussed.

That first meeting and the discussions that followed went off smoothly, but a concern lurked in the background. Pakistan was to host the Champions Trophy in 2008, but terror attacks forced the ICC to call the tournament off. As it turned out, The Marriott, a prominent hotel in Islamabad, Pakistan's capital, was attacked in September 2008, when the tournament was scheduled to take place. Cricket in Pakistan was even more directly impacted six months later, when the Sri Lankan team was waylaid by terrorists outside the Gaddafi Stadium in Lahore.

That horrific incident had its consequences. The ICC withdrew the co-hosting rights of Pakistan for the 2011 World Cup, much to the dismay of cricket-lovers in that country. A new working group was constituted and the Tournament Directorate moved to the Cricket Centre at Mumbai's Wankhede Stadium, which housed the headquarters of the BCCI. The matches which were to be played in Pakistan were divided amongst India, Sri Lanka and Bangladesh. As per the revised structure, India was to host 29 games, Sri Lanka 12 and Bangladesh eight. All the League games of the Pakistan team were scheduled in Sri Lanka. Bangladesh was to host one quarter-final, Sri Lanka two quarter-finals and one semi-final, and India, one quarter-final, a semi-final and the final. The BCCI, Sri Lanka Cricket (SLC) and the Bangladesh Cricket Board (BCB) accepted the request of the PCB that it be paid the amount it would have received had the matches not been moved. Thus, the co-hosts did not receive the hosting fees for the additional matches they were getting to host.

There was one significant difference between the ICC CWC 2011 and the World Cups that India had co-hosted earlier. In 1987, as well as in 1996, it had been the responsibility of the co-hosts[1] to organize and conduct the tournament and manage its various aspects, which ranged from engaging a title sponsor to selling the television rights. The ICC had changed its outlook since. The seventh World Cup, which was played in the United Kingdom (UK) in 1999, was the first which did not have a title sponsor and was referred to as the 'ICC Cricket World Cup'. Since then, the ICC had been in charge of the run-up, planning and execution of the quadrennial tournament, with the host nations providing only the venues and logistic support and helping with security issues. The ICC singularly managed all the key aspects such as selling the television rights, getting sponsors on board, managing the media, design and centralized printing of tickets and even the supervision of the preparation of the wickets at the venues.

Mr Pawar, who became the president of the ICC in 2010, was the chairman of the Central Organising Committee (COC) for the ICC CWC 2011 and Haroon Lorgat, the chief executive officer (CEO) of the ICC, its convener. The Organising Committee also comprised the presidents and secretaries of the BCCI, SLC and BCB, as well as the HTD and the event manager and commercial manager of the ICC.

It was an honour to be appointed the HTD of an event of this magnitude. Having served in the same position during the ICC Champions Trophy in 2006, which India had hosted, I had an idea of the role and responsibilities it entailed. The flip side was that, by the time plans were changed and I was

---
[1]India and Pakistan in 1987 and India, Pakistan and Sri Lanka in 1996.

appointed, it was already April in 2009. There were less than two years to go for the tournament at that stage. However, I was backed by Mr Pawar. I had enjoyed working with him in the MCA and later the BCCI, and there was no question of backing away from this challenge.

The COC, in its first meeting, had discussed the concerns which had emerged during the previous World Cup, especially the poor spectator turnout and the pricing of tickets. The early exits of India and Pakistan from the ICC CWC 2007, which had been played in the Caribbean, had hit the tournament hard in terms of the spectatorship. In fact, the relevance of the 50-overs' version of the game itself was being questioned in the lead-up to the ICC CWC 2011. However, we were confident that there would be no dearth of enthusiasm in our part of the world.

The format was changed from what it had been in 2007. The ICC CWC 2011 was to feature 14 teams, which would be divided into two groups of seven teams each. Each team would play the other six in its group in a round-robin league[2] and the top four teams from each group would qualify for the quarter-finals. The four quarter-finals would be followed by two semi-finals and the final. Mr Pawar requested the office-bearers of the host boards to ensure that the match tickets were affordable. The boards of the hosting nations were also advised to reserve a certain number of tickets of those matches that did not involve the co-hosts, so that local schoolchildren could watch the matches free of cost, thus increasing spectatorship.

The ICC had created a budget for the hosts to engage professionals to discharge different responsibilities for a period of eight months preceding the tournament. The senior office-bearers of the BCCI and I felt that it would be better to ask the professionals who were then working for the BCCI to take on additional duties for the World Cup, instead of hiring outsiders.

---

[2] Each team to play all the other teams in its group.

The managers and assistant managers of the BCCI were only too delighted to get to work on the game's ultimate event. It meant that they practically did two jobs for a period of eight months, but never complained. Their passion and commitment were exemplary.

The senior professionals led from the front. Suru Nayak, the former Test cricketer who handled Cricket Operations at the BCCI, was appointed the tournament director (India). Suraj Dandeniya and Mohammed Ali Ahsan Babu were his Sri Lankan and Bangladeshi counterparts, respectively and they had their own teams working under them. Devendra Prabhudesai, who handled media relations and corporate affairs at the Board, was assigned the role of ICC media manager (India). Mr R.K. Das, former head of the Central Industrial Security Force (CISF), who had worked on the 2010 Commonwealth Games in Delhi before joining the BCCI, came on board as the security advisor and Milind Rege, the former Mumbai captain, was appointed the tournament manager. Kedar Gupte, an employee of Air India, came in to handle the logistics and travel arrangements and Jayant Jhaveri, who had retired as the deputy general manager (DGM), Bank of Baroda, took on the responsibility of maintaining the accounts for the tournament. He was to function as per the ICC's protocols pertaining to spending, which were quite strict.

Sri Lanka and Bangladesh got things off to a flying start. Whether it was the placement of banners and welcome desks in the arrival lounges of airports, the erecting of arches at the hotels and on the route from the hotels to the match venues, the provision of foolproof security arrangements and the refurbishing of the venues themselves, the governments of both countries went out of their way to back their respective cricket boards. Mahinda Rajapaksa, the president of Sri Lanka, even recommended the creation of a new venue at Hambantota, his home town. The engineering expertise of a Chinese team, which was in the region for another project, was sought and a magnificent facility constructed. On our inspection visits to Hambantota, the Sri Lankan government provided us a helicopter ride so that the time spent travelling was reduced.

I have to admit that we, in India, did not match up to the publicity and promotional activities which were carried out in Sri Lanka and Bangladesh. We could not erect welcome arches in the cities which were to host the matches. Despite receiving assurance from the minister of civil aviation, we could not place welcome desks at the Delhi and Mumbai airports, as we were asked to cough up a huge sum of money for the same. That apart, the concessions and customs duty exemption granted to us were withdrawn by the Sports Ministry because the BCCI refused to register itself as a National Sports Federation.

There were other concerns as well. Just a couple of months after India was confirmed as a host, the government introduced a new visa rule, as per which a person who had exited the country, could re-enter only two months later. We had to take up this issue with the Union Home Ministry and draw its attention to the fact that there would be frequent travelling in and out of India during the tournament by the teams, officials, spectators, broadcast teams, media, and of course, fans. To our relief and delight, the Home Ministry officials assured us that the certain groups—the details of which would be provided by us—associated with the tournament would be exempt from this rule. Spectators who possessed valid tickets and were travelling from country to country, would also be allowed re-entry.

The other important issue was securing income-tax exemption on the ICC's earnings from the event. The government had granted the same for the Champions Trophy in 2006 and we were confident that the Finance Ministry would do likewise for the World Cup as well. The exemption was officially granted only in July 2011, well after the tournament had been completed, as the ICC took its time to answer a few queries raised by the Finance Ministry. I must state here that a trust deficit was created mainly due to the fact that the ICC was not forthcoming about the sponsorship agreements on which it wanted tax exemption. The Finance Ministry insisted on looking at the sponsorship agreements and rightly so. It turned out that all the sponsors had a clause in their agreements to gross up the payment in the absence of tax exemption. The Finance Ministry therefore granted exemption only for the income from the media rights.

The BCCI decided to allot the games to be played in India to all the permanent Test venues, other than Kanpur. Eight cities—Mumbai, Ahmedabad, Chennai, Bengaluru, Kolkata, Delhi, Mohali and Nagpur—were thus nominated. League matches featuring India were highly sought after, of course. This issue was resolved by asking the associations managing the venues to choose between an India game and a knockout game. Ahmedabad and Mohali opted for knockout games, with Mumbai already slated to host the final. The Indian team was to play its first game of the tournament at Mirpur in Bangladesh and the remaining five at home. Lots were drawn to assign each of the five matches to venues.

However, it wasn't always smooth sailing with the ICC. Its representatives were always on tenterhooks, not knowing how the BCCI and its member associations functioned. While we knew that our associations invariably delivered on time, although they often did not stick to a pre-decided schedule, it took the ICC a while to comprehend this. The ICC representatives also kept asking us what would happen if Pakistan were to make it to the final. It was a worrying thought, considering the fact that the Shiv Sena, a prominent political outfit headquartered in Mumbai, had 'embargoed' the Pakistani cricket team from playing in the city, but we managed to stave the ICC off by telling them that we would cross the bridge when we came to it.

The ICC team, which was headed by Chris Tetley, the event manager, was keeping track of the preparations on a bar chart, which represented the different verticals related to the tournament and was updated daily. There was a lot to learn from the professionals in the ICC and the way they went about their tasks.

Every single point was documented. The host tournament director, the three tournament directors, the host liaison manager and the events manager would meet once a month and a progress report would be submitted to the ICC every fortnight. The ICC also undertook reconnaissance visits to the nominated venues, first in late 2009 and subsequently, in November–December 2010, a couple of months before the tournament got underway. The reconnaissance team comprised the professionals who were handling cricket operations, media, broadcast and TV production, pitches and security. At every venue, this team met representatives of the host association's organizing committee and discussed the preparations and timelines. The BCCI can learn from the ICC how the latter trains individuals, including those designated as volunteers, at every venue to ensure the smooth conduct of the matches.

The ICC team had planned promotional events in all the three host nations. These included, the launch of the tournament logo, the announcement of the draw, the unveiling of the tournament's mascot and the start of the countdown to the tournament. The 30-day countdown for the ICC CWC 2011 officially began at the Bombay Stock Exchange (BSE), exactly one month before the first game. Mr Pawar and Mr Lorgat rang the historic BSE opening bell at 9:15 a.m. sharp, thereby announcing the markets open for trade for the day. Lorgat then handed over the World Cup Trophy, which was to be presented to the winning team, to Mr Pawar. The trophy was kept at the Cricket Centre. The official broadcaster and event sponsors had also lined up promotional events in each of the three countries, such as a 'Trophy tour' through the cities which were to host the matches. ESPN Star Sports, the official broadcaster, organized a talk show in Delhi, where I had the honour of sharing the dais with Imran Khan, Kapil Dev and Arjuna Ranatunga, the three World Cup-winning captains from Asia, as well as Vivian Richards, who represented the West Indies, the winners of the first two editions of the tournament, in the absence of Clive Lloyd. While Mahinda Rajapaksa, the then president of Sri Lanka, chaired the function at which the dates and schedule of matches to be played in his country were announced, Ms Sheikh Hasina, the then prime minister of Bangladesh, declared the tournament open at a spectacular ceremony in Dhaka on 17 February 2011.

We, in India, had three venues which were being refurbished for the World Cup. Of these, the M.A. Chidambaram Stadium at Chennai posed no worries. It was the other two that gave us sleepless nights. The rebuilding of the Wankhede Stadium, which was to host the final, was to have started in late 2007, but it did not begin until the end of the inaugural season of the Indian Premier League (IPL) in June 2008. The rebuilding was marred by numerous delays. The pressure got to everybody, from the members of the MCA to the president of the ICC (and the MCA) himself. At one point, Mr Pawar even considered looking at the D.Y. Patil Stadium, situated at Nerul on the outskirts of Mumbai and host of the IPL finals in 2008 and 2010, as a backup. However, I convinced him that we would pull it off. The efforts of all those who worked around the clock to get the Wankhede Stadium ready in time for the tournament did not go in vain.

Kolkata's iconic Eden Gardens, which was to host three league games, including the marquee encounter between India and England on 27 February, was another concern. The reconnaissance team discovered on its visit in December 2010 that the structural work had not been completed. The venue was given additional time to speed up the refurbishing, but to no avail. The ICC team which inspected the three venues on the eve of the tournament comprised a structural expert, who felt that the Eden would not be ready in time for the India–England match.

The decision to shift the game out of Kolkata greatly upset Mr Jagmohan Dalmiya, the president of the Cricket Association of Bengal (CAB). An extraordinary individual who had contributed to making the BCCI the force it was in international cricket, Mr Dalmiya had also made a huge impact at the ICC during his stint as its president from 1997 to 1999. He called me when I was in Bangladesh for one of the preparatory meetings and asked me if he should request the ICC to reconsider its decision. He felt that BCCI politics had something to do with the ICC's decision (his group had lost the BCCI elections to Mr Pawar's group in 2005). I explained to him that the ICC had taken the call on the basis of the feedback given by its experts. It was very unfortunate. I remember telling the ICC officials that in a different day and age, Mr Dalmiya would not have allowed them to enter his office, forget the stadium.

Shashank Manohar, the then BCCI president, suggested that the India-England game be shifted to Bengaluru. I then spoke to Anil Kumble and Javagal Srinath, who were the president and the secretary of the Karnataka State Cricket Association (KSCA), respectively. Along with their respective teams, they rose to the occasion and did a splendid job. One of the instructions passed on to them was that all those who had purchased tickets online for the game at Kolkata, needed to be accommodated first.

Virender 'Viru' Sehwag got the ICC CWC 2011 off to a blazing start. He struck Shafiul Islam for a boundary off the first ball of the tournament and went on to score 175, as India rattled up a score of 370-4 against co-hosts Bangladesh at Mirpur. Virat Kohli also scored a century and India went on to win by 87 runs. The notable thing about Viru, as we knew him, was that he was the only player in the tournament to not sport a number on his jersey. He hadn't been sporting one in bilateral series either and decided to carry on in the same vein in the World Cup.

Even as I travelled from venue to venue during the tournament, I kept track of the happenings on the field. The Indian team did well in the league phase, winning four games, losing one and tying the game against England. The victory over Australia, the defending champions, in the quarter-final at Ahmedabad, convinced one and all that Dhoni's side was the frontrunner for the title.

The start of that game was dramatic for me. Milind Rege, Suru Nayak and I were travelling in a car to the stadium when we got stuck in the traffic. It turned out to be a long and frustrating wait. Finally, we told the driver to ply on the opposite side of the road, which was clear. Sure enough, we were stopped by the traffic police. We showed our identity cards to the officer in charge and told him that it was imperative that we reached the venue before the toss. When he asked us why, we told him that the balls which were to be used in the match were with us! Fortunately for us, he did not ask us to show him the balls. That is how we made it in time.

Australia won the toss and set a target of 261 runs. India were given a good start by Sachin Tendulkar and Virender Sehwag, but the innings stuttered in the middle overs. Yuvraj Singh then essayed a gem of an innings to take his team home and set up a semi-final clash with Pakistan at Mohali. The celebrations on the streets of Ahmedabad after that game were unbelievable. It took us more than a couple of hours to reach the hotel from the Sardar Patel Stadium[3], which is situated on the outskirts of the main city. I then took an early morning flight to Delhi,

---

[3]The venue was rebuilt and renamed the Narendra Modi Stadium in 2021.

from where I boarded a chartered flight to Dhaka, where New Zealand was to take on South Africa in another quarter-final. With me on the flight was Mr Pawar.

We were watching the quarter-final at the Sher-e-Bangla Stadium when I received a call from the office of Dr Manmohan Singh, the then prime minister of India. The caller came straight to the point—Dr Singh would attend the semi-final at Mohali with Yousaf Raza Gillani, his Pakistani counterpart.

I briefed Mr Pawar and we then called Mr I.S. Bindra and Mr M.P. Pandove, who were in charge of the Punjab Cricket Association (PCA), to give them the news. The game was five days away at that stage, but we had to start preparing for it right away. Five hundred paid tickets were made available to the Pakistan fans and the Indian government granted visas to the ticket holders travelling from the Wagah border.

Certain areas at the PCA Stadium in Mohali were reserved to accommodate the entourages of both the leaders. The PCA had to contact all those who had paid substantial sums to book the corporate boxes at the ground and request them to move out. They were assured of alternate seating arrangements, of course. Much to our relief, the people in question understood the gravity of the situation.

The security arrangements at Mohali were unprecedented. I had never seen or experienced anything similar in my years as an administrator. Unfortunately, the conversion of the venue into an impenetrable fortress resulted in the food vans meant for the players, being stopped outside the stadium by the police on the day of the game. Normally, the food is laid out on the table by the time a team arrives at the stadium, but the tables in the dressing rooms were laid bare on the morning of 30 March 2011. We did whatever we could, even going to the food stalls in the main pavilion to procure burgers, sandwiches and wafers for the players, who were understandably restless. The vans did reach the ground eventually, but very late. The players had no time to help themselves to the food before they took to the field. It wasn't exactly the best way to start a World Cup semi-final.

More surprises were in store, for the players and also, for yours truly.

In ICC tournaments, there is only a 10-minute interval between the playing of the national anthems of both the teams' nations and the commencement of the game. Hence, those 10 minutes mean a lot to the players. They utilize them to focus and mentally prepare themselves for the battle to follow. So, when they were told to stay on the field to exchange introductions with the prime ministers, all the players, both Indian and Pakistani, were understandably, very upset. If being deprived of food prior to the game wasn't bad enough, losing those precious minutes just before the start of play was worse. Unfortunately, there was nothing that could be done. Only five minutes were left when the handshaking affair ended, and we had to literally beg the members of the entourages to hurry off the field. It was embarrassing.

The prime ministers ended up watching the entire game. India won by 29 runs and the celebrations on the streets of Mohali were reminiscent of those in Ahmedabad. We reached the airport on time for our chartered flight to Mumbai, but were made to wait. No flights could be cleared for take-off until the plane carrying Dr Singh had landed in Delhi, as per security protocol. We ultimately took off at around 2:00 a.m.

I had received a message from the chief secretary of the Government of Maharashtra regarding a meeting at Mantralaya, or the Secretariat, on the morning of 31 March. Smt Pratibha Patil and Mr Rajapaksa, the presidents of India and Sri Lanka, respectively, were to attend the final in Mumbai on 2 April and the requisite arrangements had to be made. I reached the Mantralaya, which was not very far from the BCCI headquarters and the Wankhede Stadium, where a senior member of Smt

Patil's staff was waiting for me. We proceeded to discuss the modalities. Wiser after the Mohali experience, I turned down a suggestion that members of both teams be introduced to the presidents after the national anthems were played. I explained that not only did the ICC not encourage that practice, but even the players themselves were not very comfortable with it. When asked why that had been permitted at Mohali then, I replied that it was an aberration. The official then proposed that the president of India present the World Cup trophy to the winning team, only to be vetoed by me again. I told him that doing so was the prerogative of the ICC president. The official was displeased, but I told him that I was merely following the rules and regulations laid down by the ICC.

Officials from the Ministry of Home Affairs informed us that they had received alerts of a possible terrorist attack during the final. The officials wanted to know details of the tickets sold, especially the ones which had been sold online. Police officers were accordingly deputed to sit alongside the vendors who were distributing the tickets sold online. Security was beefed up, with snipers placed on the buildings adjoining the Wankhede Stadium. Every nook and corner of the stadium was sanitized. The MCA had installed CCTVs within the stadium and at all the gates which came handy for the Mumbai Police to monitor from the control room in the stadium.

Arup Patnaik, Mumbai's then commissioner of police, had agreed to engage the services of the CISF at the entrances of the stadium and the stands. This was a notable first. All the matches I had been involved in at the Wankhede Stadium since 1981 had been managed by the Mumbai Police and local volunteers.

The inclusion of the CISF lent a new dimension to the proceedings. The CISF took charge of the stadium entry gates at 8:00 a.m. and every person, including the police, had to step out of the stadium and then re-enter. Mr Pawar and I were stopped at the entrance of the main pavilion when we were taking a round on the morning of the game. We were politely told by the jawan on duty that he was merely following the instructions issued to him. He and his colleagues would take orders only from their commandant, who came over a little later and allowed us entry. Every single individual who entered the stadium that day had to show their ticket and was frisked, regardless of whether they were a minister, a VIP or a commoner. Never before, in my memory, had every single valid ticket holder managed to enter the Wankhede Stadium, 15 full minutes before the first ball was bowled. Generally, a few hundred valid ticketholders would be stranded and denied entry whenever the Wankhede Stadium hosted a One-Day International (ODI).

An issue which cropped up on the day before the final needed prompt intervention. The ICC had a system as per which it issued accreditations centrally for every knockout game. There were changes in the list of the accredited individuals, depending upon which team qualified. This was especially true for mediapersons from overseas, who were following their respective national teams. The police commissioner called me on the afternoon of 1 April and declared that the police would not entertain accreditations issued by the ICC. He told me in no uncertain terms that nobody would be permitted to enter the venue without a pass issued by the Mumbai Police.

This meant that with less than 24 hours left for the final, we were looking at a situation where in the media and the TV production crew, among others, would not be allowed inside the Wankhede Stadium for the World Cup final. I had no option but to ask Mr Pawar to intervene. He spoke to the Home Ministry, which convinced the commissioner to reverse his decision.

I can never thank the Home Ministry enough for its support before and during the tournament. Its concerns did not end with the conclusion of the World Cup, as I was to discover in later years, when I received calls from the Ministry, asking if I had any information on some Pakistani journalists who had been issued visas to cover the World Cup and had disappeared after entering India. I am afraid I could not be of much help in that matter. As tournament director, my job was to ensure that their visas were in order and nothing more. It was then that I realized how difficult it was for the government to trace people from Pakistan.

The Wankhede Stadium looked magnificent on the day of the final. The new structure resembled a flying saucer. The dressing rooms were spacious, the spectator stands embellished with bucket seats and the media box, huge. The venue hosted the league games between New Zealand and Canada and then the encounter between the Kiwis and Sri Lanka, before being readied for the final.

The MCA team had worked relentlessly behind the scenes. One of the highlights of their handiwork was an air-conditioned marquee at the Mumbai University ground, just behind the North Stand of the stadium, which was managed by Mr Shripad Halbe and his team. Spectators who had purchased tickets in the North Stand of the denomination of ₹35,000, could avail food and drinks in the marquee. A smaller marquee was also set up in the MCA Lounge in the Garware Pavilion, which accommodated the holders of the highest-priced tickets for the big game, which were of the denomination of ₹50,000. The MCA officials were assisted by volunteers, who were spread out all over the stadium. They did a phenomenal job!

The atmosphere at the Wankhede Stadium on the afternoon of 2 April 2011 was electric. I felt charged and emotional when the national anthem was played at the start of the game. Needless to say, all the Indians and Sri Lankans in the ground felt the same way, along with those who were watching on their televisions.

'Scoreboard pressure' can be a factor in a final and both teams wanted to bat first to avoid the same. The coin had to be tossed twice when the call of Kumara Sangakkara, the Sri Lankan captain, was not heard clearly by Jeff Crowe, the match referee, even as Dhoni felt that he had won the toss. Sangakkara won the re-toss and elected to bat first.

Zaheer Khan bowled an excellent first spell and India had things pretty much in control before Mahela Jayawardene came in to essay a magnificent innings. His century enabled Sri Lanka to score 274-6, a competitive score for a final. India started poorly, losing Virender Sehwag without a run on the board. Sachin Tendulkar, playing his sixth World Cup, seemed to be in good nick, but the stadium went deathly quiet when Lasith Malinga, who had dismissed Viru earlier, struck again, having Tendulkar caught by Sangakkara. The chase was put back on track by Gautam Gambhir and Virat Kohli. People were surprised when Dhoni promoted himself over the in-form Yuvraj at the fall of Virat's wicket, but the Indian captain knew best. He and Gambhir batted brilliantly till the Delhi opener was bowled, only three runs short of what would have been a memorable century. It was appropriate that Yuvraj, who was declared the 'Player of the Tournament' minutes before the end, was on the pitch when victory was achieved.

There was a lot of activity in the Garware Club House even as Dhoni and Yuvraj were taking India home. At around 9:30 p.m., the police commissioner reminded us of the court ruling, as per which loudspeakers were to be switched off at 10:00 p.m. With India doing well and the patriotic songs being played between overs doing their bit to pump up the spectators, the shutting down of the sound system would have been anti-climactic. Mr Pawar and I then spoke to Mr Prithviraj Chavan, the chief minister of Maharashtra, who was seated in the President's Box. Could the World Cup final be treated as a special case? Mr Chavan heard us out and sent for the commissioner, whose expression as he entered the enclosure said it all. 'You must have told him something,' he said to me. I could only smile in response. Mr Chavan then persuaded the commissioner to make an exception for the ongoing game and even suggested that we speak to the chief justice of the Bombay High Court, who was also present in the President's Box, totally engrossed in the game. The commissioner relented and that was how we could use the sound system till the presentation ceremony ended. We will always be grateful to Mr Chavan for his help.

The heads of state of India and Sri Lanka, governor and the chief minister of Maharashtra apart, the MCA President's Box was occupied by other VIPs, like ministers from the central government, Members of Parliament, industrialists and guests of the ICC and BCCI, among others.

After receiving the trophy, the Indian team did a lap around the ground, with Sachin, who had played his sixth World Cup, perched on the shoulders of his teammates. He had been a childhood hero for most of them, and they dedicated the victory to him. The celebrations continued in the dressing room. I remember Dhoni asking for Gautam, alias Sudhir Kumar Chaudhary, the team's number one cheerleader, to be permitted entry. The captain emphasized the importance of according respect to those who were committed to the Indian team. Sudhir, who, by then, had travelled all over the world to cheer for the Indian team, was overwhelmed when he was allowed to hold the trophy.

The boys were thrilled to hear that the BCCI president had announced a bonus of ₹2 crore to each of the players and ₹50 lakh to every member of the support staff. This was in addition to the ICC's prize money of $3,00,000.

One of my many memories of that night is of being accosted by a prominent member of the Indian team when I was in the dressing room to tell me that the 'monopoly' of the 1983 team was over. The reference was to the World Cup-winning team of 1983, whose members would be sought after by one and all every four years when the World Cup was around the corner.

Be that as it may, the 1983 World Cup win can never be forgotten. It infused not only the cricketers, but also their fans, with self-belief. Some of those fans went on to follow the footsteps of their heroes. Indian cricket changed irrevocably after what Kapil's Devils achieved on 25 June 1983.

The champions of 2011 were hosted by the Honourable President of India for a tea party at the Raj Bhavan, the official residence of the governor of Maharashtra, the day after the World Cup final.

Even as the celebrations were on all over India, a section of the media ran a story that the World Cup trophy was in the custody of the Mumbai customs. It was claimed that the customs officers had intercepted a member of the ICC staff who had brought the trophy to Mumbai and the one which was presented to the Indian team was a replica. However, this wasn't the case. The ICC has a trophy which, for perpetuity, is kept in their headquarters and used only for promotional activities. The trophy which is awarded to the winner is created only before a tournament. This trophy had been handed over by the ICC to the BCCI for safekeeping, prior to the final. Shri Uddhav Thackeray, the current chief minister of Maharashtra, called me to check the veracity of the claims. He told me that Balasaheb, his father and founder of the Shiv Sena, wanted to know the facts before penning his column in *Saamna*, the newspaper he edited. I duly passed them on and was moved when the newspaper backed our point of view.

In conclusion, I have to say that the Indian team was determined to avenge the humiliation of 2007. Stumpy, the mascot of the ICC CWC 2011, was unveiled in Sri Lanka in August 2010, when the Indian team was engaged in a bilateral series in the country. Sachin and Dhoni met me in Sri Lanka and requested a meeting with the BCCI president to discuss their strategies and the team composition they had in mind for the World Cup. On my return to India, I spoke to Shashank, who agreed to meet the duo in Nagpur. I have no doubt that this meeting helped the Board president ensure that the selectors were on the same page as the captain, when they sat down to pick the squad for the World Cup.

The ICC CWC 2011 was a huge success. The quality of cricket was excellent, the TV viewership was double of what it had been in 2007 and the spectator turnout incredible. Tetley, in his report to the ICC's Board, had this to say about the ICC CWC 2011: 'It has been widely acclaimed as the most successful CWC till date. The office of the host tournament director and the host organizing teams of the three countries deserve praise for the delivery of an event, which by general consent and according to standard measurements, can legitimately be remembered as one of the best cricket events in history.'

India's victory was the proverbial icing on the cake. I was proud of what my team of managers and volunteers in the three boards had achieved off the field, and proud of what the Indian cricket team had accomplished on it. 2 April 2011 was the happiest day of my life, the apogee of my career as a cricket administrator. The Wankhede Stadium, my 'karmabhoomi' (land of action) for decades, will be remembered forever for the first-ever victory in a World Cup final by a team on its own soil.

2
FORMATIVE YEARS

'Prof. Shetty is one of our most loved members of the staff. He is an able, competent and conscientious teacher and takes great interest in the intellectual development of his students. By his sincerity, devotion, hard work and dedication to the cause of teaching, he has won the hearts of his students and they love him immensely. I regard Prof. Shetty as one of the most valuable assets of our college in all aspects.'[4]

—Prof. A.J. Borde, former principal, Wilson College

I was second of seven sons, born to Shivaram and Sharada Shetty. We lived in Mazgaon, one of the oldest parts of the city of Mumbai. I consider myself lucky to have been born and brought up in a city that encourages ambition and enterprise.

Mumbai is a metropolis which never sleeps and provides everybody who is willing to work hard with opportunities to earn a living. Yes, we 'Mumbaikars' do complain about various things, like the flooding during rains, the poor condition of the roads, traffic jams and the challenge of commuting long distances in overcrowded trains, but for me, Mumbai is still an extraordinary city. My work with the BCCI took me all over the

---

[4]This was part of the recommendation to the University Grants Commission (UGC) for sanction of study leave for my M.Phil.

country and I can proudly say that Mumbaikars are a blessed lot. We are far better off than other Indian cities in terms of public transport, uninterrupted power supply, an assured supply of drinking water and the best healthcare facilities. An attribute typical of a Mumbaikar is resilience. Be it floods or terrorist attacks, the city has been quick to bounce back. The COVID-19 crisis is also a case in point. The Municipal Corporation of Greater Mumbai (MCGM), the city's healthcare workers and the police deserve all the praise they have earned for tackling one of the most challenging health crises in history.

My family belongs to the Bunt community. My father came to Mumbai, like hundreds of others, from the Udupi district of Karnataka, and joined the hotel industry at a young age. He finally came to own a restaurant in the same chawl[5] where we lived. Those who have lived in a chawl will tell you that it is a universe in and of itself. Different households make up one extended family and partake in each other's joys and sorrows. One of the high points of life in a chawl is the celebration of festivals. During Ganeshotsav[6], most of the residents would install idols of the deity and we children would go from home to home to sing aartis (hymns in praise of the Lord). We shifted to an apartment when I was 12 and honestly, I felt out of place for a while. It was not easy to adjust to life outside a chawl.

As is the case with all middle-class families in the country, my parents accorded top priority to education. They did not spare any effort to ensure that we grew up as responsible citizens. It is sad that my parents did not live long enough to see us prosper in our respective careers. One of my brothers is a qualified chartered accountant. Another did his master's programme in the United States (US) after completing his B.E.

---

[5]It is a structure of one-room or two-room flats, generally with common toilets and bathrooms.
[6]The annual festival dedicated to Lord Ganesh.

in Electronics from Manipal University. He lives in Silicon Valley. My youngest brother did his Master of Dental Surgery (MDS) and moved to the UK, where he is a consultant in maxillofacial surgery. The other three also graduated from their respective universities. One of them entered the restaurant business while the other two joined our corrugated paper packaging unit in Bengaluru.

My brothers and I studied at the St Joseph's High School in Umerkhadi (Dongri), which was walking distance from our house. The school, which was run by Jesuit priests, focused on discipline and ethics. Academics apart, the importance of doing the little, seemingly insignificant things properly, was emphasized. The tie, which was part of our uniform, was a case in point. It had to be knotted the right way. All the students were supposed to wear uniforms made of cotton and polished shoes were a must. Those who would be found wearing a uniform made of an expensive fabric such as terrycot or terylene would be sent home. The idea was to ensure that students who belonged to relatively affluent families and could therefore afford terrycot or terylene were not envied by those whose families were not as well off and could not afford them.

Two teachers who made a huge impact on me were Mr Iyer, who used to teach Mathematics and Ms Doyle, who taught English. Both had dedicated their lives to the profession and continued to teach us well past their retirement.

For me, an experience in the sixth standard was a turning point. Ms Saldanha, one of our teachers, insisted that I participate in an elocution competition which had been organized on the occasion of Independence Day. I was shy and hence, reluctant to do so, but she prevailed. She helped me draft a speech and rehearse the same. Speaking in front of a live audience was a massive confidence booster. I went on to become the head prefect of the school. I would conduct the morning school assembly and later, I was also asked to do some administrative work. Ms Saldanha transformed my life with her perseverance. I will never forget her.

After passing my Secondary School Certificate (SSC) Board examination, I chose to study Science at Wilson College, one of the oldest educational institutions in western India. Founded in 1832, the college shifted to its present location in 1889. The college building, which was constructed at a cost of ₹1 lakh at the time, is a Grade III Heritage structure and is situated opposite Girgaum Chowpatty in South Mumbai. The first few vice chancellors of the University of Mumbai, which was established in 1857, were 'Wilsonians'.

Alumni of Wilson College have made their mark in diverse fields, like politics, theatre, medicine, bureaucracy and sports. Students of the college were actively involved in the freedom movement in the first half of the twentieth century. One of them was Usha Mehta, the eminent Gandhian, who ran an underground 'ham' radio station (Congress Radio) during the Quit India movement of 1942. B.G. Kher, another Wilsonian, became the first chief minister of the erstwhile Bombay State after Independence. He hoisted the national flag at Mantralaya, the State Secretariat, on the morning of 15 August 1947 and then drove to Wilson College to do likewise.

The Scottish missionaries who ran the college were sympathetic towards the students who were active in the freedom movement. This tradition continued even after Independence. When Prof. K.K. Theckedath, one of my teachers, was arrested during the Emergency of 1975, the college management refused to be intimidated. A decision was taken to pay his wife his monthly salary for the entire period when he was in prison.

Morarji Desai, who had graduated in Physics from Wilson, was elected India's prime minister in 1977. I got an opportunity to observe him from close quarters in my capacity as the program manager, when he was felicitated by the college, shortly after becoming prime minister.

The college was served by some extraordinary teachers, over the decades. One of them was Dr H.J. Taylor, a teacher of Physics, who had worked with Nobel Laureate, Ernest Rutherford. Dr Taylor, I am told, was a part of the team that designed the sound system of India's Parliament Hall. He was later appointed the first vice chancellor of Gauhati University.

The one constant in my formative years, apart from studies, was cricket. The game was an integral part of my life, ever since I can remember. My school did not have a cricket team, but we played a lot of tennis-ball cricket in the lanes and streets. I also became a regular, like several others, on the maidans of South Mumbai in watching local cricket matches. The 'A' division matches of the inter-club Kanga League and inter-corporate Times Cricket Shield, which were mostly played on the grounds on the Kennedy Sea Face (Marine Drive), attracted huge crowds. The leading cricketers of the time would play these games and the Times Cricket Shield would also feature cricketers from other parts of the country. Inter-school and intercollegiate matches were also well attended. I remember watching an intercollegiate final between Siddharth College and St Xavier's College at the Bombay Gymkhana in the late 1960s, where the crowd was easily in excess of 10,000. That game featured a diminutive opening batsman who went on to rewrite the record books. In fact, I ended up watching many of the matches he played in, on the maidans.

Admittedly, in my school days, I was a bigger fan of the Australian cricket team than the Indian team. My attraction for the Indian team started with the debut of Gundappa Viswanath against the Australians in 1969 and it grew with the advent of Sunil Gavaskar on the international scene in 1971. This was the age in which a cricket fan's best friends were the radio and newspapers.

The first Test match I watched live was the one against Bill Lawry's Australians at the Brabourne Stadium in 1969. I stood in a queue for almost five hours and bought a 'season' ticket for the East Stand for a cost of ₹25, a substantial amount at the time. The ticket gave me access to the stadium for the entire duration of the game, which was an enjoyable affair, till S. Venkataraghavan was declared out and one of the radio commentators criticized the decision. The spectators, many of whom were carrying transistors, caught onto the commentator's words and rioted. A stand was set on fire and we were driven out of the stadium by the police. However, sanity prevailed the next day and the game resumed.

Indian cricket came of age in 1971 when Ajit Wadekar led the national team to back-to-back series triumphs in the West Indies and England. The chief architects of the victory in the West Indies were Dilip Sardesai, who scored 642 runs in the series and Gavaskar, who amassed a record 774 runs in his very first series. He never looked back, going on to score 35 international hundreds and becoming the first batsman to score 10,000 runs in Tests.

The spinners, who had also excelled in the Caribbean, then gifted the nation another series win in England. Residents of Mumbai lined its streets to welcome the Indian team on its return from England. The Bombay Cricket Association (BCA) organized a motorcade with Ajit Wadekar, the victorious captain, in an open car, followed by the rest of his team in cars behind. I was part of the crowd which stood at Lamington Road (now known as D.B. Marg). We cheered as the players drove past us and flower petals were showered on them from the buildings. It was an unforgettable experience! Little did I know then that I would be involved in planning a similar welcome for an Indian cricket team, 36 years later!

Wadekar's team was felicitated at a packed Brabourne Stadium later that day and I was among those watching from the East Stand. A huge stage had been set up on the ground, facing the clubhouse, and speeches were made by several dignitaries. The twin wins of 1971 transformed the outlook of not only India's cricketers, but also the fans.

I graduated in 1973, majoring in Chemistry, and then, completed my MSc in Physical Chemistry two years later. Subsequently, I did my M.Phil in Chemistry from Mumbai University in 1988 and enrolled for my PhD in Chemistry at the Institute of Science, Mumbai. However, cricket administration got the better of me and I could not focus on my research.

Back in 1974, when I was in the second year of MSc, I got an opportunity to work as the assistant warden of St Andrew's House, one of the two boys' hostels at Wilson College. A.J. Borde, the principal and Ashok Patet, the warden, advised me to 'be the students' friend' but at the same time, keep a distance'. I served in that capacity till 1980. The hostel was cosmopolitan, with a number of foreign students staying there, as well as students from the interiors of Maharashtra. My stint as the assistant warden gave me the opportunity to not only interact with youngsters hailing from diverse backgrounds, but also understand and address their concerns. This hostel experience and the teacher-counsellor workshops I attended, set the tone for my subsequent forays into teaching and administration.

The college authorities appointed me as a full-time lecturer of Chemistry in 1975, after I completed my MSc. Teaching was my first love and I spent a lot of time with the students on the campus, engaging with them in cultural and sporting activities. I served on the local managing committee of Wilson College for 20 years, from 1986 to 2006. I eventually opted for voluntary retirement as an associate professor, after joining the BCCI.

I was inducted into the College's Gymkhana Committee as the staff-in-charge for cricket in 1975. I felt proud to be in august company. Wilsonians who had made a mark in cricket, on or off the field, included former Test cricketers such as L.P.

Jai (also Mumbai's first Ranji Trophy captain), Ramesh Divecha and Dilip Sardesai, Dr H.D. Kanga, after whom the Kanga League was named, Anandji Dossa, the statistician and Suresh Saraiya, the commentator. The Wilson College Gymkhana was situated on a plot of land which had been allotted to the college in 1910, on the Kennedy Sea Face, a kilometre or so away. So steadfast was the College's commitment to sports that Dr Dugald Mackichan, who was the principal when World War II broke out, refused to surrender the ground to the government, which wanted to use it to erect tents for soldiers.

With the benefit of hindsight, it can be said that my innings as a cricket administrator commenced in 1975, the same year in which I was appointed staff-in-charge of cricket at Wilson College. A phone call from Prof. Madhukar Vinayak (M.V.) Chandgadkar started it all. He was the secretary of the BCCI at the time and also taught at the R.A. Podar College of Commerce and Economics in Mumbai. He was a part of the teachers' union and of course, the BCA, as it was known at the time. Prof. Chandgadkar advised me to register myself as the representative of Wilson College for the upcoming elections of the BCA. I went on to represent the college at the Annual General Meetings (AGMs) of the BCA (later renamed MCA) from 1975 to 2013 and will always be grateful to the principals and the college management of that period for having faith in me.

Coincidentally, 1975 turned out to be a watershed year for cricket in Mumbai.

In the first two decades after Independence, the Cricket Club of India (CCI), which owned the Brabourne Stadium (inaugurated in 1937), had functioned as the de facto elder brother of the BCA. Despite being a private club, the CCI enjoyed a special status in Indian cricket, as it was a founder-member of the BCCI. Anthony de Mello, the first secretary of the BCCI and later its president, had also headed the CCI in later years. The CCI had allotted office space in its North Stand to different sports federations, including the BCCI and the BCA. This was a magnanimous gesture by the club, as there wasn't any money in sports then and none of the federations would have been able to afford the cost of office space in what was Mumbai's central business district. The BCCI operated from a couple of rooms on the first floor of the North Stand and the BCA from the ground floor.

When it came to international cricket, matches would be allotted by the BCCI to the BCA, which was the body that oversaw cricket in Mumbai. As the BCA did not have a stadium of its own, it had worked out an arrangement with the CCI, as per which, Test matches allotted to it would be played at the Brabourne Stadium. In those days, the BCCI used to levy a surcharge on tickets. This surcharge had to be collected by the associations hosting the Tests and then deposited with the BCCI. It was hence the responsibility of the BCA, as the host association, to collect the surcharge and give the same to the BCCI, whenever Tests were played in Mumbai.

The Gymkhanas, which were a part of the BCA, were allotted tickets in the West Stand of the Brabourne Stadium for Test matches. The CCI would give around 10,000 additional tickets to the BCA, in the North and East stands for its clubs and for sale. These tickets were the BCA's primary source of income, with the affiliated clubs being given tickets at concessional rates. As the years passed, the BCA started demanding more tickets from the CCI. There were heated discussions and arguments between the two sides on the eve of every Test match in Mumbai in the 1960s. However, the CCI prevailed every time. The Brabourne Stadium was theirs, after all.

Matters came to a head in the late 1960s, when the CCI was headed by Vijay Merchant, the Indian cricketing legend, and the BCA by S.K. Wankhede, the finance minister in the Government of Maharashtra. The CCI, once again, refused to increase the BCA's quota of tickets and this time around, the BCA decided that enough was enough. All the BCA was asking for was 3,000 more tickets, but the CCI in its infinite wisdom, vetoed the request. Mr Wankhede declared that it was time to become independent. He was supported by M.W. Desai, the vice president of the BCA, who was also the deputy municipal commissioner of Mumbai. They convened an AGM and declared their intent to build a new stadium.

It was a bold decision. The BCA, at that stage, had no money, but Mr Wankhede was a determined man. He used his good offices as minister to acquire the Lloyd's Reclamation ground at Churchgate, less than half a kilometre from the Brabourne Stadium. This ground had been originally given to the University of Mumbai, which had utilized only a part of it.

When you think of a plot for a cricket stadium, you visualize a vast, open space, but that wasn't the case as far as the Lloyd's Reclamation ground was concerned. The space that the university had let go was abutted by residential buildings on the west, the university pavilion on the north, the Bombay Hockey Association stadium on the south and railway lines on the east. The BCA decided to go ahead nevertheless.

There were multiple attempts by different agencies and people to throw a spanner in the works, but Mr Wankhede and his colleagues were up for the challenge. Among those who supported the BCA was Balasaheb Thackeray, who would visit the site often and boost the confidence of the BCA officials. Cricket and Balasaheb went back a long way. In his days as a cartoonist at the Free Press Journal, he would commute to work by train in the company of cricketing stalwarts such as Madhav Mantri, Ramakant Desai and Bapu Nadkarni, all three of whom were to be actively involved with the BCA in the years to come.

The House of Tatas gave the BCA some money, as did the Garwares. The North Stand and clubhouse of the new stadium were named after them respectively, as a result. Interestingly, the sports minister in the Government of Maharashtra, who formally allotted the land to the BCA, was none other than Mr Sharad Pawar, who, in later years, became the president of the Association.

The members decided to name the stadium after Mr Wankhede and he richly deserved the honour. The Wankhede Stadium became Mumbai's third Test venue in January 1975, when Mansoor Ali Khan Pataudi's Indians took on Clive Lloyd's West Indians in the fifth and final Test of what had been an enthralling series. The series was tied at 2-2 and the final Test was the decider. The game witnessed tall scores by both sides in the first innings, but the West Indies stepped up a gear in the second innings and eventually won the series 3-2. The only blip was a riot-like situation that had developed on the second day when the police manhandled a spectator who had run onto the field to congratulate Lloyd for completing his double century. The stands had erupted and the match had to be halted, but normalcy was restored after appeals by the BCA officials and the police. The game resumed on the third day.

The BCA displayed magnanimity by naming the West Stand of the new stadium after Vijay Merchant. Had Mr Merchant and his colleagues at the CCI displayed a bit more flexibility, the history of Mumbai Cricket would have been different. I salute the grit and determination of Mr Wankhede and his colleagues and the members of the BCA, who stood behind him. If they had not taken such a bold step, the BCA would never have been able to stand on its own feet and have a stadium and an office of its own.

Mr Merchant remained a respected figure, not only for his achievements as a cricketer, but also for his philanthropic pursuits. He was amiable and articulate. His radio programme, which used to be broadcast on Sunday mornings, was extremely popular. It pains me to recall one of the rare occasions when someone as unflappable as him was upset.

Wilson College had invited him for a talk in the early 1970s, soon after the end of his eventful tenure as India's chairman of selectors. He spoke eloquently and also offered to answer questions posed by the students. One of the questions put to him was that of the casting vote, which he had exercised in favour of Wadekar at the expense of Pataudi, when the captain for the tour of the West Indies in 1970–71 was to be chosen. Mr Merchant stated his desire to provide a frank reply and asked if there was a journalist in the audience. After he was reassured that there wasn't, he spoke about the injustice meted out to him on the eve of the Indian team's tour of England in 1946. Back then, he was India's top batsman and in terms of merit, the frontrunner for the captaincy. However, in what was a dramatic twist, the national selectors had named Iftikhar Ali Khan Pataudi as the captain, although the latter had not played competitive cricket for a long time.

Mr Merchant explained to the gathering that he did not want history to repeat itself. He said that Iftikhar's son, Mansoor, had not delivered as a captain for a long time and Wadekar, the then captain of Mumbai, deserved the job on merit. He also said that he did not feel that he had done anything wrong and the success of the team in the West Indies and later England, under Wadekar's captaincy, had vindicated his stance. Unfortunately, Mr Merchant's reply appeared in the *Loksatta*, a leading Marathi daily, the following day. Needless to say, he and our principal were not very happy.

In 1975, I, too, got my first managerial assignment in sports. I accompanied the Mumbai University's five-member badminton team to the All-India Inter University Championship at Aurangabad. Our team, which comprised Pankaj Dhume and Sudhanshu Hukku, the top two national players of the time, and Shyam Divan, now a leading senior advocate, won the title. My first assignment in cricket was in 1988, as manager of the West Zone Universities team, led by

Shantanu Sugwekar, for the Vizzy Trophy played in Mumbai.

L.P. Jai had led Wilson College to victory in the intercollegiate tournament in the pre-Independence era, an outstanding achievement at a time when the competition featured teams stretching from Madras (now Chennai) to Karachi, in what is now Pakistan. However, subsequent generations of Wilsonians had struggled to emulate the achievement. We had always had a reasonably good cricket team, but we would invariably falter at the semi-final stage.

I did what I could to create a good team by suggesting that we go out of our way to admit successful schoolboy cricketers to our junior college. This strategy paid off, with Wilson College winning the junior college championship during 1980–81 and 1981–82. Our junior college team comprised players such as Prakash Karkera, Deepak Jadhav, Rajdeep Sardesai[7], Jayprakash Jadhav, Salim Kamaluddin, Shahid Ansari and Faisal Kadri. Vasant Amladi, one of the most respected cricketing gurus, agreed to be our coach. He was assisted by Mr Suryakant Chaudhari. The senior team, which comprised the likes of Vimal Bhatia, Sandeep Talim, Anil Naik, Kaustubh Wagle, Shailesh Sanzgiri and Kiran Temkar also reached the semi-finals of the degree college tournament twice, during the same period.

My association with cricket was bolstered by the senior sports administrators of the time. They were very kind to me. In 1982, Mr V.B. Prabhudesai, the then secretary of the BCA, called me to his office and informed me of my nomination on the Bombay University Cricket Tournament Committee, a position I held till 2004. In the late 1990s, I was made a member of the Sports Advisory Board of the Bombay University, where I served for five years.

A landmark event occurred in June 1983. Kapil's Devils stunned the cricketing world, India included, by beating the

---

[7]Future journalist and recipient of the Padma Shri.

mighty West Indies in the World Cup final. We did not have a TV at home and watched the game at our neighbour's place. I joined the people in my locality who came out on the streets and played drums and lit crackers to celebrate the victory. The felicitation of the team at the Wankhede Stadium, which I attended, rekindled memories of 1971.

Indian cricket was never the same again, on or off the field.

3

MY CRICKETING ALMA MATER

Becoming an official of the BCA was never on my mind. In fact, my association with the BCA got off to a rather rocky start. We were on opposite sides of a confrontation, two years after I started attending its AGMs.

The educational system in Maharashtra was restructured after 1975. The '11+4' system (11 years of school followed by four years of college) was replaced by the '10+2+3' system (10 years of school, two years of junior college and then three years of degree college). Inter-school tournaments in Mumbai were being run by the Mumbai Schools Sports Association (MSSA) and those for the degree colleges were being managed by the university. However, there was nothing for junior college students, who fell in between. I was part of a group of teachers that sought to address this gap by forming the Junior College Sports Association (JCSA) in 1977–78. In later years, I served as the secretary of the JCSA from 1988 to 1993 and was the organizing secretary of the junior college cricket tournament for nearly two decades.

There was much drama in the very first season of the intercollegiate cricket tournament. The winner was to receive a trophy named after Dr P.T. Solomon, the noted coach. R.A. Podar College qualified for the final and waited for the result of the other semi-final between Ramnarain Ruia College and Lala Lajpatrai College. Ruia won, but Lala Lajpatrai lodged a protest, claiming that the opposition had fielded a player who was older than the permissible age limit of 19 years. A committee was formed to investigate the charge and it found the accusation to be true. The JCSA accordingly decided to award the semi-final to Lala Lajpatrai.

However, the BCA intervened in its capacity as the parent body, with whom the tournament was registered. We were summoned to the BCA office and informed that Ruia had not committed the violation intentionally and it was nothing more than an oversight on the college's part. We were told to reverse our decision, but we stood our ground and reminded the BCA that we were only following the eligibility rules. Our view was that, while it was mandatory for a tournament registered with the BCA to abide by the playing conditions laid down by the latter, it was the prerogative of the JCSA, as the body which was conducting the tournament, to take a call on whether a player was eligible or not to participate in the tournament. However, the BCA did not budge, but neither did we. The final wasn't played as a result.

Thankfully, both parties moved on. I became a regular visitor to the BCA office in the years that followed, to discuss matters related to the conduct of the junior college cricket tournament and secure approvals pertaining to the match schedule and the appointment of umpires and scorers, among other things. My nomination on the Bombay University Cricket Tournament Committee in 1982, at the behest of Mr Prabhudesai, marked the start of my administrative role in the BCA, which lasted three decades.

Before I go any further, it is necessary to take a look at the origins of organized cricket in Mumbai. The year 1892 marked a watershed for cricket in Mumbai, or Bombay, as it was then known. Bombay started hosting an annual 'Presidency' match between the Europeans (Britons who were serving or settled in Mumbai and surrounding areas) and the Parsis, the first Indian community to take to cricket. This annual affair became a Triangular tournament in 1907, when Hindus entered the fray. It became a Quadrangular when Muslims joined in 1912. It finally became a Pentangular in 1937, when Christians, Anglo-Indians and Jews came together to form a team which was called 'The Rest'.

The Pentangular laid the foundation of the institution that is Mumbai cricket. Cricket lovers ignored its communal overtones and came together to savour the sport. The tournament gave local cricketers the opportunity to play with and against stalwarts from across the country, who flocked to Mumbai to play as they loved its competitive nature. Till it was abolished in 1946, the Pentangular was more popular than the Ranji Trophy, the country's premier domestic competition, which was instituted in 1934–35.

Since the start of the Pentangular as an annual Presidency match in 1892, every generation of Mumbaikars has produced stars, who have inspired youngsters to follow in their footsteps. The seniors have handed over the baton to their understudies, who, in turn, have handed it down to their juniors. The relay continues, over a century later.

The Bombay Presidency Cricket Association, whose objective was to manage and run cricketing activities in the city, came into existence in 1928, and its constitution and rules were adopted in 1930. When it comes to celebrating the jubilees of the association, it is considered from this year. The Bombay Presidency Cricket Association was renamed the Bombay Cricket Association in 1935. It was rechristened the Mumbai Cricket Association in 1996.

Mumbai has won the Ranji Trophy 41 times and figured in the final 46 times in all, in 86 seasons of the competition[8]. This includes a record 15 consecutive wins from 1958–59 to

---

[8] The 87th season of the Ranji Trophy in 2020–21 was called off because of the COVID-19 pandemic.

1972–73. Dilip Sardesai, the former India and Mumbai great, used to proudly say that Mumbai won the title for the entire duration of his first-class career! The enormity of Mumbai's achievement can be gauged from the fact that Karnataka, the second-most successful team in the history of the Ranji Trophy, have won the title eight times, which is less than one-fifth of Mumbai's tally. Speeches have been made and books written about the 'khadoos'[9] spirit that characterizes cricketers from the city. Mumbai has gifted India over 70 international cricketers since 1932. This includes three of our country's greatest batsmen in Sunil Gavaskar, Dilip Vengsarkar and Sachin Tendulkar, and 10 India captains: Vinoo Mankad, Gulabrai Ramchand, Pahlan Ratanji 'Polly' Umrigar, Ajit Wadekar, Sunil Gavaskar, Dilip Vengsarkar, Ravi Shastri, Sachin Tendulkar, Ajinkya Rahane and Rohit Sharma.

Never one to rest on its laurels, the BCA/MCA has never spared any effort to unearth talent. The annual summer camps, which are conducted by the association in April–May every year, free of cost, are eagerly awaited by cricketing hopefuls. Not everybody gets to play in the inter-school tournaments and hence, they look forward to the summer camps, to get noticed.

The quality of cricket played on the maidans, the lifeline of Mumbai cricket, has historically given the city's cricketers a head-start over their counterparts from other parts of the country. Once upon a time, club cricket in Mumbai was extraordinarily competitive. Senior players would miss club games only if there was no choice. There are stories of how top international cricketers would report to the maidans for club matches, barely hours after returning from tours with the Indian team. The passion displayed by the seniors rubbed off on their juniors. The players were fiercely loyal to their respective

---

[9]There is no one English equivalent of this word; it implies a combination of determination, stubbornness and resilience, all rolled into one.

clubs. No wonder then that institutions such as Shivaji Park Gymkhana, Dadar Union Sports Club, MIG Cricket Club, Parsi Cyclists, Karnataka Cricket Club, National Cricket Club, Fort Vijay and Shivaji Park Youngsters, to name just a few, are spoken of in awe, even today. The dedication of those who represented these clubs and also those who managed these institutions produced outstanding cricket and cricketers.

Sadly, the 'loyalty' factor has worn off in recent times. The penchant of players to move from one club to another has had an adverse effect on cricket in the city. In recent years, maidan cricket has suffered because a majority of the top players have registered themselves with three or four clubs. With only 11 players able to represent a team at any given point of time, some prominent ones end up missing matches. This has had a detrimental impact on the cricket that is played. I squarely blame the cricketers who prefer to sit out rather than play, for this decline in cricketing standards.

In 1986, I was made a member of the BCA's tournament committee, whose responsibility it is to oversee the hundred-plus tournaments registered with the association. It turned out to be a great experience as I came in direct contact with players and officials. Their insights on the way things stood and how they could be improved, were invaluable.

Some of the tournaments played in Mumbai, like the Harris Shield and Giles Shield, the intercollegiate tournament of the Mumbai University and the inter-club Purshottam Shield are more than a century old. The inter-office Times of India Cricket Challenge Shield is over 80 years old. The inter-club Padmakar Talim Shield, which was instituted in the early 1950s, was the first-ever limited-overs tournament in the world.

The king of all the inter-club tournaments is of course, the Dr H.D. Kanga League, the first edition of which was played in 1948. The Kanga League is the only tournament which the MCA conducts directly for its member clubs. All the other tournaments are conducted by the member clubs, with the BCA laying down the rules and regulations, preparing the schedules, allotting grounds and appointing match officials.

The Kanga League is one of a kind, played as it is in the second half of the monsoon, on uncovered pitches in slushy maidans. The impeccable batting technique which generations of Mumbai batsmen have been known to possess is said to be an outcome of the Kanga League, where the bowlers (and conditions) make the ball talk and the batsmen have to fight for every run. That the tournament is played the way it is has befuddled people from outside the city.

Anil Kumble, India's leg-spinning legend, was invited to distribute the caps to the teams as a part of the golden jubilee celebrations of the Kanga League in 1998. We took him to the Azad maidan, where he was shocked to see as many as 22 matches being played simultaneously on adjacent plots. He asked how was it that the players knew who was playing which game! The fact is that the Mumbai cricketer is no different from his fellow Mumbaikars. Like them, he is adept at adjusting and adapting to whichever situation presents itself.

The MCA has been supported by unsung heroes as well, who have devoted their time and energy to the game they loved. One such character was my dear friend Vinod Vasudeo and the other was Kulkarni, or 'Mhatarya,'[10] as he was known in cricketing circles. These two gentlemen would distribute blank scoresheets at match venues in the mornings and collect the same in the evening, along with photographs of those who had done well. They would then visit the offices of newspapers to report on the happenings of the day and deliver the images. Mind you, they did all this during local tournaments, including club games, and expected nothing in return. They just happened to love the sport and were passionate about it. In their own

---

[10]'Mhatarya' means 'old man' in Marathi.

way, they contributed to the growth of the sport in the city and helped the administrators in organizing tournaments. The Mumbai media has traditionally taken a lot of interest in grassroots-level cricket as well, covering club, school and college games with enthusiasm and spotlighting the most consistent teams and players.

Then, there is the incredible Mumbai cricket grapevine, which comprises players, umpires, groundsmen, officials and even onlookers and passers-by on the maidans. The eye for talent which these people have, is complemented by the alacrity with which the word spreads and the cricketer in question finds himself at the receiving end of encouragement and support.

If the Kanga League is Mumbai's premier inter-club tournament, then the Times of India Cricket Challenge Shield, which is run by the 'Old Lady of Boribunder', is the city's most prominent and prestigious inter-office tournament. Over the decades, the Times Shield has witnessed memorable performances by teams representing organizations and corporates and yielded thousands of job opportunities to young cricketers. The 'A' Division of this tournament was highly competitive and just one rung below the Ranji Trophy, in terms of the standard and quality of cricket. In a bygone era, when international cricket wasn't played for over 300 days a year, the top cricketers from across the country would turn up to represent the organizations that had recruited them, in the Times Shield.

The matches, which used to be three-day affairs, would draw large crowds, mostly in thousands, and a good performance would invariably elicit the attention of the Ranji Trophy selectors. There is no doubt that the Times Shield matches made cricketers from Mumbai more competitive. There could not have possibly been a more effective way for a cricketer to prepare for a Ranji Trophy season than the Times Shield.

My association with the Times Shield began in 1990, and I am proud to say that I continue to be a member of the tournament's committee, 31 years later. The Times Shield apart, inter-office tournaments like the Merck Shield for pharmaceutical companies, Shipping Shield Cricket Tournament, Tata Inter-Offices, Inter-Hospital Cricket Tournament and Insurance Shield Cricket Tournament are played under the aegis of the MCA. These tournaments have helped cricketers get jobs.

During my stint on the BCA's tournament committee, we had a debate with the managing committee of the association, on Dilip Vengsarkar, the India and Mumbai captain at the time. He had expressed his displeasure at an umpiring decision in a Times Shield match at the Wankhede Stadium by kicking the stumps. The Tournament Committee, of which Pravin Barve was the secretary, deliberated on the matter and recommended disciplinary action against Vengsarkar in its report to the managing committee. The office-bearers of the association did not appreciate this, but we in the tournament committee stuck to our guns and took a stand that it was up to the managing committee to take the final call on the issue.

There was a lot to admire in the BCA. At that time, there were two groups vying to control the association: the Prabhudesai Group and the Umrigar Group. The elections, which I had observed and actively participated in since 1975, were fought bitterly, but the rancour ended when the elections ended. The members of both groups would come together and run the association to the best of their abilities. Cricket always came first.

Mr S.K. Wankhede had accomplished the unthinkable in the 1970s, having given the association its own stadium and office space. However, he was not one to rest on his laurels. The manner in which he would conduct the AGMs and other meetings as the president, was exemplary. He would handle delicate matters and soothe ruffled feathers with aplomb. Assisting him was a competent team, comprising several former cricketers. I don't think there was any other cricket association in the country, barring Karnataka, which had so many international cricketers in its management. Over the years, I worked with the likes of Madhav Mantri, Bapu Nadkarni, Naren Tamhane, Ramakant Desai, Polly Umrigar, Dilip Sardesai, Ajit Wadekar, Dilip Vengsarkar, Sandeep Patil, Lalchand Rajput, Chandrakant Pandit, Sudhir Naik, Suru Nayak and even Sunil Gavaskar, who was the vice president of the association for six months. There were many first-class cricketers as well, who served the BCA with distinction. Among them were Vilas Godbole, Milind Rege, Subhash Bandiwadekar, Tukaram Surve, Gopal Koli and Sanjay Patil. Madhav Gothoskar, the former Test umpire, also served as a member of the managing committee of the association.

These individuals contested the association's elections and did everything they could for the betterment of the sport in the city. Their commitment was exemplary. Former cricketers who were not selectors would watch even the junior-level matches, including school games and then, share their observations with the selectors. A Ranji Trophy game at the Wankhede Stadium would witness a reunion of old colleagues, all of whom would watch the proceedings from the Garware Pavilion. They would interact with the players—their successors—during the intervals and at the end of the day's play, and pass on priceless advice. No wonder then that Mumbai reigned supreme at the domestic level for decades.

Senior umpires such as A.M. Mamsa, Madhav Gothaskar, Piloo Reporter, M.Y. Gupte and Dara Dotiwalla made themselves available to train the next generation of umpires. Simply put, there was no compromise on quality. I must also mention the contribution of Anandji Dossa and Sudhir Vaidya, who rendered yeoman service to the game of cricket as statisticians in an era in which they had to do the job manually. The BCA published Sudhir Vaidya's compilations of statistics pertaining to Mumbai cricket and its players in domestic tournaments.

Mr Wankhede headed the BCA till 1987, which was when the Ministry of Youth Affairs and Sports introduced a rule, as per which office-bearers of sports bodies could not continue in the same post after eight years in office. He expected the BCA to overlook the rule, considering all that he had done for the association, only to be disappointed when the General Body of the BCA chose to adopt it. He passed away a year later. The BCA apart, the Tamil Nadu Cricket Association (TNCA) was the only other cricket association in the country to adopt the rule. Of course, this stipulation was amended by both associations in later years to ensure the continuation of Mr Sharad Pawar and Mr N. Srinivasan as presidents of the MCA and the TNCA, respectively.

India and Pakistan co-hosted the World Cup in 1987. The Wankhede Stadium staged two matches: the league encounter between India and Zimbabwe and the semi-final between India and England. I did not have much of a role to play during those games, but I did make the most of the opportunity to observe how the BCA officials went about organizing the games. They worked hard and were complimented for their efforts. Disappointingly, India, the defending champions, lost to England in the semi-final. My friend Prakash Kelkar was in charge of the ballboys for the World Cup games and he told us the story of how the 14 year-old Sachin Tendulkar pestered him to get to stand near the dressing room, so that he could watch the international cricketers from close quarters. Nobody had imagined at that time that the teenager would represent India in the next World Cup in 1992 and go on to become a legend.

Mr Prabhudesai passed away in 1988 and Bal Mahaddalkar took charge of his group. The BCA elections were due in 1990, and I was invited to join the Mahaddalkar group and contest for a place in the managing committee. Our group swept the elections that year, winning all the seats, except one. I won my first election and was appointed the secretary of the Tournament Committee, of which I had been a member since 1986.

By this time, many of the cricketers I had interacted with while organizing the cricket tournament for junior colleges had attained cricketing maturity. I saw players like Lalchand Rajput, Chandrakant Pandit, Raju Kulkarni, Sanjay Manjrekar, Sameer Dighe and Jatin Paranjape, to name just a few, climb up the ladder from intercollegiate cricket to the Mumbai Ranji Trophy team and then the Indian team. All these players hailed from middle-class backgrounds and they had come up the hard way, training for hours, playing as many matches as they could and in some cases, travelling long distances to and from the grounds. They possessed the drive and the hunger to succeed. It was not at all surprising that they went on to have successful careers.

Working under Madhav Mantri, who succeeded Mr Wankhede as the president of the BCA in 1987, was a learning experience. Mr Mantri would always be seated in the first row of the Managing Committee box during international and Ranji Trophy games at the Wankhede Stadium. He would take his seat five minutes before the start of play and leave only after the end of the day's play. An epitome of discipline and professionalism, he headed the association till 1992, when he lost the elections to Manohar Joshi. What he did the very next day bore testimony to his integrity. He resigned as treasurer of the BCCI, stating that he had no right to continue as an office-bearer of the parent body if his own association had rejected him. His colleagues in the BCCI pleaded with him to change his mind, but he could not be persuaded.

Another MCA official whom I admired greatly was Vilas Godbole. So popular was he that he used to contest the elections as an independent candidate and win. I first interacted with him in the early 1980s, when he was named manager of Mumbai's under-19 team. The squad, which comprised a few boys from Wilson College, was travelling for a tournament by train and I had gone to the Bombay Central Station to see them off. It was there that I realized how challenging a manager's job was. Only a limited number of seats had been reserved and the rest of the team was to travel unreserved. The manager had to ensure that everybody boarded unhindered. He then had to look after the boys for the entire duration of the trip. Godbole did a fine job as manager and administrator and was an inspiration.

My entry into administration also gave me the opportunity to interact with Sunil Gavaskar, my hero. He was passionate about Mumbai cricket and never hesitated to call a spade a spade. I remember an incident during a domestic game at the Wankhede, years after he had retired. He spotted V.V.S. Laxman in the Mumbai dressing room, wearing the lion-crested Mumbai cap. Mr Gavaskar was upset and told me to convey to Laxman that wearing the MCA cap was a matter of pride for all those who had represented the city and someone who had not played for Mumbai should not be wearing the Association's cap. I then had a word with Laxman, who realized his mistake and took off the cap.

The BCA was at the receiving end of Mr Gavaskar's criticism in 1990–91, the season which marked the diamond jubilee of the association. Mumbai qualified for the Ranji Trophy final, our first since 1984–85, and we were to play Kapil Dev's Haryana. The game was due to be hosted by the Haryana Cricket Association (HCA), but we felt that it would be appropriate if we hosted the final in our diamond jubilee year and both the BCCI and HCA acceded to our request. The game turned out to be a thriller. Haryana took the crucial first innings lead and then set Mumbai a target of 355 with a little over two sessions left on the last day. Mumbai started poorly, losing three wickets with only 34 runs on the board, but then, we were brought back into the game by Sachin Tendulkar and Dilip Vengsarkar. Sachin fell for a splendid 96, but Dilip carried on. The match went down to the wire and we needed only three to win when Abey Kuruvilla, the last man, was run out in a mix-up. We were gutted. Dilip could not control his tears and neither could many of us. A member of the Haryana team, who had represented India for years, commented that he had never seen Dilip cry when India lost matches.

In an article for a local newspaper that he wrote after the game, Mr Gavaskar slammed the BCA for having the final shifted to Mumbai. His contention was that the players ought to have been spared the additional pressure of playing a final at home in the diamond jubilee season. He had a point. Some years later, Mr Gavaskar criticized us for including Munaf Patel as a guest player in the Mumbai Ranji team. According to him, only the players who toil in local tournaments and perform, ought to get the opportunity to represent Mumbai.

A happier memory of the diamond jubilee season is a commemorative game between Mumbai's former cricketers and those from the Rest of India, which was played at the Dadoji Konddev Stadium in Thane. The luminaries who represented the Rest of India paid glowing tributes to Mumbai cricket and its maestros at a party after the game.

I contested for the post of joint secretary in the BCA elections in 1994 and lost. I was therefore not part of the committee which was formed to organize the 1996 World Cup league game between India and Australia at the Wankhede Stadium. However, I was asked to help Mr Shripad Halbe, a Committee member, to oversee the marquee, which had been erected on the university ground behind the North Stand, for the game. Holders of 1,000 tickets, each of which cost $100, had been accommodated in a special enclosure in the North Stand. They had access to this marquee and the refreshments which had been arranged in it. Both the marquee and the enclosure in the North Stand were being managed by the International Management Group (IMG).

It was my first experience of being directly involved in the conduct of a World Cup game and I got to observe how the IMG representatives worked. They were consummate professionals and there was plenty for us to learn from them. No volunteer, other than those from their team, had access to the marquee and the enclosure in the North Stand. The arrangements were excellent. It was here that I first met Catherine Simpson of IMG, one of the key individuals behind the organizing and conduct of the IPL in later years. I remember M.F. Husain trying to enter the enclosure and being stopped because he did not have a ticket for the same. Ramesh Chauhan, the owner of the Bisleri and Thums Up brands, saved the day by vacating his seat for the celebrated artist.

The action on the field was also rivetting. That game was also the first day-night encounter at the Wankhede Stadium. Mark Waugh scored a classy 100 for Australia and then Sachin essayed a blinder for India, but the Australians won by 16 runs.

My early days in the BCA also gave me a taste of 'BCCI politics.' Manohar Joshi, the Shiv Sena leader, who defeated Mr Mantri in the BCA's presidential elections in 1992 and became the chief minister of Maharashtra in 1995, hit the nail on the head, when he said that even a politician as seasoned as he found the 'politics' in the state associations and the BCCI, a lot more challenging than state and national politics! Both he and Mr Pawar experienced BCCI politics in the years to come. Mr Joshi had a piece of advice for me too. He strongly recommended that I should never join politics because I was far too outspoken.

4
ON 'BOARD'

A Marylebone Cricket Club (MCC) squad, financed by Maharaja Bhupinder Singh of Patiala, one of the foremost patrons of Indian cricket in its fledgling years, toured the subcontinent in 1926–27. Arthur Gilligan, who had led MCC in nine Test matches prior to the tour, was the captain. It is believed that the performances of the Indian cricketers which he witnessed in the first-class matches on the tour, especially the belligerent century scored by C.K. Nayudu for the Hindus against the visitors at the Bombay Gymkhana, convinced Gilligan that India was ready for Test cricket.

However, a country could not become a Test-playing nation without an apex organization which would promote and run the sport. The Board of Control for Cricket in India (BCCI) was founded in December 1928 at a meeting held at the Roshanara Club in Delhi. Grant Govan, an Englishman, was its first president and Anthony de Mello, its first secretary.

In an article for its Golden Jubilee souvenir, Prof. M.V. Chandgadkar attributed the birth of the BCCI to four primary reasons:

(a) The growing popularity of cricket on the subcontinent, with the number of matches being played by even the locals, only increasing as the years passed.
(b) The birth and evolution of clubs and gymkhanas, which acted as springboards.

(c) Several wealthy patrons, who dedicated their time and money to the promotion of the game.

(d) The zeal, enthusiasm and dedication of the founding fathers, who converted their dream into reality.

One of the earliest founding fathers of Indian cricket was Lord Harris, the governor of Bombay province[11], in the 1890s. He had been a cricketer in his youth and had captained England at the international level and Kent in the county championship. He advocated that the organizations and clubs which were running the game in different parts of India (then undivided) should come together to form an official body, which would administer cricket in the land. As the governor of Bombay province, he allotted land on Mumbai's western seafront to the three principal religious communities—the Hindus, Muslims and Parsis—to set up their respective gymkhanas for sporting (primarily cricket) activities. These gymkhanas still stand and continue to function as cricketing nurseries, nearly 130 years after they were established. Lord Harris's contribution to cricket in Mumbai was acknowledged in 1897, when an inter-school tournament was instituted in his name. The Harris Shield is still going strong.

Lord Harris was the chairman of the ICC[12] in 1930, when India became a Full Member of the body and thus became eligible to play Test cricket. The ICC's decision to admit India was unanimous.

India made its Test debut, two years after becoming a Full Member of the ICC. The Maharaja of Patiala took the lead in financing a tour of England in 1932. In keeping with the

---

[11]The Bombay province comprised parts of the modern Indian states of Maharashtra, Gujarat and Karnataka, as well as Sind, which is now in Pakistan.
[12]The ICC at the time stood for Imperial Cricket Conference, which was founded in 1909. It was renamed the International Cricket Conference in 1965 and then the International Cricket Council in 1989.

times, royalty was accorded top billing, with the Maharaja of Porbandar and his brother-in-law, Prince Ghanshyamsinhji of Limbdi, being appointed captain and vice-captain, respectively. The fact that both the captain and the vice-captain were far from proficient cricketers, unlike most of the players they were to lead, was not considered. However, when it came to the all-important Test match—India's first—merit prevailed over royalty. The captain and vice-captain stepped aside to allow Cottari Kanakaiya (C.K.) Nayudu, the leading Indian cricketer of the era, to captain the team.

The rest, as they say, is history.

The founding fathers of the Board and their immediate successors were visionaries. Some of the decisions they took in the early years had a huge bearing on the evolution of the game in India.

First, they decided that the BCCI would be an autonomous body and would not depend on government funding. The Board would create its own resources. Second, they worked hard at the grassroots level. They understood that it was critical to have a solid foundation. The Board often struggled to make ends meet, but never compromised on the development and promotion of cricket across the land. The constitution of the BCCI was drafted and crafted meticulously, as well as the rules and regulations which governed it. The seeds were thus sown for the BCCI to become the best-managed sports federation in the country. The BCCI has always had a federal structure. While the Board frames the guidelines, playing conditions and rules, it is the state units that run the actual cricket and spot and nurture talent across the country.

When we look at the annual budget and outlay of the BCCI today, we need to also remember the strict fiscal discipline which was maintained in the early days. Two individuals who held a firm control on the finances of the Board till 1990 were Z.R. Irani (BCCI treasurer for 32 years) and M.A.

Chidambaram (BCCI treasurer for 24 years). Irani also served as the vice president of the BCCI for three years before being elected as the president for three years, from 1966 to 1969. Chidambaram served as the president from 1961 to 1964 and then took over as the treasurer. When he relinquished his post as the treasurer for good in 1990, he was working on a budget of a few lakhs. Unbelievable, but true! International cricketers made a meagre ₹50 per match and a Ranji Trophy player got ₹5 per match day, till the 1960s. Those were tough times for cricketers.

Apart from the financial help extended by its patrons, the BCCI's only other source of income in the early days was Test matches and tour games played by visiting sides. The five permanent Test centres—Mumbai, Chennai, Kolkata, Delhi and Kanpur—were supposed to pay the BCCI guarantee money, as well as a surcharge on the tickets sold (four annas[13] per ticket per day). Of the sum collected in the process, 50 per cent was distributed among the members of the Board and the remaining 50 per cent was kept in a reserve fund, to be utilized on tours undertaken by the Indian team. The BCCI also had to pay hefty amounts in terms of guarantee money to teams such as England, Australia and the West Indies, to get them to tour India. Today, of course, things have changed. A series involving India enables other cricket boards to sell their broadcasting rights for handsome amounts of money, which in turn helps finance their cricketing activities. No wonder that other boards look forward to series against India and even plead for the same!

In the 1950s, even when funds were scarce, the BCCI paid the state units ₹1,000 each for coaching assistance and ₹1,500 to enable them to participate in the Ranji Trophy. The BCCI had thought of welfare schemes for its cricketers and umpires

---

[13]One rupee was equivalent to 16 annas.

as early as the 1950s, and even started a benevolent fund with an initial corpus of ₹5,000.

An interesting discovery which I made while going through the papers of the Board was that till 1953, the captain of the Indian team was elected at the AGM of the BCCI! In fact, some of the contenders for the post would represent their respective associations at the AGM. The clout that the captain of Team India enjoyed on the Board in those days, can only be imagined.

Two significant decisions were taken in 1953:

(1) The state units would nominate a representative from among their respective managing committees to attend Board meetings. No active first-class player would be permitted to be a representative.
(2) The power to appoint the captain of the national team would be vested with the national selection committee.

The 1950s saw a number of cricketers applying to the Board for 'professional' status. The BCCI defined a professional cricketer thus: 'Someone who ordinarily devotes his time to cricket in India and earns his main livelihood playing cricket and/or coaching cricket.'

Vinoo Mankad, Dattu Phadkar, Baloo Gupte and Vijay Manjrekar were among the first to get that status. A professional was paid ₹1,500 as a tour fee, while the others got ₹1,000.

Just for the record, the documents of 1953 also mention the princely amount of £300, which the Board paid to the Haslingden Cricket Club in England to get Mankad to represent India in the Test series in England in 1952. It is a known story that Mankad, who was contracted to Haslingden, a club in the Lancashire league, asked Col. C.K. Nayudu, the then chairman of selectors, for a guarantee that he would be picked in the Indian squad for the tour of England, so that he could then inform Haslingden about his unavailability that season. However, Nayudu refused to give him a guarantee, notwithstanding the fact that Mankad was India's premier cricketer of the time. An upset Mankad withdrew from the tour as a result and joined Haslingden, only to receive an SOS from the BCCI after the Indian team was routed in the first Test of the series. Mankad then drove to London for the second Test at Lord's. He was at his best in that Test, opening the batting in both innings and scoring 72 and 184, respectively. In between, he bowled 73 overs and took 5-196 in England's first innings. He then bowled 24 overs in the second innings and took two wickets.

Col. Nayudu figures prominently in the 1953 documents as well; the BCCI decided to celebrate his 60th birthday by raising funds for him. The media (only print at the time) was requested to publicize this fund-raising initiative. It reminded me of the crowd-funding ventures which are organized in different sectors today.

This was also the year in which the selectors started receiving what was called 'smoke money'. The BCCI used to take care of the travel and accommodation of the selectors, of course. However, the selectors, led by Col. Nayudu, asked for additional payment for personal expenses. The Working Committee of the Board then sanctioned a 'smoke money' allowance of ₹10 per day per selector for a period of eight days: one day before the game, the day after the conclusion of the game and the six days in between (there used to be a rest day during the Tests in those days). This allowance later came to be known as the DA (short for 'Daily Allowance').

The Board's financial health did not improve by much in the following years. The members of the teams which won series in the West Indies and England in 1971 under the captaincy of Wadekar, received a bonus of ₹1,500 (per series) each.

I started following the working of the BCCI in the late 1980s, after being nominated to the Tournament Committee of the BCA. This was soon after the Board teamed up with its Pakistani counterpart to organize the World Cup in 1987 and silenced all those who had doubted the capabilities of the two countries to work together.

Mr N.K.P. Salve, who was primarily responsible for bringing the World Cup to the subcontinent, narrated to me the story of how the co-hosts confirmed the title sponsorship. The BCCI had managed to get Dhirubhai Ambani to agree to Reliance Industries becoming the title sponsor of the tournament, but the closure of the agreement was held up on the advice of the Prime Minister Rajiv Gandhi's office. It was sealed only after getting a clearance from the PMO.

While the Reliance World Cup 1987 was a success, the failure of the co-hosts to make it to the final had resulted in many people losing money. Tickets had been purchased at high prices for what was expected to be a final between India and Pakistan at the Eden Gardens, Kolkata, but both sides lost in the semi-finals to England and Australia, respectively. Many of those tickets were then sold at throwaway prices.

Nevertheless, the 1987 World Cup gave the BCCI the confidence to host more events, and two years later, the Board organized the Jawaharlal Nehru Cup, a six-nation tournament, to commemorate the birth centenary of India's first prime minister. Pakistan won the tournament, beating the West Indies in the final at Kolkata.

The BCCI elections were due in 1990. B.N. Dutt from the East Zone had served two terms as the president of the Board and was seeking a third, but his colleagues in the Board were reluctant to let him continue and Mr Madhavrao Scindia filed his nomination against B.N. Dutt. Scindia was representing the HCA from the North Zone. The interesting bit was that Scindia had represented the Railways, an association which is part of the Central Zone, in BCCI meetings till then. Scindia defeated B.N. Dutt and became the president.

History was to repeat itself three years later, when it was the West Zone's turn to nominate the president of the BCCI.

The BCA had decided to support Dnyaneshwar Agashe of the Maharashtra Cricket Association in his bid to be elected president. A few days before the BCCI's AGM, we were contacted by Mr P.M. Rungta, a former BCCI president, who had the reputation of being a 'kingmaker'. He was someone who used to be in great demand, on the eve of every BCCI election, with representatives of several state associations making a beeline for him. I met him at the Cricket Club of India along with my colleagues Ravi Savant and Ravi Mandrekar (incidentally, we were called the 'three musketeers' of the BCA). We were taken by surprise when he advised us not to nominate Bal Mahaddalkar, the head of our group, as our association's representative at the AGM.

We heard Mr Rungta out and left. We even spoke to the media about his conversation with us and did not think too much about it, until a few days later, when Manohar Joshi, our president, proposed that Naren Tamhane represent the BCA at the BCCI's AGM, instead of Mahaddalkar. The president's instructions prevailed.

To cut a long story short, Tamhane did attend the AGM, but he was not reachable at all and efforts to contact him failed. There were no mobile phones in those days and we could not reach him on a landline. By then, we got to know that I.S. Bindra had become a member of the Baroda Cricket Association and thrown his hat in the ring for the president's post, as the representative of an association from the West Zone! Bindra thus contested the elections and beat Agashe.

1991 was a watershed year for the BCCI. The release of Nelson Mandela from a South African prison the year before triggered the dismantling of the country's policy of apartheid, for which it had incurred the wrath of the rest of the world. Among the many sanctions slapped on the country was a 'sporting' ban. The BCCI proposed South Africa's readmission into the ICC at the Council's Annual Conference in June 1991, more than 20 years after the country had last played an official Test series. The proposal was seconded and accepted. A few months later, the newly constituted United Cricket Board of South Africa (UCBSA) gratefully accepted the BCCI's invitation to tour India to play three ODIs. It was a historic series, as never before had India played South Africa in an official cricket match. The people of South Africa were obviously eager to witness their team's return to international cricket.

The office-bearers of the BCCI, used as they were to paying Doordarshan, India's state broadcaster, to telecast international cricket played in the country, were stumped when the South African Broadcasting Corporation (SABC) expressed its interest in 'purchasing the telecast rights' of the three ODIs. The office-bearers checked if they were authorized to sell the rights in the first place and discovered that the rights did belong to the Board. They deliberated and thought of quoting $20,000 for the rights, only to be stunned. The SABC offered 10 times that amount before the representatives of the Board spoke.

For the BCCI, it was a moment of truth.

Among those who realized that the Board had been taken for a ride for several years, were Bindra and Dalmiya. These two individuals then took it upon themselves to ensure that the BCCI monetized the TV rights optimally. Just over a year later, the BCCI roped in TransWorld International (TWI), the television arm of IMG, to capture the 1992–93 series against England for posterity. The Singapore-based Star TV network, which had started broadcasting in India by then, bought the telecast rights for the series. The TV coverage of that series was sleek and miles ahead of Doordarshan's standards.

TWI was subsequently signed on to cover a multi-nation limited-overs tournament, which the Cricket Association of Bengal, headed by Mr Dalmiya, was planning in the latter half of 1993, to commemorate its diamond jubilee. The BCCI was involved in the deal, of course. The league games of the tournament were to be played at different venues across the country and the semi-finals and final were to be played at Kolkata.

This was when Doordarshan, which had enjoyed a monopoly on cricket telecasts in India for several years (and had been charging the Board to cover the matches), realized what was happening, and sought the central government's help to scuttle TWI's operations. The matter went to the Honourable Supreme Court (SC) and in what was a historic judgement for the BCCI,[14] the SC ruled that the BCCI had control over the telecast rights of cricket matches which were organized by it and played in India. Doordarshan would not enjoy a monopoly and would have to bid for the rights like any other network.

Doordarshan did not give up and sought the central government's help in getting the customs to hold back TWI's equipment at the airports. The SC had to intervene again and ordered in a hearing held late in the night that the equipment be released immediately and no hindrance be posed to TWI.

The SC ruling set into motion the BCCI's transformation into a financial colossus in the years to come.

The first BCCI meeting I attended was a working committee meeting at the Cricket Club of India, Mumbai, in February 1997. I was the representative of the MCA, having been elected as its secretary in 1996. The meeting was held a few months after the successful conclusion of the Titan Cup, an ODI tri-series involving India, South Africa and Australia, which India won, beating South Africa in the final. Raj Singh Dungarpur, who had been elected the president of the Board in September that year, was in the chair. Stalwarts such as Dalmiya, C. Nagraj and P.M. Rungta were also in attendance.

---

[14]The SC delivered its final judgement on the matter in February 1995.

I raised an issue pertaining to the Titan Cup. The BCCI had a long-term contract with Pepsi for series sponsorship, but Pepsi had sublet the sponsorship of the tri-series to Titan. Strangely, Pepsi had still been given pouring rights at all the venues. The MCA, which hosted the final at the Wankhede Stadium, had received an attractive offer from Coke, Pepsi's rival, for in-stadia pouring rights. However, Pepsi objected to Coke's presence, with the support of the BCCI. The MCA committee gave in, but charged Pepsi ₹5,000 for every stall that was put up on the day of the game.

I asked the office-bearers if it was appropriate for the Board to give Pepsi additional rights when it had sublet its sponsorship to another party. I also questioned why Pepsi had been allowed to sublet the sponsorship in the first place. Rungta reacted by saying that Pepsi was the original sponsor and had been associated with the Board for a long time. Hence, an exception could be made for them, he said.

There was a break a little later and I went to the washroom. It was there that I ran into Mr Dalmiya. He told me that I had made a pertinent point and ought to hold onto it.

The discussion continued after the break. Jyoti Bajpai, who was representing the Uttar Pradesh Cricket Association (UPCA), supported me and said that what had happened was in violation of the Monopolies and Restrictive Trade Practices Act. It was then decided that the Board would have to be more careful henceforth.

The sacking of Chandrakant Pandit as the captain of Central Zone during the Duleep Trophy, was also discussed at the meeting. He had been deposed after his team lost a game to the West Zone. The Madhya Pradesh Cricket Association (MPCA), whom Pandit represented in the Ranji Trophy, was not very happy with his removal and Chandu Sarwate, who was Central Zone's representative on the national selection committee and was representing MPCA at the meeting, registered a protest on behalf of the association. The media was on the MPCA's side, having termed the reason for the sacking as 'flimsy'. The working committee of the Board decided to look into the matter and write to the Central Zone selection committee. However, nothing of that sort happened.

There was turbulence in the Board at the time, with two old associates having become bitter rivals.

If TV rights were a game-changer for the BCCI in the early 1990s, then Bindra and Dalmiya were the primary facilitators of that change. They were a team when they took on the likes of Chidambaram, Chinnaswamy and Sriraman in Board meetings in the 1980s. They did not succeed initially, but they kept trying and were eventually successful. The duo was at the forefront of the subcontinental combine's bid to host the World Cup in 1996. The triumvirate of India, Pakistan and Sri Lanka emerged triumphant at the end of a marathon and acrimonious meeting of the ICC in 1993.

However, the relationship between the two soured in 1996. I believe that the flopping of the opening ceremony of the 1996 World Cup, which took place at the Eden Gardens, Kolkata, Dalmiya's home venue, and the differences that arose between them over the annual Sahara 'Friendship' Cup series between India and Pakistan in Canada, had something to do with their fallout.

Bindra, a former IAS officer, was an excellent administrator, but he never had the votes to back him. He was always dependent on Dalmiya for the same. When the BCCI decided to contest the ICC's Presidential elections in 1996, Bindra was the first choice, as he was the BCCI president at the time. However, he was reluctant to contest, as he felt that he had no chance of winning. At that time, the Full Members of the ICC had two votes each and both Australia and England had the veto power. The BCCI then nominated Dalmiya, who was up for the challenge.

Dalmiya, originally a businessman, prepared meticulously. His calculations were spot-on. He drew up a list of the Associate Members of the ICC, who generally did not travel to London for the ICC meetings, as they could not afford the travelling and accommodation costs, which they were supposed to bear themselves, as per the ICC's rules. He then identified 15-odd representatives of the Associate member nations, most of whom were of Indian origin, and got in touch with them to seek their support. He requested the BCCI to bear their travel and accommodation expenses and the Board sanctioned £30,000 for the same. These representatives of the Associate member nations thus attended the meeting, much to the shock of Australia and England.

The elections took place and Dalmiya won, but Australia and England exercised their veto power and argued that he had not won a two-thirds majority among the Full Members. They even ensured that the result was not announced.

At this stage, Bindra, who had attended the ICC Board meeting, told the members of the BCCI that Australia and England would not object if he were to be nominated for the post of ICC president instead of Dalmiya. However, the BCCI members disagreed and reiterated their support for Dalmiya, who had won the election fair and square. The stand-off persisted for a year, after which Dalmiya's election was announced and the veto power of the English and Australian boards withdrawn. He thus, formally took over as the ICC president in 1997, although the elections had taken place a year before. It was a three-year term. He quit as the secretary of the BCCI and Jaywant Lele took over from him.

There had always been groups and politics within the Board, but personal attacks like those that were launched after Bindra and Dalmiya became adversaries, had never been seen before. It would not be wrong to say that the feud between the two hurt the BCCI greatly.

Bindra's frustration was reflected in his letters to the Central Bureau of Investigation (CBI), the Government of India, and his interviews on TV and comments on match-fixing in the wake of the controversy that exploded in 2000. It was he who told the media that Kapil Dev was the player who had allegedly offered money to Manoj Prabhakar to 'underperform' in a cricket match in 1994.[15]

That statement resulted in Bindra being issued a show-cause notice by the BCCI. He was accused of bringing disrepute to the Board and the possibility of suspending him was discussed. A compromise was eventually thrashed out, with him agreeing to stay away from Board meetings for a couple of years. He returned to the Board in 2005, when Sharad Pawar was elected the president, and played a key role in the submission of the bid document and PNA for the ICC CWC 2011. The ICC appointed him as an advisor when Mr Pawar became it's the president in 2010. Bindra also became a confidant of Lalit Modi, who incidentally, was a vice president of the PCA, besides being the president of the Rajasthan Cricket Association.

---

[15]'It was Kapil who tried to tempt Prabhakar: Bindra,' Rediff.com, 4 May 2000, https://www.rediff.com/sports/2000/may/04bindra.htm, accessed on 26 November 2021.

5

EMERALD ISLAND, 1997

Sri Lanka is a beautiful country and a great tourist destination. I have been fortunate to have visited the country on several occasions, especially just before and during the ICC CWC 2011, in my capacity as the HTD. Sri Lankans are hospitable and enjoy their cricket. The stadiums are always packed to capacity and music is an integral part of the proceedings.

Back in 1997, I was pleasantly surprised when Jaywant Lele, the Board secretary, informed me about my appointment as the manager of the Indian team, which was to undertake a tour of Sri Lanka in the middle of the year. I was then the joint secretary of the MCA and managing its cricketing activities.

My principal at Wilson College approved my request for leave, but said that I would get only half my salary for that period. I then approached Manohar Joshi, who was then the chief minister of Maharashtra and also the president of the MCA. It was kind of him to get the Maharashtra Public Universities Act, 1985 amended, so that an employee of the university or affiliated college, who had been named manager of a national team, would get his full salary during the period when he was on leave.

The 43-day tour comprised the Asia Cup, followed by a two-Test series and then a three-match bilateral ODI series against the home team. At that stage, I hadn't interacted a lot with non-Mumbai players and was looking forward to the same. Madan Lal, a member of the team which had won the World Cup in 1983, was the coach and Sachin Tendulkar, the captain. The support staff also comprised Dr Ali Irani, who was officially the physiotherapist, but was unofficially the all-in-one, as he managed the workouts of the team and coordinated the dressing-room requirements. He had backers in the Board. I even received a letter during the tour that he would conduct the training sessions of the players, not the coach.

Sachin was already abroad and was to reach Colombo directly. The rest of the team was to assemble in Chennai and then fly to Colombo. Four of us—former captain Mohammed Azharuddin, paceman Abey Kuruvilla, left-arm spinner Nilesh Kulkarni and I—were to travel to Chennai from Mumbai. Riots suddenly broke out in north-east Mumbai the day before we were to leave and there was a call for a 'bandh' in the city. For the second time since my appointment as the manager, I had to request the CM for help. He had a word with the local authorities, and the Mumbai Police ensured that we reached the airport on time.

The civil war in Sri Lanka was still raging and the External Affairs Ministry had briefed us on the dos and don'ts before our departure. This exercise was repeated when we landed in Colombo. There was a threat perception to the Indian team from the Liberation Tigers of Tamil Eelam (LTTE) and understandably, security was tight. To minimize the risk, all our matches were scheduled in Colombo and we stayed at the magnificent Taj Samudra for the entire duration of the tour. Our movements were restricted and we were confined to the hotel on non-match and non-training days. By the time the tour ended, most of us knew the place inside out. We could have walked through its corridors blindfolded and not lost our way! In a way, those of us who toured Sri Lanka in 1997 can claim to have been in a 'security bubble', which was not too different from the bio-bubble that teams have had to stay within, during the COVID-19 pandemic. In what was an odd coincidence, our local manager was a jailor by profession!

My experience of interacting with youngsters as a teacher and a hostel warden at Wilson College certainly helped in matters related to management. Syed Saba Karim, who had been selected to keep wicket in the Asia Cup, was upset when he read comments attributed to Sachin, wherein the latter was supposed to have said that he would have preferred Nayan Mongia in the side. I had a quiet word with Saba on the same.

In those days, the players shared rooms, with only the captain being entitled to a single room. However, Azharuddin got a room to himself through his contacts at the hotel. As he was allotted a single room, Navjot Singh Sidhu, another senior member of the squad, also got a single room.

The mid-1990s weren't exactly the best of times for the game. Allegations of dalliances between players and bookmakers, and betting and match-fixing would surface every now and then and raise more questions than answers. The central government had also questioned the Board on the same. Dalmiya was among those who felt that a credible individual ought to look into the allegations and conduct an enquiry. Accordingly, the Board constituted a one-man committee comprising Shri Y.V. Chandrachud, a retired Chief Justice of the Supreme Court, to delve into the rumours and ascertain the authenticity of the stories that were floating around. Justice Chandrachud was in the process of meeting cricketers, journalists and even cricket fans to glean information, when we were in Sri Lanka.

At the opening ceremony of the Asia Cup at the R. Premadasa Stadium, Sachin was upset to discover that the Indian flag had been hoisted upside down at a couple of places in the stadium. We called the local manager and told him to rectify the mistake immediately.

We lost to Sri Lanka in our first game of the Asia Cup and the next fixture against Pakistan was abandoned due to rain. The equation was such that we had to beat Bangladesh by a big margin in our third and last league match to qualify for the final. However, our preparations for the game were overshadowed by a story which appeared in *Outlook*, a weekly magazine, in which Rashid Latif, the Pakistani wicketkeeper-batsman, had made certain claims.[16] The story featured his references to some cricketers who happened to be a part of the Indian team in Sri Lanka. There was a furore and the Indian journalists who were in Colombo to cover the cricket, demanded an explanation.

The players had been prohibited from interacting with the media. I spoke to the journalists on behalf of the team and made it clear that the ongoing tournament was our priority. The BCCI had already appointed Justice Chandrachud to look into all the allegations and both Latif and the magazine had the option of sharing whatever material they had with him to substantiate their claims.

By that time, Azharuddin, who was one of the players mentioned in the story in *Outlook*, had shown me a fax, which I was told had been sent to him by Latif, as a clarification of sorts. Latif had mentioned in the fax that he had merely named the Indian cricketers as being among his friends and had not accused them of any sort of misconduct. Some of the journalists were aware of Latif having sent this fax and they enquired about the same. Their information network was certainly impressive! I called the journalists over to my room and reiterated that we had nothing more to add to the story.

To get the players to re-focus on cricket, Madan Lal and myself thought of requesting Mr Gavaskar, who was part of the TV commentary team, to talk to the team before the game

---

[16] Aniruddha Bahal Interviews Rashid Latif, 'Azhar, Jaddu Used To Call Me', *Outlook*, 30 July 1997, https://www.outlookindia.com/magazine/story/quotazharjaddu-used-to-call-mequot/203930, accessed on 26 November 2021.

against Bangladesh. He was initially reluctant and told me that he had not entered the dressing room since his retirement. But we persisted and convinced him. His talk had a positive and encouraging effect on the players.

We beat Bangladesh and made it to the final of the Asia Cup, where we lost to the hosts, who were on a roll those days. There was a lot that we learned from them, on and off the field, as the tour went on.

There were changes in the team after the Asia Cup. The arrival of Nayan Mongia, Rajesh Chauhan and Vinod Kambli for the Tests and bilateral ODIs coincided with the publication of an interview given by Madan Lal, the coach, to *The Hindu*. When I received Mongia, Chauhan and Vinod in the lobby of Taj Samudra, each one of them handed me a copy of the newspaper and asked me to read the coach's interview. I did and was shocked. The interview was laced with uncomplimentary remarks about most of the players, which was certainly not an ideal thing to do in the middle of a tour. For instance, the coach had said with reference to one of the players that he did not know whether the latter was a batsman or a bowler. I contacted Vijay Lokapally, the journalist who had done the interview and was covering the tour. He told me that he had shown the text to Madan Lal and had been given a go-ahead for publication.

The interview had its consequences. We played a three-day game prior to the first Test, during which, none of the players, save for the captain, talked to the coach. The dressing room was an awkward place to be in and I did what I could by calling for a meeting on the evening of the first day, in an attempt to diffuse the tension. I also backed the players in a conversation with Mr Raj Singh Dungarpur, the then Board president. I told him that the coach ought to have kept in mind the fact that most of the players were as committed to the team and the sport as he was in his days as a player. He could have elaborated upon his misgivings with regard to the players, if any, in his report to the Board after the tour. Anyway, the damage had been done.

A reaction from the players was only to be expected. The coach was upset when one of the players he had criticized in *The Hindu* interview, made a gesture, thrusting the handle of his bat in the direction of the media box after completing a century in one of the ODIs. I advised Madan Lal not to assume things and focus on ending the tour on a harmonious note instead.

Mr Lele's visit to Sri Lanka, with Aunshuman Gaekwad accompanying him, led to the speculation that the Board was planning to replace the coach. Aunshuman did replace Madan Lal a few months later, but his visit to Sri Lanka had nothing to do with that. He had come to invite the Sri Lankan players for his benefit match.

The first Test, played at the R. Premadasa Stadium, witnessed runs and records. We batted first and declared at 537-8. Nilesh Kulkarni, who was making his debut, became the first Indian to take a wicket off his first ball in a Test, when he had Marvan Atapattu caught by Mongia. However, he went wicketless thereafter. Sanath Jayasuriya and Roshan Mahanama batted on to add a record 576 for the second wicket. The Sri Lankans obviously wanted Jayasuriya to surpass Brian Lara's 375, the highest individual score in a Test, but the left-hander fell for 340 when Sourav Ganguly caught him off Rajesh Chauhan. Sri Lanka's 952-6 was the highest score by a team in a Test. One of the lighter moments of that game was someone quipping that while Nilesh's first ball was a 'wonderball', his subsequent deliveries were 'thunderballs'! Nilesh took it in the right spirit.

The bowlers fared a lot better in the second Test, which was played at the SSC Ground in Colombo. Sachin and Azhar scored their second centuries of the series and Sourav, the third of his Test career. However, the game was drawn, which meant that the Test series ended in a 0-0 stalemate.

We had not done well on the over rate front in the Test series. The inevitable happened at the end of the second Test, when John Reid, the ICC match referee, called me and handed me a letter. It mentioned that we had lagged behind by nearly 28 overs—a huge number. The players were slapped with a '180 per cent fine', which meant that they were to lose their entire match fee for the series. I called a team meeting, which I began by thanking all the players for playing the two Tests for free. At this stage, Vinod Kambli, who had been in the reserves and not played either of the Tests, raised his hand. The character that he was, he provided a humorous spin to the proceedings by reminding all of us that while the over rate had been slow, he and the other reserve players had ensured that there was no delay in carrying drinks on the field. Hence, they ought to be spared the penalty! I clarified that the penalty was to be paid only by the members of the playing XI.

Speaking of Vinod, I happened to be sitting next to him on the flight back to India. When the disembarkation forms were distributed just before we landed in Mumbai, he asked me what he should write in the 'purpose of visit' column of the form. He said that he hadn't played a single game on the tour and therefore did not know what to write!

He may have had the last word on those two occasions, but there were times on that tour when Vinod found himself at the receiving end. One morning, when we were in the breakfast room, Ajay Jadeja informed me that Gianni Versace, Vinod's favourite designer, from whose label Vinod had purchased a lot of accessories, including a belt for $600, had passed away. Ajay wanted me to condole Versace's death when Vinod joined us for breakfast. I was not inclined to do so, but Ajay told me that the players would participate willingly. I gave in and requested the team to observe a minute's silence when Vinod came for breakfast. The players kept a straight face throughout.

The team management had decided we would have a team

dinner on the night before every game, with a senior player picking up the tab. Vinod was one of the seniors and his turn to treat his teammates came during the ODI series. After we had had dinner, Sachin announced that he was ordering Bacardi Rum. I thought he was joking, but he was serious. He then told me that wanted to wash his hands with Bacardi Rum. 'The person whose turn it is to pay the bill, has Rum every night. He should realize how much money he is wasting as a result of that habit,' the captain explained.

The tour gave me an opportunity to get to know Sachin and Vinod, both of whom were Mumbai boys, better. We had long conversations, during which they narrated stories of their days at Shardashram High School, the record partnership in the Harris Shield semi-final of 1987–88 with which they attained stardom, the pranks they played and the firings and pastings they got from Ramakant Achrekar sir, their coach. Vinod ought to have played a lot more for India. A serious leg injury during a tri-series in early 1998, which put him out of action for a year, was a setback from which he never really recovered.

The tour selection committee, which comprised the captain, vice-captain and coach, would meet in my room to pick the playing XI for the matches. 1997 was a time when Rahul Dravid had been branded a 'Test specialist'. Madan Lal certainly felt that way and was not in favour of Rahul playing ODIs. However, Anil Kumble, the vice captain, thought otherwise. He returned to my room after one of the meetings and pleaded with me to ensure that Rahul played in the ODIs. Anil emphasized that Rahul was the future of Indian cricket and deserved more opportunities. Ultimately, Rahul did play all three ODIs. He was admittedly struggling in the shorter version at the time, but he was a quick learner, who proved in the years to come that while form was temporary, class was permanent. He scored 10,000-plus runs in both forms of the game and proved his critics wrong.

It was a tough tour, on and off the field. On non-match days, we had no option but to stick to the hotel, as outings were out of the question due to security concerns. Our only outings on that month-and-a-half long tour as a team were for a dinner hosted by the Indian High Commissioner and the flag-hoisting ceremony at the Indian High Commission on Independence Day. I did manage to go around Colombo and visited the elephant nursery and the Buddha Temple at Kandy, thanks to the arrangements made by Hussain Dawoodbhoy, one of my past students, who was settled in Colombo.

I discovered on the tour that Sidhu, who was in the room opposite mine, was an avid reader. He had brought with him a set of books on Swami Vivekanand. Players such as Anil Kumble and Rahul Dravid spent a lot of time discussing cricketing issues with Greg Chappell, Barry Richards, Gavaskar and Ravi Shastri, all of whom were part of the TV commentary team and had also been put up at the Taj Samudra.

It would have been nice to end the tour on a happy note. However, that was not to be. We came close to overhauling a target of 303 in the first ODI, but lost by two runs. We then lost the next two games as well and the reigning World Champions took the series 3-0.

As I mentioned earlier, there was a lot that we learnt from our opponents. Both teams were staying on the same floor of the hotel and we interacted with the senior members of the Sri Lankan team. It was through these meetings that we understood the need for a specialist trainer for the Indian team. Both Arjuna Ranatunga and Aravinda de Silva explained how the appointment of Alex Kountouris as the trainer had helped them extend their respective playing careers. Kountouris, they said, had studied the players and planned out individual workout schedules, keeping in mind every player's capability and his role in the team.

We also enquired about the graded payment structure

introduced by the Sri Lankan board, which took into account the relative seniority of every player. This was in stark contrast to the policy followed by the BCCI at the time, which would pay the same amount to all the players regardless of one's seniority. We also got to know from the Sri Lankan players that their government had exempted the members of the 1996 World Cup winning team from paying duty if they were to import a car. However, not many members of the team had availed of this benefit.

In 1997, the Sri Lankan board certainly gave the impression of being a lot more professional in comparison to the BCCI, as far as its administrative set-up and offices were concerned. I met up with officials of the Sri Lankan board to understand their cricketing structure. Interestingly, they had a separate board in place to manage school cricket in the country and this had yielded good results. The ICC World Cup win of 1996 had created a lot of interest and support for the game and the same was visible in the development plans that their Board had chalked out.

One of the prominent figures I met on the tour was Zaheer Abbas, the cricketing legend from across the border, who was the manager of the Pakistani team in the Asia Cup. We met again a few months later, during an exhibition game between an Indian XI and a Pakistan XI at Puttaparthi, the home of Sri Sathya Sai Baba, in the southern Indian state of Andhra Pradesh. Gavaskar, who had organized the game, took us for a 'darshan' of His Holiness. Sri Sathya Sai Baba met us and gifted Zaheer a locket, which bore an inscription from the Quran. Zaheer was surprised and he showed me the locket when we drove to Bengaluru together, after the game.

Having spent a lot of time with Sachin in Sri Lanka, I had sensed that he was disturbed. He wasn't enjoying the captaincy and I was by no means the only individual who felt that all wasn't well. There were times when information pertaining to the trajectory of games that we were yet to play, would reach us and leave us wondering. Sometimes, members of the media would tell us things that they had heard. The timing of some dismissals, especially in the ODIs, was weird, to say the least.

The captain, the coach and I wanted to brief the senior office-bearers of the Board about these incidents and seek their inputs on the future course of action, after returning to India. If indeed there was some foul play, then it was essential to take steps to nip it in the bud. We sought an appointment with Rajbhai, as the Board president was known. Madan Lal could not make it as his flight from Delhi was cancelled, and Sachin and I went to meet Rajbhai and Lele at the Cricket Club of India.

We discussed the tour, the Rashid Latif interview and the rumours, that had been doing the rounds. Imagine my shock then to receive a call later that night from none other than Azharuddin, enquiring about our meeting with the BCCI president and secretary.

I was angry and disgusted. The entire purpose of the meeting had been defeated. I called Mr Dalmiya and told him that henceforth, no manager would be frank with the Board. Our discussion was supposed to have been confidential, with only the four attendees in the know of things. How was it then that a fifth person got to know what had been discussed? Mr Dalmiya heard me out and agreed that this should never have happened.

My heart went out to Sachin. The apparent ineptitude of some of his teammates on the field had left him frustrated. Unfortunately, it took a while—three more years, to be precise—for people to realize that the ineptitude of some of the players was deliberate.

6
MENTORS

From 1987 to 1997, the BCCI office in Mumbai was run by an 'institution' named Pahlan Ratanji Umrigar. Polly kaka, as the world knew him, had served Indian cricket with distinction as a player, captain, manager, selector and curator. He had been the secretary of the BCA for eight years before being appointed the executive secretary of the Board. In later years, he was a deserving recipient of the BCCI's Col. C.K. Nayudu Lifetime Achievement Award.

It was an honour to interact with an individual of his stature. He was committed to his role and responsibilities, and unlike many people who had not achieved even a quarter of what he had as a cricketer and a gentleman, he did not have a fragile ego. I have seen Polly kaka sitting on the floor of the old BCCI office with the employees, and personally numbering the files. Every single item in the BCCI office, from the documents to the trophies won by the Indian team, was either documented or recorded, as per his instructions. He made it very easy for his successors to function effectively. The many tasks he took upon himself included, manually compiling the lists of beneficiaries for the Cricketers Benefit Fund Series (CBFS) in Sharjah, supervising the payment of ex gratia of ₹500 per match to all cricketers who had played 10 or more first-class matches and creating a medical benevolent fund scheme for retired cricketers and umpires.

Polly kaka would attend meetings of the Board and actively

participate in them on cricketing matters. His passion for the sport was palpable. When everybody in the Board was sold on the idea of staging the 1996–97 Ranji Trophy final under lights, his was the lone voice to oppose the move. The points he raised had not occurred to anybody else. He reminded the members that the white ball would lose its colour and have to be changed a lot earlier in the innings than the Red Cherry ball, and most importantly, no rules had been framed for a day-night multi-day match. There was also the small matter of insects invading the stadium after the sun went down. The players would have to contend with them for five days.

However, Madhavrao Scindia, a former BCCI president, had already been promised that the match would be played at Gwalior, his hometown, under lights, and so it was. Mumbai took on Delhi in the game and we at the MCA did what we could to help our team prepare for the game, by providing them with white balls and allowing them to practise under the lights at the Wankhede Stadium. Mumbai won the game on the first-innings lead.

Polly kaka was also not in favour of the Board's decision to allow school dropouts to participate in age-group junior tournaments of the Board. The contention of the office-bearers was that someone who was not academically inclined but was a talented cricketer should not be denied the opportunity to make a mark, just because he wasn't going to school or college. Polly kaka felt that the move could backfire, in that there was a possibility of more teenagers being tempted to drop out of school. Missing out on formal education would have an adverse effect on their overall development. This was a serious issue, which some cricketers were likely to grapple with after retiring from active cricket. The BCCI would then have to look at how they could be helped.

Polly kaka had a point. However, not many agreed with him back then. An outcome of that decision of the Board was the steady deterioration in the standard of university cricket. A lot of quality players opted out of higher studies and preferred to play the BCCI's age-group tournaments instead. The decline of inter-university cricket, where the likes of Dilip Sardesai, Sunil Gavaskar and Sanjay Manjrekar, to name just a few cricketers, had made an impression in their formative years, was unfortunate. Mr Sardesai was, in fact, picked to represent India on the basis of his performances in the inter-university tournament. He made his Ranji Trophy debut for Mumbai later.

Polly kaka's association with his beloved sport continued till his demise in 2006. When the MCA acquired a plot in Mumbai's Bandra-Kurla Complex (BKC) to build a ground, academy and clubhouse in the early years of the new millennium, there was only one individual we could think of, who could help us convert a marshy tract of land into a cricket arena. I, along with C.S. Naik, the CEO of the MCA, requested Mr Pawar to speak to Polly kaka. For months, the great man toiled on that plot of land, transforming it slowly, but surely. He was assisted by M.S. Rao and Deepak Murkar. He was provided transport by the MCA, but he did not charge a farthing for his efforts. I don't think anybody else would have done what he did so selflessly, at his age. The BKC ground, which has hosted hundreds of local matches, plus domestic and international (Women's T20) games since, owes its existence entirely to Polly kaka.

I remember an occasion when things did not go according to plan, despite Polly kaka's efforts. The Wankhede Stadium was to host a Test match against the touring New Zealand team in the 1988–89 season. It was to be the hundredth Test of Vengsarkar, then the captain of India and Mumbai. Polly kaka, who was in charge of the wicket preparations, was told by the Indian team management to ensure that there was not a single blade of grass on the strip, so that the threat posed by Richard Hadlee could be nullified. Polly kaka then instructed the ground staff to get disposable razors from a nearby store and used them to shave off all the grass! However, Hadlee still took six wickets in the first innings and four in the second innings.

I continued to attend BCCI meetings as a representative of the MCA after my return from Sri Lanka. In what can only be described as a lucky break, Mr Dalmiya took me under his wing. He went out of his way to make me understand how the Board functioned and advised me to work on the different committees of the Board. I think he had been impressed with the points I had raised in the Working Committee meeting in February 1997.

Thanks to him, I served on the Umpires, Finance, Junior Cricket, Vizzy Trophy and Tour Programme and Fixtures Committees of the Board, over the next few years. I was also made a part of the Board's Constitutional Review Committee, which comprised the incumbent office-bearers and a few former office-bearers such as C. Nagaraj, Ranbir Singh and P.M. Rungta. My joy knew no bounds when I was inducted into the cricket academy committee, which was to discuss the establishment of a National Cricket Academy. This committee consisted of the Board's office-bearers,[17] Mr Gavaskar and Mr Brijesh Patel. Mr Dalmiya also made me do a stint in the New Area Development Committee, whose brief was to oversee the cricket development in the north-eastern states and union territories, including the Andaman and Nicobar Islands.

Mr Dalmiya was heading the ICC at the time and did not hold any official post in the Board. However, he would attend the Board meetings as a representative of the CAB. I made it a point to observe him, as there was a lot to learn from him. He was a very good listener and an even better talker. He was sharp, decisive, an outstanding administrator and a master strategist, who ensured that his group retained control of the Board even when he was away at the ICC. Mr Dalmiya

---

[17]President, Secretary, Treasurer and Joint Secretary.

was also fortunate to have an excellent executive assistant in Kunal Kanti Ghosh, who was methodical and good at drafting.

Mr Dalmiya took great pride in his background. There is a lovely story of his first visit to the ICC headquarters after taking over as the president in 1997. The ICC operated from a couple of rooms at the Lord's Cricket Ground at the time, with a CEO and skeletal staff. The only cabin in the office was occupied by the then CEO. When Mr Dalmiya first visited the office after taking over, he was told that there was no cabin for the president, as the latter did not come to the office on a day-to-day basis. Mr Dalmiya then declared that the CEO's cabin would be the ICC president's office and the CEO would sit outside.

He took the presidentship of the ICC very seriously. There is reason to believe that Shane Warne and Mark Waugh's brush with a bookie in 1994, which was pushed under the carpet by the administrators of the time, came to light in 1998, only because of Mr Dalmiya's scrutiny of the ICC's documents.[18]

He prioritized the financial health of the ICC, which was precarious when he took over. The 'Knockout'[19], a biennial limited-overs tournament that featured all the Test-playing teams, was his brainchild. The inaugural edition, hosted by Bangladesh in 1998, was a blockbuster. To Mr Dalmiya goes the credit of making the ICC financially robust. From not being able to hire staff for its London office as it could not afford the salaries, to becoming a cash-rich organization based in Dubai and run by professionals recruited from all over the world, the ICC has come a long way.

Mr Dalmiya facilitated the promotion of Bangladesh as a Full Member of the ICC and got the Full Members from Asia

---

[18]'Waugh, Warne speak on bookies scandal,' ESPNcricinfo, 9 December 1998, Rick Eyre for ESPNcricinfo.
[19]It was renamed the Champions Trophy in 2002.

to support his proposal that every third World Cup be staged in the subcontinent. Needless to say, it was accepted. He was also responsible for the formation of the Asian Cricket Council (ACC) in 1983 to develop and promote cricketing activities of the Asian Countries. On the flip side, Mr Dalmiya copped flak for 'protecting' Shoaib Akhtar of Pakistan, when the latter was accused of having an illegal bowling action.

Mr Dalmiya's tenure as the BCCI president from 2001 to 2004 was highly eventful and challenging when it came to the Indian team's participation in bilateral tours and ICC events. The annual retainerships for international cricketers and enhanced payment to domestic cricketers were introduced during his tenure.

In the second test between India and South Africa in South Africa in 2001, Mike Denness, the ICC match referee, penalized six Indian players for different offences. Four of the players were rapped for 'over-enthusiastic appealing', Sourav Ganguly, the captain, was pulled up for 'not controlling his players' and Sachin, one of the most respected names in the game, was accused of ball tampering. This caused a massive uproar in India and Mr Dalmiya, who had just been elected the BCCI president, took up the cudgels on behalf of the team. The Board threatened to withdraw from the tour and declared that the Indian team would not play the third Test unless the referee was changed. The ICC refused to agree to this. However, the South African Board[20] sided with the BCCI and the third Test was played with a new referee in place. The ICC reacted by withdrawing the 'Test' status of the game and declaring it an unofficial five-day game.

The BCCI was not impressed when the ICC objected to the Sahara logo being displayed on the jerseys of the players.

---

[20]The United Cricket Board of South Africa (UCBSA) was formed in 1991. Cricket South Africa (CSA) was established to run professional cricket in the country in 2002, while the UCB ran amateur cricket. The UCB merged with CSA in 2008.

This happened after the ICC signed on South African Airways as an official sponsor of the ICC CWC 2003, which was to be co-hosted by South Africa. The fact was that one of the key business interests of Sahara, the sponsor of the Indian team at the time, was airlines. It is important to note that Sahara paid the BCCI the full sponsorship fees even though their logo was not used in two ICC events—the Champions Trophy 2002 and the CWC 2003—so that the players did not lose out. Prior to 2004, the international cricketers were entitled to 60 per cent of the sponsorship money, which was a substantial amount.

ICC had an agreement with Global Cricket Corporation (GCC) for the media and commercial rights of the ICC events for the period from 2000 to 2007 and had unilaterally agreed to impose certain restrictions on the players' appearances in advertisements before, during and after ICC events, without even discussing the same with the players. This was ostensibly done to eliminate the possibility of 'ambush marketing'. The Indian players, many of whom had already signed lucrative endorsement deals with the competitors of the ICC's official sponsors, took umbrage and refused to sign the player terms of the ICC. The BCCI stood by the players and even picked an alternate squad, in case the ICC did not change its stand. Thus, there was uncertainty over the Indian team for the ICC Champions Trophy 2002 and the ICC CWC 2003.

GCC then demanded damages from ICC, claiming that it had suffered huge revenue losses due to the uncertainty over the Indian team's participation in the tournaments. The ICC passed those damages on to the BCCI, who refused to pay the said amount of $70 million. Mr Dalmiya contacted all the sponsors of the ICC and got letters from them, in which they stated that they had no claims against the BCCI. In 2006, the ICC finally gave in and decided to claim $7 million from each of its 10 Full Members.

Mr Dalmiya always consulted Mr Gavaskar on cricketing matters. Whether it was the setting up of the National Cricket Academy, playing conditions related to domestic cricket, the appointment of the coach of the Indian team or even dealing with a sensitive issue like the face-off between Sourav Ganguly and Greg Chappell in 2005, Mr Gavaskar's participation and inputs were always sought and valued.

The annual conclave for the captains and coaches of all the Ranji Trophy teams was Mr Gavaskar's idea. He felt that it would be prudent to seek their feedback on how the cricket season had panned out and what changes could be incorporated for the next season. Mr Gavaskar continued to advise the Board even after Mr Pawar took over as the president and he also served on the IPL Governing Council. He chaired the Technical Committee of the Board for almost 15 years under different regimes, apart from heading the ICC Cricket Committee from 2000 to 2008. The man was and is a genius, committed to cricket.

The first BCCI President I worked with was Raj Singh Dungarpur. I have yet to meet someone who loves the sport more than he did. A member of the Rajasthan team, which had lost seven Ranji Trophy finals to Mumbai in the 1960s, he took special permission from the Board to create a replica of the trophy, which he installed in the lounge of the Cricket Club of India. I remember him telling me that every time he saw the replica, he momentarily felt as if he, too, had won the trophy in his playing days.

Relations between the MCA and the CCI, which had been frosty till the 1970s, were cordial during Rajbhai's stint as the CCI president. He followed junior-level cricket closely and always made the Brabourne Stadium available for inter-school and intercollegiate matches, free of charge, for the MCA. His team's reverses against Mumbai in the 1960s notwithstanding, he was an admirer of Mumbai cricket and would always say that Indian cricket would stay healthy only if Mumbai cricket stayed healthy. He felt strongly about cricketers, former as well as contemporary. He looked after former cricketers, especially those from a bygone era, who had fallen on hard times. Rusi Modi, the great Mumbai and India batsman of the late 1940s, used to live at the CCI. Rajbhai used to pay him and Salim Durani, the charismatic all-rounder of the 1960s and his Rajasthan teammate, a monthly stipend. That apart, all the expenses that Mr Salim Durani incurred at the CCI were borne by the club itself on Rajbhai's instructions. I remember an afternoon when I was sitting with Rajbhai on the lawns of the club and Mr Durani dropped in. He told Rajbhai that he wanted to become a member of the CCI. It was obvious that someone had instigated him. Rajbhai heard him out and then explained the ramifications of such a move. If he were to become a member, other people would accompany him to the club. Who would bear their expenses? Rajbhai assured Mr Durani that he would continue to take care of him.

Rajbhai told me an interesting story about Salim Durani. Having been born in Afghanistan, he did not fit into the BCCI's eligibility criteria of the 1950s, the decade in which he grew up. The Board then decided to allow him to choose the state he wished to represent in the Ranji Trophy. He chose to play for Rajasthan and the rest is history.

Rajbhai's fondness for Sachin was well known. He was the chairman of the national selection committee when Sachin was picked in the Indian team for the tour of Pakistan in 1989–90. A year and a half earlier, Rajbhai had convinced his colleagues at the CCI to amend a rule which forbade minors from entering the clubhouse. The 15-year-old Sachin had just been inducted into the CCI's team, after all.

Azharuddin was another of Rajbhai's favourites. When the Board announced a life ban on the former India captain in November 2000, Rajbhai, who was at the meeting in which the bans were discussed and imposed, wept inconsolably, I am told.

He had a big heart and was generous with his words. Shortly after the end of his term as the BCCI president and Dr A.C. Muthiah's taking over, there was a Board meeting in Delhi. This was the time when the Dalmiya-Bindra rivalry was at its peak. I was interviewed by a news channel after the meeting and as was expected, most of the questions I was asked pertained to the alleged controversies regarding the Board. I emphasized that, while differences did exist between some of the members, they did not affect the functioning of the Board. After returning to Mumbai, I received a message from Rajbhai, asking me to come over to meet him at the CCI. He gifted me his fountain pen and a card, on which he penned words of praise. I was touched by his gesture.

Rajbhai was well versed in the history of the sport. When the final Test of the 1992–93 series against England was being played at the Wankhede Stadium and India was in the process of completing a clean sweep, it was Rajbhai who reminded everybody of the Anthony de Mello Trophy[21], which had been instituted for series between India and England in India. The trophy was with the Cricket Club of India and he brought it himself to the Wankhede Stadium for the presentation ceremony.

As the Board president, Rajbhai raised the issue of international cricketers not playing enough domestic cricket, on multiple occasions. The late 1990s was a time when the BCCI had committed to several limited-overs series and tournaments all over the world, which made it impossible for the players to make themselves available for their domestic sides, save the odd game here and there. This had robbed the Ranji Trophy

---

[21]The England Cricket Board (ECB) instituted the Pataudi Trophy, to be presented to the winner of Test series between India and England in England, in 2007.

of some of its competitiveness. However, not much could be done on that front.

Rajbhai was not authoritative by nature and it was therefore not easy for him to run the Board, with its groups and the other issues it had to contend with. He was more or less dependent on Mr Dalmiya, with whom he fell out at the turn of the millennium.

One of his weaknesses was his love for cricketers from overseas. His decision to appoint Bob Simpson, the former Australian captain and coach, as the 'mentor' of the Indian team for the 1999 World Cup, was baffling, considering that Aunshuman Gaekwad and Brijesh Patel, two former India Test cricketers, were already on board as coach and manager respectively. I thought it was an awkward situation for everybody concerned. The presence of too many authority figures in a team can backfire and that is exactly what happened, in my view.

I also did not agree with his decision to appoint Geoff Marsh, another former Australian coach, as an 'advisor,' whose brief was to travel all over India to 'study the domestic cricket structure.' Frankly, there was (and is) nothing wrong with our domestic and junior cricket structure and hence, there was no need to conduct such a study, leave alone seeking external help to do the same. Mr Gavaskar, who was the chairman of the National Cricket Academy at the time, was also not happy and let his feelings be known. That led to some bitterness between Rajbhai and him, which resulted in Mr Gavaskar putting in his papers.

I had an unforgettable experience in 1998–99. The Indian team was on tour and a couple of players had suffered injuries. After the selectors had picked their replacements, Mr Lele, the secretary, was to brief Rajbhai, the president, before the names were announced, as per protocol. I called Rajbhai, who was in London at the time, to connect him to Mr Lele. A female voice answered the phone. Rajbhai then came on the line and asked me if I knew whom I had just spoken to. I replied in the affirmative. The lady was none other than Lata Mangeshkar.

Rajbhai was succeeded by Dr A.C. Muthiah, the son of M.A. Chidambaram. Not many members knew much about Dr Muthiah, who headed the TNCA at the time. His election was planned and executed by Mr Dalmiya. Relations between the two were harmonious till 2001, which was when equations in the Board started changing. The catalyst for the change was Mr Pawar's election as the president of the MCA. All those who were not on Mr Dalmiya's side, threw their weight behind Mr Pawar. It was at this point that Dr Muthiah began to resent Mr Dalmiya's hold over the Board, despite not holding any post at the time. He wanted to emulate his father and be his own man when it came to taking decisions.

The office-bearers had taken cognizance of the report which I had submitted after the Sri Lanka tour of 1997 and Dr Muthiah requested me to work on the graded contracts for the players. I met Sachin Tendulkar, Anil Kumble, Sourav Ganguly and Rahul Dravid when they were at a camp at Bengaluru and explained the need to present a proposal to the Board. Anil and Rahul took the lead and did a lot of work behind the scenes, preparing multiple drafts and even seeking legal opinion. Ironically, it was in 2001, just before Dr Muthiah lost the presidential election to Mr Dalmiya, that I told him that we had a proposal ready.

When the players finalized the draft of the presentation, I suggested that we show it to Mr Gavaskar and seek his feedback. The players agreed and I contacted Mr Gavaskar, who invited me to the office of Professional Management Group, his company. He went through the draft and then offered to drop me to the Board's office, on his way to the Bombay Gymkhana for his daily bout of badminton. On the way, he expressed his happiness at the fact that an attempt was being made to structure the fees of the players. He called it a welcome change from the days when some Board administrators behaved as if they were paying the players from their own pockets. I was moved when he complimented me and my role in the initiative, in his column for *The Sportstar*.[22]

Mr Gavaskar was a special invitee at the Working Committee meeting of the Board, where Anil Kumble was to present the graded payment proposal. Dr Muthiah and the other officials were of course unaware that the Little Master had already gone through the proposal. After Anil was done, Dr Muthiah sought Mr Gavaskar's views. What he said took many people by surprise.

Mr Gavaskar began by saying that he was happy that the players had taken the initiative to work out the payment structure themselves. He then told the gathering that the money belonged to the players and they could have very well decided what to do with and how to allocate it. However, they had opted to approach the Board and seek its opinion. They deserved to be complimented for the same, he said. He also praised the players for recommending that the money be distributed among their counterparts in domestic cricket.

You could have heard a pin drop when Mr Gavaskar made these points.

The revised player contracts were to be announced by Dr Muthiah at the AGM in 2001, but their implementation was delayed till 2003, as the new regime, headed by Mr Dalmiya, asked for time to study the proposal. Mr Dalmiya eventually announced during the 2003 World Cup that the Board would share 26 per cent of its revenue with the players (13 per cent with international cricketers and the remaining 13 per cent between senior and junior domestic cricketers). The

---

[22] 'On the Write Line by Gavaskar: Payments and psyche', *The Sportstar*, 9 June 2001, pp. 20–21.

significance of this decision can be gauged from the fact that Cricket Australia (CA) was sharing 25 per cent of its revenues with its cricketers at the time. The annual player retainerships were thus implemented and revised payments came into force from the 2004–05 season.

Like Mr Dalmiya, Dr Muthiah had immense trust in me. He named me the chairman of the Board's affiliation committee, which comprised Shivlal Yadav, the former Test cricketer, and Sharad Diwadkar, who had succeeded Polly kaka as executive secretary of the Board. We visited the three newly constituted states of Uttarakhand, Chhattisgarh and Jharkhand, which had been carved out of Uttar Pradesh, Madhya Pradesh and Bihar, respectively. We studied the cricketing activities and existing infrastructure in the states and submitted our recommendations along with suggestions to further develop cricket in these regions, to the Board.

Meeting Lalu Prasad Yadav, the former chief minister of Bihar who was also heading his state's cricket association, was an experience in and of itself. He took us around his house in Patna and showed us the cattle-sheds. There appeared to be a close bond between him and his cows and buffaloes. He would talk to them and they would respond with their moos. He snubbed his supporters who wanted him to pose for a picture with a bat in his hand and called Smt Rabri Devi, his wife, who was the chief minister of the state then, to come over and tell the media how the state government would extend all possible help to the Bihar Cricket Association. Incidentally, Patna had staged a league game of the 1996 World Cup when he was chief minister.

After Patna, our next stop was Jamshedpur, which was now a part of the newly created state of Jharkhand. There, we were to meet the two groups vying to be recognized as the official cricketing representatives of the state. Shivlal and I boarded a train to Jamshedpur. It departed on schedule, late in the night. We had barely dozed off when it stopped in the middle of nowhere, at around 1:00 a.m. Suddenly, a group of about 15 entered our coach, shouting slogans in support of Lalu Prasad Yadav and the Bihar Cricket Association. It was pitch dark outside and quite scary. Soon, Shivlal and I had lots of garlands around our necks even as the other passengers were wondering what was going on. The group then requested us to alight from the train for a group photograph. We were unsure, but frankly, we did not have much of a choice! We were assured that the train would leave only after we had boarded it again. Sure enough, the guard came with a lantern in hand to check if we were back on board and only then, did the train start moving. That experience made us realize who was calling the shots in Bihar, regardless of whether he was the chief minister.

Lalu Prasad Yadav visited the Wankhede Stadium to watch an international match a few weeks later, and reminded me of the affiliation. After the game, he walked all the way to the gate to board his car and enjoyed the company of the outgoing spectators on his way out!

Dr Muthiah asked me to manage the under-15 Indian teams for the Asia Cup in Malaysia and the World Cup in England, in 2000. The sides were coached by Roger Binny, one of the chief architects of the 1983 World Cup triumph, who, in his report, predicted that at least two players—Irfan Pathan and Ambati Rayudu—had it in them to represent India. The players in question did not let him down. That apart, the assignments were embarrassing for both Roger and me, as some players were clearly overage. I reported the same to Dr Muthiah. It was hugely gratifying to get an opportunity to work on eliminating this bane of Indian cricket, in subsequent years.

My stint as the manager on the Sri Lanka tour of 1997 and interactions with leading players on the graded payment structure had enabled me to establish a rapport with most of them. Apparently, some of them spoke to Dr Muthiah, who called me to the CCI one evening in late 2000 and informed me that the players wanted me to become the 'permanent manager' of the team. Dr Muthiah said that both he and Rajbhai, who was also present, endorsed the players' view in this regard. However, I was not keen. By then, I had seen enough of the Board to know how it functioned. I still had 11 years of my teaching career left and did not want to risk being in a 'neither-here-nor-there' situation, given the turbulence in the Board. Sachin called me the next day requesting me to take up the assignment, but I explained to him why I could not.

An individual who worked with both Rajbhai and Dr Muthiah as the secretary of the Board was Jaywant Lele. He was among those who invested a lot of time and energy in laying the foundation of the powerhouse that the BCCI has become today. Mr Lele wore his heart on his sleeve and believed in speaking his mind. He meant well, but because of his bluntness, was often misunderstood. He achieved much during his stint in the Board; however, it is unfortunate that he is remembered only for a statement by him, to the effect that India would lose 0-3 in Australia in 1999–2000.

The Indian team was scheduled to fly to Australia from Mumbai. Mr Lele and I had gone to the Orchid Hotel, where the players had been asked to report, to bid them farewell. Shortly after the team left for the airport, we were told by the hotel authorities that a few members of the squad had not settled their bills. Apparently, they had told the hotel staff that the Board would do so. This did not go down well with Mr Lele, and rightly so. The members of the team had been given a DA to make such payments, after all.

Mr Lele decided then and there that the money would be recovered by deducting the match fees of those who had defaulted. Dr Muthiah, the president, called Mr Lele the next day and told him that he had assured Kapil Dev, who was then the coach of the team, that the Board would settle the bills.

Mr Lele promptly reminded the president that the secretary of the Board was its executive head, as per its constitution, and the president was only the functional head of the Board. Hence, the secretary's decision could not be reversed!

It was two years since Justice Chandrachud had completed his enquiry and submitted a voluminous report to the Board. Nothing concrete emerged from his findings. Many people whom he had met said a lot of things, but they had no evidence to back their claims. It was not a police investigation, after all. No player was questioned, as that could have boomeranged on the Board. It was claimed by many, after the enquiry had concluded, that all was well.

They were in denial. What happened in early 2000 was deeply disturbing, to say the least.

7
A FRESH START

The turn of the millennium was a tough time for Indian cricket, on and off the field. When the time came to appoint a new captain after the 1999 World Cup, Ajit Wadekar, who was chairing the selection committee, thought of reinstating Sachin Tendulkar. While the move made sense, the fact was that Sachin himself was not keen. He had not enjoyed his first stint as the captain of the Indian team in 1996–97 and had even requested me to inform the selectors that he wasn't interested in another go at the job. I did what I was told, but Mr Wadekar and his colleagues still went ahead and named him captain. Sachin was taken by surprise, but he then gallantly decided to give the captaincy another shot. His second term started on a happy note, with a series win over New Zealand at home, but the tour of Australia turned out to be a disaster. One of the strongest teams of all time defeated us 3-0.

By then, Sachin had had enough and he announced his decision to step down after the end of our next assignment: a two-Test series against South Africa. He gave it everything against Hansie Cronje's side, but we still went down 0-2. Sourav Ganguly, who had served as the vice-captain on the tour of Australia, was handed the reins for the ODI series against South Africa, which we won 3-2.

It was after that ODI series that the Delhi Police released transcripts of alleged telephonic conversations between Cronje and bookies.[23] The BCCI, like everybody else, brushed off all talk of match-fixing when the reports first came out. While stories related to unethical practices had been doing the rounds for half a decade prior to the disclosures of the Delhi Police, Justice Chandrachud, who had been appointed by the Board to look into the claims, had not come up with anything significant. That was good enough for some members of the Board, who declared that nothing was amiss.

Of course, everything changed when Cronje admitted his guilt. The spotlight then shifted to the cricketers whose involvement with bookmakers had been spoken about in hushed tones in earlier years. Memories of matches which we ought to have won but had surprisingly lost, were rekindled.

The cricket-loving community felt let down. Things got worse as the days passed. Kapil Dev, the man who had led us to World Cup glory in 1983 and was now the coach of the national team, broke down in a TV interview, shortly after being named by Mr Bindra as the player who had tried to bribe Manoj Prabhakar into underperforming in an ODI against Pakistan in the mid-1990s. Questions were asked in Parliament and the government ordered the CBI to conduct an investigation and submit a report.

Among the first to be summoned by the CBI to its Delhi HQ was Mr Lele, the secretary of the Board, who had scoffed at the allegations when the story had initially broken. He was asked to report to the CBI HQ at 11:00 a.m. He reached on time, but was then made to sit in a room, all by himself. He was told that he would be called in for questioning soon. Two hours passed, but he wasn't called. He then asked the officials if he could go out for lunch. Their reply was curt: 'We know

---

[23]Partab Ramchand, 'How the match fixing drama unfolded', Espn Cricinfo, 11 April 2000, https://www.espncricinfo.com/story/how-the-match-fixing-drama-unfolded-84318. Accessed on 26 November 2021.

that you BCCI officials only eat at the Taj. Tell us what you want and it will be delivered to you from the Taj.' He was told that he could not leave the office. He then had lunch and continued to wait. Finally, at around 5:30 p.m., he was told that he could leave. He would be called some other time, the officials said. This was the CBI's way of playing on the nerves of the people it intended to question.

More individuals, including players, were summoned and questioned by the CBI, in the days that followed.

Sharad Diwadkar was the executive secretary of the Board at the time and Mr Dalmiya had requested me to help him out, as and when required. I remember going to the BCCI office one afternoon in August 2000 to collect some documents. The Indian under-15 team was to fly to England for the World Cup later that night and I was its manager. I entered the office to find a team from the CBI there and the BCCI staff sitting quietly. I was not allowed to enter Diwadkar's room and had to call him on the intercom. I dialled, and the phone was answered by another CBI official, who asked me who I was and what was the purpose of my visit. He seemed satisfied with my replies and allowed me to enter. Diwadkar was seated inside with two officials, one of whom was questioning him on the structure of the Board and its affiliated units, and the other was going through files.

One of the fallouts of the CBI's investigation was the end of the 'Sharjah era'. The venue, which the Indian team would visit at least twice a year for limited-overs tournaments, was believed to be a hotbed of unscrupulous elements and activities. The government advised the Board to cancel all upcoming tours of the cricketing oasis. The Indian team thus did not play at Sharjah after October 2000. I was also given to understand that some of the senior players had felt uncomfortable playing in Sharjah and had sounded the BCCI out about the same, and were therefore happy to not have to go there.[24]

This was bad news for the cricketers whose names had already been approved by the Board as beneficiaries of the tournaments planned in Sharjah till 2002[25]. In 2008, the BCCI compensated all the cricketers who were scheduled to receive the benefit in tournaments in Sharjah in 2001 and 2002.

The CBI interrogated the cricketers, administrators and, of course, the bookies, during the course of its investigation. Among the matches which came under scrutiny was the 1990–91 Ranji Trophy quarter-final between Mumbai and Delhi. That game was played at a time when the season in England was about to start. It had been claimed that the Delhi players who were contracted to play in the leagues in England, had deliberately allowed Mumbai to take the first-innings lead, so that Delhi would be eliminated from the tournament and they would thus be able to fly to England. The CBI censured the Delhi players, but did not recommend action against them.

The CBI indicted some of the biggest cricketing names in the country in its report. The BCCI was also criticized for not 'controlling' its affiliated units and failing to control the proliferation of limited-overs tournaments all over the world, from Sharjah to Toronto. The CBI even sought the opinion of Harish Salve, the then solicitor general of India and Justice Manoj Kumar Mukherjee, a former SC judge, on whether criminal charges could be filed against the guilty, the cricketers included. However, the charges were not filed.

Dr Muthiah, the BCCI president, referred the CBI's report to the Disciplinary Committee of the Board, of which he was a

---

[24]'Report on cricket match-fixing and related malpractises, October 2000,' Central Bureau of Investigation, New Delhi, Rediff.com, 1 November 2000, https://www.rediff.com/cricket/2000/nov/01full.htm. Accessed on 6 December 2021.

[25]Eminent former and contemporary cricketers would receive financial rewards for their contribution to the sport during tournaments played at Sharjah. The scheme was called the Cricketers Benefit Fund Series (CBFS).

member, along with vice presidents Kamal Morarka and K.M. Ram Prasad. The Board also decided to conduct an independent enquiry on the basis of the findings of the CBI and appointed K. Madhavan, the former director of the CBI, to do the same.

Mr Madhavan met all the individuals who had been named in the CBI's report and then submitted a fresh report to the Board. He felt that there was a case against four players, as well as an individual who had been part of the support staff for several years. Dr Muthiah was of the view that the Board needed to take action against those indicted, but there was a section which felt that the Board should not be too harsh. Morarka, for instance, did not agree with the president. However, Dr Muthiah and K.M. Ram Prasad were on the same page and their recommendations were eventually accepted and adopted. Azharuddin and Ajay Sharma were banned for life, Ajay Jadeja and Manoj Prabhakar were banned for five years each and strictures were also passed against Dr Ali Irani.

The bans were announced on 5 December 2000, when the Indian team was playing an ODI against Zimbabwe in Ahmedabad. I was in the city for the game and was accosted by three senior players after the news came through. They asked me how a fifth player, whose alliance with bookies they had suspected all along, had escaped the axe. I had to explain to them that the evidence against the player in question was not consequential.

How strongly the senior players felt about colleagues who were suspected to be fixing matches, can be gauged from what I had witnessed a year before. Two players, both of whom were viewed with suspicion, were picked as replacements when a couple of members of the team touring Australia, suffered injuries. However, the team management refused to accept the replacements. The selectors backed down on one of the replacements, but insisted on sending the other. This player did fly to Australia, but it was made clear to him that he was not welcome, and he eventually returned to India. Dr Bhargava, the manager, had a tough time sorting out the mess.

Although the Board did take action against those found guilty of match-fixing, I will credit the senior members of the Indian cricket team of 2000 for restoring the credibility of the sport. After all, the players were the face of Indian cricket, as far as those who loved and followed cricket were concerned. For the cricket-loving public, it did not really matter who was running the Board.

It was therefore vital for the players to make a statement. Fortunately, we had men of integrity at the helm. Sachin Tendulkar, Rahul Dravid, Anil Kumble, Javagal Srinath and Sourav Ganguly, the captain, took the initiative in bringing the smiles back on the faces of disillusioned cricket-lovers. The composure and commitment which these individuals displayed during those dark times, inspired those who had just been inducted into the side. The Indian team performed brilliantly in the ICC Knockout Trophy at Nairobi in October 2000, going all the way to the final. The senior players were complemented by Zaheer Khan and Yuvraj Singh, who made their international debuts in the tournament and went on to serve the country with distinction for over a decade. A few months later, the national team achieved an incredible Test series win over an Australian team, which had won a record 15 Tests in a row before coming to India. We lost the first Test in Mumbai in less than three days and were asked to follow-on in the second Test at Kolkata. A seventeenth consecutive win for Australia, and their first Test series win on Indian soil since 1969–70 seemed imminent, but Rahul Dravid and V.V.S. Laxman sculpted one of the greatest comebacks in sporting history. Harbhajan Singh, who, like Laxman, had been in and out of the side before that series, took 13 wickets at Kolkata and then 15 in the decider at Chennai. We won the second and third Tests to take the series 2-1. Cricket was back where it belonged, thanks to Sourav Ganguly and his team.

Mr Dalmiya prioritized the safeguarding of the Board's interests after being elected the BCCI president in September 2001. He strongly felt that the Board should highlight its side of the story and reply to the charges that had been levelled against it in the report which the CBI had submitted to the government. Some members of the Board did advise him to ignore the issue altogether 'as everything would be forgotten after a while', but Mr Dalmiya disagreed and opted to be proactive. He wanted the Board's side of the story to be made public, just like the CBI's report, which was in public domain.

A legal team was constituted to frame the Board's reply to the charges. Mr Dalmiya asked me to assist him in presenting the facts to the legal team, and I made quite a few trips to Kolkata during this phase. After the points had been compiled, Shashank Manohar, a member of the Board and legal luminary, was called upon to vet the same. Mr Dalmiya was close to Somnath Chatterjee, the Communist Party of India's veteran from Bengal and a sitting Member of Parliament, and was to seek his help in ensuring that copies of the Board's report were distributed to the Members of Parliament.

The new millennium also saw the long-overdue establishment of the National Cricket Academy (NCA). Several proposals were advanced and discussed, and ultimately, the committee, which comprised the office-bearers, Mr Gavaskar, Brijesh Patel and me, recommended that the NCA be based in Bengaluru, in space provided by the KSCA in the Chinnaswamy Stadium complex, till the BCCI created its own facility. There wasn't much information available then on how to go about setting up an academy and the consensus was that the Australian model be followed. The Australian Cricket Academy, which was situated in Adelaide at the time, had yielded many an outstanding cricketer since its inception in the late 1980s.

Rodney 'Rod' Marsh, the Australian wicketkeeping legend and a former director of the Australian Cricket Academy, was brought on board as the director of the NCA. He was assisted by Hanumant Singh and Vasudeo 'Vasu' Paranjape, both renowned coaches. Mr Gavaskar was to be the advisor and Brijesh Patel the director. The plan was to start off by replicating the Australian system of training cricketers, with the Australian model metamorphosing into an Indian version as we went along.

The collective wisdom and experience of Marsh, Singh and Paranjape, got the NCA off to a great start. Summer camps and specialised coaching camps became a regular feature at the academy. For instance, the likes of Bishan Bedi and Erapalli Prasanna were approached to conduct camps for spinners at the NCA and they readily agreed to do so.

Around a year after the launch of the NCA, the BCCI introduced the Talent Resource Development Officer (TRDO) system to identify and nurture talent across the country. Makarand Waingankar had submitted a proposal to Mr Dalmiya on the same. It was approved and implemented, with Dilip Vengsarkar being appointed as its head and Waingankar as the coordinator. Talent officers were appointed in different associations, with the list comprising former first-class cricketers such as Raju Mukherjee, Rajendrasinh Jadeja and Nariman Contractor, the former India captain, who was highly impressed with the system.

The TRDOs were supposed to observe every ball bowled in junior-level matches and prepare reports analysing the top performers in every game. Technical assistance was provided to the TRDOs in the form of a video analyst, who would feed the details into a specially created software. These reports were then shared with Dilip Vengsarkar and Brijesh Patel, who was then the director of the NCA. The system worked extremely well and was instrumental in the Board identifying a number of cricketers who went on to represent India. Dilip was authorised to attend meetings of the national junior selection committee to shortlist boys for camps at the NCA and also to select the national under-19 team for bilateral series or tournaments like the World Cup.

Dilip had an eye for talent and would back players, even if their own state association or the national selectors were hesitant. Paul Valthaty was a classic example. An outstanding young cricketer, he was not picked in the zonal side as the selectors did not find his performances satisfactory. He thus missed the inter-zonal tournament, on the basis of which the probables for the India under-19 team were to be selected. Dilip convinced Mr Dalmiya about Valthaty's calibre and got him picked directly, first in the probables and then in the national under-19 team.

Another significant development that occurred in 2000 was the appointment of India's first foreign coach. While it wasn't that the team hadn't done well under all those who had coached the side in the 1990s, the senior members of the team were keen on having someone who could provide a different perspective. Greg Chappell, the former Australia captain, was in the running for the job, as was Geoffrey Marsh, who had coached the Australians to World Cup success in 1999, but the man who pipped both to the post was John Wright, the former New Zealand captain. The senior players and Board had first-hand information on Wright, courtesy Rahul Dravid, who had played for Kent (the team that Wright coached) in the English County Championship in 2000. Rahul had spoken to Sourav and Sachin, both of whom concurred with his assessment of Wright.

Wright came on board without any baggage. Andrew Leipus, a qualified physiotherapist, was already with the team. Wright and he got along very well and reinforcements arrived the following year in the form of Adrian Le Roux, who was appointed trainer. Le Roux was succeeded by Greg King after the 2003 World Cup. All these individuals were consummate professionals, who earned the respect and trust of the players and got the best out of them. Wright was an excellent man manager. He was generous when it came to praise and harsh when it came to criticism. However, he never went overboard with either. His consistency was appreciated even by those who found themselves at the receiving end of a verbal rocket from him. Leipus's injury management skills were brilliant, as were the training routines brought in and managed by first Le Roux and then King.

The work put in by these men behind the scenes significantly boosted the endeavour of the players to guide Indian cricket to unprecedented heights. They were fitter than ever before and it reflected in the cricket they produced. We reached the final of the ICC CWC 2003 and retained the Border–Gavaskar Trophy on Australian soil the following season, after drawing a series which Steve Waugh's side had been expected to win 4-0. We then achieved a historic double in Pakistan in 2003–04, winning both the ODI and Test series. The dark days of 2000 were forgotten for good.

A story related to the ICC Cricket World Cup 2003 needs to be recounted here. Sahara Pariwar, the team sponsors, announced that every member of the team would be gifted an apartment in the plush Aamby Valley City, which they had created off the Mumbai-Pune Expressway, if India were to win the World Cup. We did reach the final of the World Cup, but lost to Australia. Subrata Roy, the Sahara India Pariwar chairman, then declared that the members of the team would still be honoured and gifted a seven-star deluxe apartment each. A grand function was held in Aamby Valley City, in the presence of distinguished guests like Amitabh Bachchan, the megastar, where the members of the World Cup squad were handed ownership certificates of the apartments. It was announced that the apartments would be allotted later.

There was no news on the allotment for the next one year. Some of the players brought up the issue during the tour of Pakistan and requested me to check when the allotment was to take place. When I inquired about the same after our return, I was told that a special 'World Cup Enclave' was being constructed at Aamby Valley City, where members of the World Cup team could stay for a limited period of time. One of the players informed me later that the terms of the agreement sent to them did not mention ownership rights. On the contrary, the players were expected to pay maintenance fees and other charges for using the facility!

There was an unpleasant event in 2003. Sharad Diwadkar was offended by something that the personal assistant of S.K. Nair, the Board secretary, said to him, and decided to resign. We tried to reason with Diwadkar, but he did not budge. A proud, self-respecting individual, he explained that there was no way he could continue as the executive secretary after being insulted by the assistant of an office-bearer.

It was therefore expected that a new executive secretary would be appointed at the AGM of the Board, which was to be held in Kolkata, later that year.

With Mr Pawar having become the anchor of the anti-Dalmiya group in the Board by that time, it was obvious that the MCA, which I was representing at the AGM, would not side with Mr Dalmiya's group, which was in a majority. Hence, I was surprised when Mr Dalmiya called me to meet him on the day before the AGM and told me that he wanted me to become the joint secretary of the Board. He would convince his group not to object to my candidature, he said.

Mr Pawar was aware of Mr Dalmiya's affection for me and he had no issues with my taking up the post. Thus, I became an office-bearer of the Board for the first time. Mr Dalmiya also proposed during the AGM that I could also look after the Mumbai office of the Board. The members agreed and I was given additional charge as the executive secretary of the Board.

The challenge before me was to live up to the standards set by my predecessors in that position. Mr N.D. Karmarkar had served the Board as the assistant secretary from 1948, when the office moved into the North Stand of the Brabourne stadium, till 1980. He was succeeded by Prof. Chandgadkar, who officiated in the redesignated post of Executive Secretary from 1980 to 1984. Polly kaka was appointed in 1987 and succeeded by Diwadkar, a decade later.

While I was happy to take over as the executive secretary, I did not want to give up my teaching job and made it clear that I could go to the Board's office only in the afternoons. I accordingly suggested that my post be an honorary one. The members agreed to the same. Luckily for me, my home in Mazgaon and workplace (Wilson College) were relatively close to each other. I would go to the college in the morning and complete my classes. I would then reach the BCCI office by 2:00 p.m. and be there till 5:00 p.m., after which I would go to the office of the MCA at the Wankhede Stadium. In those days, the BCCI office handled only the postings of umpires and match officials and sent out itineraries and match schedules, apart from archiving correspondence between the Board and the outside world and storing the trophies won by the Indian team.

As the executive secretary, I was a witness to the tussle for the coveted television rights in 2004. The Board made the most of its 1991 realization that it owned the television rights, in the years that followed. The rights for all matches played in India from 1994 to 1999 were sold to TWI for ₹98 crore. Doordarshan, who had by then realized that it was missing out, entered the bidding race in 1999 and acquired the rights for the next five years for ₹230 crore. The next bid, in 2004, became a two-horse race between Zee and ESPN and and it was expected to yield the BCCI around ₹2,000 crore. It was this episode that sowed the seeds of the rift between Mr Dalmiya and Mr N. Srinivasan, who had joined the Board by then and was the chairman of the finance committee. When the tender documents were opened, it was found that Zee had quoted the higher amount. However, Mr Dalmiya felt that ESPN ought to be given an opportunity to match Zee's figure, considering that the channel had been a rights' holder in the past. Mr Srinivasan, on the other hand, felt that the Board should simply go with the party which had quoted the higher amount.

Technically, Zee was the winner and was therefore awarded the rights, but ESPN contested the decision and took the matter to court. The Board was made a party and so was Zee. The matter came up for hearing in the Bombay High Court. I was in the courtroom every day and had plenty of company. The courtroom would be packed to capacity to hear the arguments and counterarguments of K.K. Venugopal, the counsel of the Board, and Harish Salve, the son of N.K.P. Salve, the former BCCI president, who was representing Zee.

Until that point, the government had always supported the BCCI and recognized it as the only body responsible for the administration and promotion of cricket in the country. However, an affidavit was filed in the court around the time the Zee-ESPN issue was being heard in court, the contents of which were rather vague, although it did appear that the government was deviating from its earlier stand. Mr Dalmiya sensed that the government was getting restive and realized that he needed to do something before things got out of hand. He called me late in the night when the Zee-ESPN matter was being heard, and told me about the provision to cancel the bids altogether, which was a part of the tender document. I conveyed his instructions to Mr Venugopal the following morning.

I will never forget the drama that ensued. The audience

arrived, followed by the lawyers and then the judges. When the proceedings began at 11:00 a.m. sharp, Mr Venugopal announced that the Board was exercising its right, which had been explicitly mentioned in the tender document, to cancel the bid and call for fresh bids. The courtroom went deathly quiet when he said that. The silence was broken by the judges, both of whom agreed that the Board was well within its rights to do so.

Zee challenged the cancellation of the bids and appealed to the SC, where it was referred to a constitutional bench of five judges, headed by Justice N. Santosh Hegde. The Board then filed an affidavit, claiming that it was an autonomous body. One of the things the affidavit mentioned was that the Board selected a team 'to represent the BCCI and not India'. This was always going to be controversial and the Board came in for a lot of flak from the media, public and former cricketers. Eventually, the five-judge bench headed by Justice N. Santosh Hegde announced a split verdict in favour of the BCCI, in February 2005. The Apex Court ruled that the BCCI did not fall within the ambit of Article 12, as it was an autonomous body, not created by any statute, not funded by the government and was not directly controlled by the government. This was a historic judgement, as significant as the one on the TV rights a decade previously. This judgement also meant that the BCCI was not covered under the Right to Information (RTI) Act, as per the existing rules framed by Parliament.

The legal proceedings delayed the calling of fresh bids for a couple of years, during which the Board sold the rights on a series-by-series basis to Prasar Bharati, which ran Doordarshan. Telecast of international matches was compulsory, as per the ICC's norms. I have to state here that the Board did not earn the full value of the rights in this period. In case a match ended earlier than scheduled, Prasar Bharati would pay the Board a reduced amount, taking into account the revenue it had lost out on in terms of advertisements because the match had ended early.

All this changed with Mr Pawar's election as the BCCI president in November 2005. The BCCI tendered the TV rights afresh in early 2006, for the period from 2006 to 2010. Nimbus Communications won the rights after bidding an astronomical $612 million, which worked out to around ₹2,500 crore for four years.

8

ACROSS THE BORDER, 2004

India was due to tour Pakistan for a full series in early 2004. However, the spectre of terrorism loomed large and threatened to play spoilsport. The Kargil conflict between the two nations had taken place less than five years previously, and therefore cynics were convinced that the series would be called off.

From a commercial point of view, a cancellation would have been bad news, as every series between the traditional rivals is a guaranteed blockbuster and money-spinner. It all boiled down to the governments of the two countries, whose clearance was needed, when it came to bilateral series. The Pakistani government was willing but the Indian government appeared to be wary, and understandably so. India had extended a hand of friendship, only to be let down on multiple occasions. Having said that, the government had no objections to cricket matches against Pakistan in ICC and Asian Cricket Council (ACC) tournaments.

Cricket lovers in both countries were delighted when Atal Behari Vajpayee, the prime minister of India, announced that his government was open to the possibility of a series between India and Pakistan. The last Test series between the two teams on Pakistani soil in 1989–90 had been drawn 0-0 and witnessed some impressive performances by players of both sides, but there had also been a couple of unsavoury incidents. A spectator had run onto the field during the first Test at Karachi and attacked K. Srikkanth, the Indian captain. The intruder was apprehended, but not before he had torn a couple of buttons off Srikkanth's shirt. The tour went on only because the Indian team management chose to treat the incident as an aberration. Later on in the tour, an ODI at the same venue had to be called off due to the unruly behaviour of the spectators.

We in the BCCI did not want to take any chances in 2004. Senior government officials were consulted and it was decided to send a reconnaissance team to Pakistan. This team comprised Yashovardhan Azad[26], a senior IPS officer, Amrit Mathur, who had accompanied the team as the media manager on a couple of tours, and myself. Mr Azad had managed the security on Prime Minister Vajpayee's visit to Islamabad for the SAARC Summit in 2003, as well as some of President A.P.J. Abdul Kalam's trips overseas. He had also supervised the security arrangements of the Pakistani team on its tour of India in 1998–99.

The three of us flew to Lahore, where we had a preliminary meeting with Mr Shaharyar Khan, the president of the Pakistan Cricket Board (PCB) and a distinguished former foreign secretary in his country's government. He was also the first cousin of Mansoor Ali Khan Pataudi, our former captain. We also met Ramiz Raja, the former Pakistan captain and CEO of the PCB.[27] We proceeded to Islamabad, the capital, where we met Mr Shivshankar Menon, the Indian high commissioner, and sought his advice. We then visited Rawalpindi, Islamabad's twin city and one of the probable hosts. In Karachi, our next destination, we were surprised to see people lining the streets on either side and holding posters bearing the images of Vajpayee and Pervez Musharraf, the president of Pakistan. Their message was loud and clear.

---

[26]The brother of Kirti Azad, one of the members of the 1983 World Cup-winning team.
[27]Ramiz Raja is now the chairman of the PCB.

We subsequently visited Peshawar, Multan and Faisalabad. In every city, top officials of the Pakistani Army and Police briefed us on the security and travel arrangements which would be in place for the Indian team. We travelled extensively through the country, mostly by air and also by road and saw quite a bit of Pakistan. The high commissioner quipped when we met him again in Lahore, just before returning to India, that we had probably seen a lot more of Pakistan than many Pakistanis themselves! He had come to Lahore to participate in the city's traditional kite-flying festival, which is quite a spectacle. The kites are affixed to fine metal wires and flown, and contests are celebrated by firing gunshots in the air.

The final meeting of the trip, at the PCB's HQ in Lahore, was attended by officials of Pakistan's interior ministry. We were assured that the security arrangements for the Indian team would be equivalent to those provided to a head of State. We then returned to India and Mr Azad submitted our report to the Home Ministry.

Apparently, the Muttahida Qaumi Movement (MQM), a political party which was in power in Karachi, was keen to host a Test match in the port city and had even requested Shri L.K. Advani, our deputy prime minister and a resident of Karachi in his formative years, to put in a word. However, after our reconnaissance trip, we had come to the conclusion that both Karachi and Peshawar should be hosting ODIs, that too during the day, and not Test matches. Both cities were known to be volatile and we wanted our players to spend as little time there as possible. A couple of years previously, a bomb explosion in Karachi, in the vicinity of the hotel in which the New Zealand team had been staying, had resulted in the termination of that series.

Our recommendation that the Tests be played at Multan, Lahore and Rawalpindi, and the ODIs at Karachi, Rawalpindi, Peshawar and Lahore, was agreed upon. The PCB also accepted our request that the ODIs be played before the Tests.

Even as the planning was on, there were some stories doing the rounds that members of the Indian team, which was then in Australia, were concerned about their safety and hence hesitant to tour. The players were then briefed at length and Mr Dalmiya, the Board president, gave them the option to skip the tour if they had concerns. However, all the players declared themselves available. It was decided that the cricket team would be accompanied by the reconnaissance team. I was appointed the manager, Amrit Mathur was named the media manager and Mr Azad was one of two officials assigned to oversee the security arrangements.

We assembled in New Delhi a day before our departure and were briefed by officials of the Home and External Affairs ministries on the protocols which we had to follow, on the tour. The Prime Minister's Office (PMO) had planned a detour for us before we flew to Lahore the following day. We were to meet the prime minister himself at his residence before proceeding to the airport. I received a fax from the PMO, which mentioned the names of all those whose entry into the prime minister's official residence had been 'approved'. Interestingly, the PMO had struck off the names of S.K. Nair, the BCCI secretary, Jyoti Bajpai, the BCCI treasurer and Rajeev Shukla, the BCCI vice president, from the list. The officials in question were not pleased one bit, but there was nothing that could be done. The name of S. 'Ramky' Ramakrishnan, the team's video analyst, had been left out from the list which the Board had sent to the PMO for approval, and the poor guy had to sit in the bus and while away his time outside the prime minister's residence, as a result.

The prime minister spent nearly an hour with the team. We gifted him a bat autographed by the players and I told him about our reconnaissance trip and the banners we had seen in Karachi. In his address to the team, he emphasized the need to win hearts. *'Khel bhi jeeto aur dil bhi* (Win the game and also, the hearts),' he said. Just as we were preparing to take his leave, he asked the naval band to play *'Hum honge kaamyaab'* (We shall overcome). He wished us luck and the players in turn promised him that they would do their best, on and off the field. They kept their word.

The series had elicited a tremendous amount of interest and many Indians were eager to travel to Pakistan to watch the matches. The two governments deliberated and announced the issuance of more than 5,000 'cricket' visas. Cricket fans and media persons apart, film stars, several industrialists and politicians from India crossed the Wagah Border in the days that followed. Everything went off smoothly, except the Pakistani government's denial of a visa to Mr Farooq Abdullah, the former chief minister of Jammu and Kashmir.

The Pakistanis rolled out the red carpet. The BCCI was allowed to extend invitations to former India captains and representatives of the affiliated units, for matches of their choice. Arrangements were made for their travel and accommodation, and they were also given a DA by the Board. The BCCI also designed a special tie for the tour and the office-bearers carried with them mementos to present to dignitaries, including the president of Pakistan. Airtel was given special permission to operate mobile phone services in Pakistan for the duration of the series. The PCB sold the broadcasting rights to Ten Sports for a princely amount and Samsung was roped in as the series sponsor.

We were welcomed warmly in Lahore. The security arrangements were foolproof, as promised. The Elite Force of the Punjab Province (the equivalent of the National Security Guard [NSG] in India) with the caption 'No Fear' printed on their jerseys, was in charge. The bus that took us to the hotel was part of a convoy which comprised 19 other vehicles, including pilot cars (open jeeps with security personnel) and motorcyclists, a decoy bus, an ambulance, and even a fire brigade, whose presence confounded the players. Traffic was closed on both sides of the roads on our journey from the airport to the hotel. This practice was followed right through the tour at all the centres, whenever the team travelled from the hotel to the venue and back.

The day we landed, the health minister of Pakistan got in touch with me and asked if a couple of players could endorse the government's polio awareness and eradication campaign on radio. Sachin and Laxman volunteered for the same and both were felicitated for doing so, during the third Test of the series.

We stayed at the impressive Pearl Continental. When we went downstairs for dinner, we saw fans of Sachin in the lobby. He was happy to oblige their request for autographs and they quickly formed a queue. It was all done in an orderly manner. What we realized on that first evening was that the vegetarians in the team were in for a tough time. The others would also have to be careful, as the non-vegetarian delicacies on offer were delightful. We had of course conveyed to the hosts that we would not have beef. We played a warm-up one-dayer in Lahore, which we lost, before flying to Karachi for the first ODI. Ranjan Madugalle, the ICC match referee, met the captains, coaches and managers of both sides in Karachi and emphasized the need for good cricket and decorum on the field.

The Pakistan Rangers, their equivalent of our Border Security Force (BSF), which was handling the security in Karachi, had locked up the city on the day of the game. No vehicles, other than those accredited by the authorities, were allowed to ply in the vicinity of the venue on the day of the game and the spectators had to walk the last mile to the ground. The security barriers, which the spectators had to clear, comprised a facial recognition software, the aim of which was to prevent potential troublemakers from getting in. The match turned out to be a high-scoring thriller, which we won. The spectators enjoyed the cricket and it was heartening to see the tricolour being waved along with its Pakistani counterpart. Watching the game from the stands were Arun Jaitley and the Gandhi siblings, Rahul and Priyanka. They were accompanied by Rajeev Shukla.

After the match, the security officials decided to transport the members of the team to the hotel in vans, even as the bus remained a part of the convoy. This was where we encountered the first and as it turned out, only security lapse of the tour. A boy was found in the van, which was transporting Sachin and a few other players. It emerged that he was the son of an Inspector-General of Police and wanted to meet Sachin. Mr Azad took up the matter with the security officials and we were assured that there would be no such lapse henceforth.

We flew to Islamabad for the next ODI at Rawalpindi, the following morning. We checked in at the Pearl Continental there and switched on the TV, only to discover that a truck laden with a huge amount of liquid explosive had been found near the American embassy in Karachi, which was situated only 500 metres from the Pearl Continental in Karachi, where we had stayed.

We had our chances in the second ODI, but did not grab them and Pakistan levelled the series, a brilliant 141 by Sachin notwithstanding. President Musharraf hosted both the teams for a tea party at his residence the next day. He was in a jovial mood as he interacted with the players of both sides and cracked jokes, some at the expense of the Pakistani team. He described the lavish spread of food, which was rich in ghee, as 'weapons of mass destruction'.

Like Karachi, Peshawar, where we played the third ODI, had been converted into a fortress by the security agencies. This did not deter some of the players and support staff from expressing their desire to shop for carpets, for which Peshawar is known. Sachin was as popular in Pakistan as he was in India and the owner of one of the carpet shops was desperate to sell a specially designed one to him. He followed us all over the country and waited for Sachin in the lobbies of the hotels where we were staying, but did not succeed. When I mentioned this to Sachin, he told me jokingly that the carpet he was being offered was costlier than one tyre of his Ferrari! Eventually, Virender Sehwag went up to the man in one of the hotels and told him that he could have saved on all the travelling had he gifted the carpet to Sachin in Peshawar itself.

We lost at Peshawar, which meant that we would have to win the last two matches, both of which were to be played at Lahore, to take the series. We reached Lahore the next morning and got the news that rocket launchers had been fired in Peshawar after the game. This was alarming. First the truck in Karachi and now rockets in Peshawar. Would we run out of luck as the tour went on?

We won the fourth ODI, a day-nighter, thanks to a remarkable partnership between Rahul Dravid and Mohammad Kaif. The win triggered the usual allegations of match-fixing by Rashid Latif, the former Pakistan captain and a usual suspect when it came to allegations of that variety. Needless to say, no one took him seriously. We batted first in the decider, also a day-nighter, and set Pakistan a target of 294. I was amused when Sourav got into a huddle with the players in the dressing room and exhorted them to forget the 'winning-hearts' bit and do whatever it took to win the match and the series.

The captain was forced to leave the field shortly after the start of Pakistan's innings, as he strained his back while trying to stop a hit in the outfield. Rahul, the vice-captain and ODI wicketkeeper at the time, took over as a result. The Pakistanis tried hard, but we outplayed them that night. Sourav was still wincing in pain when the players returned to the dressing room in triumph, with Leipus working on his back. I said to Rahul that he would have to receive the trophy as Sourav did not seem to be in a condition to attend the presentation ceremony. However, Sourav said that he would manage.

The first phone call I received on my mobile after the game was from Lata Mangeshkar. She congratulated the team, as did our prime minister and deputy prime minister. The players were touched when the general officer commanding (GOC), Western Command of the Indian Army, sent a message the next morning, congratulating the team and saying that our series win meant a lot to the soldiers stationed at the border.

There was a large Indian contingent in the stands, with celebrities from the entertainment and corporate world also in attendance. The scenes we witnessed after the game were to be seen to be believed. Imagine Indians waving the tricolour and dancing to the beat of drums being played by Pakistanis, on the streets of Lahore! Unbelievable, but then, that is exactly what happened that night.

The hospitality of the Pakistanis was not restricted to the members of the Indian team. The fans who had travelled from India were also offered free food, free rickshaw rides and heavy discounts on purchases.

I was informed that the Pakistanis were thrilled at the prospect of Ms Dina Wadia, the daughter of Mohammed Ali Jinnah, the founder of Pakistan, coming to Lahore to watch the last two ODIs. The Wadia family is revered in Pakistan for obvious reasons. Ms Wadia came with her son Nusli and grandsons Ness and Jehangir and expressed her appreciation of the 'cricket diplomacy' which was being practised to improve relations between the two countries. When Pakistan toured India three years later, we hosted a dinner for both the teams at Mr Pawar's official residence in New Delhi. Nusli Wadia, Jinnah's grandson, was one of the invitees. The Pakistan squad waited till he arrived and each member of the team knelt before him and kissed his hand as a mark of respect.

As the manager of the Indian team, I could not help but note how much things had changed—be it the attitude of our players, their conversations in the dressing room and their approach to training sessions—since my last managerial assignment on the tour of Sri Lanka in 1997. This transformation owed itself to the professionals who constituted the support staff and the introduction of technology. SportsMechanics, our video analyst Ramky's company, had developed a software which could help analyse the happenings in an entire match, with inputs from the official broadcaster's live feed. This enabled the players to study their performances in every game. Ramky had also studied the footage of the last three series played by Pakistan and compiled video dossiers on every batsman and bowler whom we were likely to come up against. These dossiers were used by the team to strategize. It was a pleasure to see every member of the side participating in the discussions. The meetings were purposeful and the outlook of the players, positive. The support staff, which consisted of John Wright, Andrew Leipus and Greg King (Adrian Le Roux before him) had well and truly transformed the Indian team.

There were some changes in the squad for the Test series. Sourav, who had not recovered from his back injury, decided to return to Kolkata and consult a specialist. Rahul thus took charge for the first two Tests, which were to be played at Multan and Lahore, respectively.

Multan was known for its Sufi saints and as the hometown of Inzamam-ul-Haq. The stadium where the Test was to be played, was also on the outskirts of the city, and attendance was sparse as a result. We created history, winning a Test on Pakistani soil for the first time. The hosts were never in the game after we batted first and scored 675-5, with Viru becoming the first Indian to score a triple 100 in Tests. We eventually won by an innings and 52 runs, but both the triple century and the innings victory were overshadowed by an episode that could well have torn the team apart, had its protagonists not nipped it in the bud themselves.

The team's plan was to declare and give Pakistan at least an hour (15 overs) of batting on the second day. Sachin was on 194 and at the non-striker's end when Ramesh Powar, one of the reserves, was instructed to convey a message to the batsmen in the middle that the declaration would be made after one more over. Ramesh conveyed the message to Yuvraj Singh, who was on strike on the first ball of the next over, but not to Sachin. As it happened, Yuvraj was caught-and-bowled off the very first ball and Rahul closed the innings immediately. It was a classic instance of a communication gap. I personally felt that there was a lot of time left in the game and Sachin could have been given a couple of overs in which to complete his double century.

Sachin was unhappy with the declaration and visibly angry. He did not take the field that evening and expressed his displeasure at the end-of-day press conference. That set the cat among the pigeons. Sections of the media started claiming that there was a 'rift' within the team. Former cricketers in both India and Pakistan also entered the fray, some of them siding with Sachin and others with Rahul. Javed Miandad, the coach of the Pakistan team and someone who would do anything to provoke the opposition, said that he commiserated with Sachin. He even recalled his being stranded just 20 runs short of a triple century, when Imran Khan decided to declare in a Test against India in 1982–83.

Something needed to be done. I had a long chat with Sachin that evening and also spoke to Rahul. Wright also spoke to both and played a critical role in getting them to be frank with each other. Sachin and Rahul then met up the next morning and decided to look ahead rather than back.

Sourav was still with the team and due to fly to Kolkata a couple of days later. A story appeared in *The Pioneer*, an Indian daily, the next day, featuring a quote attributed to Sourav, along the lines that 'he would have waited for Sachin to get his 200 had he been captain.' Rahul was very upset when he heard of the story. Unfortunately for Indranil Basu, the journalist who had filed the story, I spotted him in the lobby of our hotel, where I was seated with Sourav and Rahul and trying to sort out the misunderstanding created by the report. I called Indranil over and confronted him in the presence of the two players. He then apologized for the quote, which he said he had added of his own volition.

We won the game early on the fifth day and the boys agreed to visit the SOS Children's Village at Multan, where the children welcomed the team with a short entertainment programme, before spending almost an hour playing with the Indian cricketers. Their joy knew no bounds.

One of my memories of the Test is being told by Ranjan Madugalle, the referee, to talk to Viru, who had had an altercation with Shoaib Akhtar on the field. When I asked Viru what had transpired between him and Akhtar, his response was hilarious. He said that the Rawalpindi Express was constantly telling him to hit him over mid-wicket. Finally, Viru asked him why he, a fast bowler, was behaving like a beggar.

Viru was a character. He was to get married after the series and told me a funny story related to the same. An official of the Delhi and District Cricket Association (DDCA) had already asked him for 10 extra invitation cards for his wedding reception. I had heard of and even encountered people demanding extra passes for matches, but someone demanding extra invites for a wedding was a new one!

While on funny incidents, I must mention one involving V.V.S. Laxman. I was in the lobby of the hotel, when our security-in-charge walked up to me and told me that he had arranged for a black horse as requested. I had no clue what he was talking about. He then took me to the parking lot, where Suman, one of the Indian photographers, was clicking pictures of Laxman, who was in his cricketing whites, sitting on a horse.

I organized a team dinner on the eve of the second Test at Lahore, in an attempt to sort the declaration issue out, once and for all. However, the players had moved on already, much to my relief. We lost the Test, despite a fine hundred by Yuvraj Singh, who had replaced Sourav in the XI. Some key umpiring decisions went against us when the Pakistanis batted, and that left Anil Kumble, among others, furious. When the team came in for a lunch break, Anil saw a packet of sweets on the table. He summoned a steward, handed him the packet of sweets and told him to deliver the same to Steve Bucknor, the umpire who had negatived most of our appeals. I had to intervene and stop the steward from doing so.

The extra time we got to spend in Lahore gave us the opportunity to look and move around. There was an invitation from the Lahore University of Management Studies. Rahul Dravid, V.V.S. Laxman and Lakshmipathi Balaji, whose hitting in the slog overs in the ODIs had made him a sensation in Pakistan, went over and interacted with the students, who turned up in large numbers.

Imran Khan, who is now the prime minister of Pakistan, invited us to his Cancer Hospital in the city. The players went around the facility and met members of the staff.

We also visited the Wagah Border to witness the 'Beating the Retreat' ceremony, where the Indian and Pakistani flags were simultaneously lowered at sunset, watched by people on either side. Watching the ceremony from the Pakistani side was a novel experience. The players were permitted to walk all the way up to the line that separated the two countries, and Sachin came up with the idea of clicking a photograph with one leg on the Indian side and the other on the Pakistani side. This was not appreciated by an official of the Pakistani army.

The players had got used to the surroundings by then and were a lot more comfortable. Some of them had asked their spouses to join them for the Test series. Masood bhai, our liaison manager, went out of his way to indulge the players. He organized sightseeing and shopping excursions for them. In Lahore, we were invited by one of the locals who had a huge DVD shop. A few of the players went and were told by the owner to pick whichever DVDs they wanted, free of cost. I must add here that we witnessed one of the biggest piracy industries in operation. Everybody was busy duplicating DVDs of recently released Hindi films.

During the Lahore Test, I received a message that Fazal Mahmood, one of Pakistan's all-time greats, wanted to see me. When I went over to the box where he was seated, he told me that he wanted to meet Sachin. I invited him to our dressing room at the end of the day's play. He just held Sachin's hand for some time and told him that he was a big fan of his. When I introduced him to Rahul, Mr Mahmood started telling him about Sachin and how he had watched most of his innings on television.

Sourav's return for the final Test at Rawalpindi necessitated a change in the XI. As Yuvraj had done well in the previous game, it was decided to leave Akash Chopra out. But then, who would open the batting with Viru, was the question. Sourav surprised all of us by announcing at the press conference on the day prior to the Test that he would open. However, it was Parthiv Patel, who had been struggling a bit behind the stumps, who went in with Viru, after we had dismissed Pakistan cheaply on the first day. We thought that John Wright had Parthiv's wicketkeeping on his mind when he took the youngster aside for a chat at the lunch interval on the first day. It turned out that Parthiv told John during that conversation that Sourav had asked him to open the innings.

Viru fell on the first ball, but Rahul was solid and he and

Parthiv took us through to the close. Sourav and I were sitting on the balcony of our dressing room, when play ended for the day. A little later, we saw the media contingent from Bengal making its way towards the press conference hall for the end-of-day interaction. All the journalists looked dejected. Sourav told me the reason. In their reports the day before, all of them had highlighted his decision to open the batting and his 'sacrificing' his middle-order slot for Yuvraj. However, Parthiv's opening the batting that afternoon had put them in a fix. They were now wondering what to say to their respective editors back in Kolkata, who would surely demand an explanation from them!

Rahul scored an epic 270 and we went on to win the Test by an innings and 131 runs. It was one of Team India's biggest-ever Test wins and that it sealed a series win in Pakistan was the icing on the cake. It was the first time since 1986 that India had won both the ODI and Test series on a tour.

There was an embarrassing moment for me during the game, when Sachin and I were following Mumbai's progress in the Ranji Trophy semi-final against Railways. I was getting score updates on my phone and we were discussing the game when Yuvraj, accompanied by Viru, came up to us and challenged me to tell them what India's score was in the ongoing Test match, without looking at the scoreboard. I had to admit that I was unaware of the same.

Shivshankar Menon, our high commissioner, was at the ground on all the days of the Rawalpindi Test. He had been a great help during the series and reconnaissance trip. He had treated the team to dinner earlier on the tour and had arranged for sumptuous meals for the vegetarians in the team during the final Test. His presence in our dressing room during the final session of the Test attracted the attention of Shoaib Akhtar, who had spent a substantial part of our innings off the field, due to a hand injury. Much to the exasperation of the Pakistani team management, Akhtar requested me to speak to Mr Menon about clearing his visa application for India at the earliest, as he had an advertisement shoot lined up.

The final highlight of what had been a historic tour was Mr Shaharyar Khan's address to the team at the hotel, just before our return to India. He spoke eloquently and praised the manner in which the boys had carried themselves both on and off the field. He hailed them as true ambassadors of cricket and India. I made some long-lasting friendships with Mr Shaharyar Khan himself, as also Zakir Khan, Subhan Ahmed, Asad Mustafa and Sami Ul Hasan, all of whom worked for the PCB.

Our travel plans had to be advanced as the Test ended on the fourth day itself. Indian Airlines was kind enough to organize a special flight to Delhi at short notice. The seats which were left after the players and support staff had been accommodated were offered to the Indian media. The scenes at the airport in Delhi were chaotic, with some over-enthusiastic politicians having arranged a reception for us to gain mileage. We turned them down and focussed on organizing flights for all the non-Delhi players to reach their respective hometowns, instead.

I enjoyed the experience of managing some of the best cricketers in the world on what was a successful and historic tour. The only time I got angry was when some of the players went for a party hosted by the Punjab chief minister's son, outside the hotel at Lahore, without seeking the permission of the security team. I had to issue a stern warning to the errant players as it was clearly a security breach.

The success of the tour raised hopes of more bilateral tours between the neighbours. It was a no-brainer that 'India v/s Pakistan' would be much bigger than the Ashes. The BCCI and PCB also decided to play an annual first-class game between the Ranji Trophy champions and the winners of the Quaid-E-Azam Trophy, Pakistan's premier domestic competition, for the Mohammad Nissar Trophy. Mohammad Nissar, a giant of a cricketer, literally and figuratively, had taken the new ball for India in its inaugural Test in 1932 and become the first Indian to take five wickets in a Test innings, in the game. In fact, he also took a 'five-for' in his sixth and last Test, against England at the Oval in 1936. A decade later, he opted to settle in Pakistan after Partition. Three editions of the Mohammad Nissar Trophy were played in all. In 2006, the UPCA defeated Sialkot in Dharamshala; in 2007, Mumbai defeated Karachi Urban in Karachi and; in 2008, Sui Northern Gas Pipelines defeated DDCA at Delhi.

The next four seasons witnessed three more Test series—two in India (2004–05 and 2007–08) and one in Pakistan (2005–06)—before relations between the two countries nosedived all over again after the terrorist attack in Mumbai in November 2008.

Bilateral cricketing relations between the nations resumed in December 2012, when Pakistan toured India to play two T20 Internationals and three ODIs. The success of this mini series prompted the BCCI and the PCB to plan a tour of Pakistan by an Indian team in 2014, subject to the clearance of the Government of India. However, this tour did not materialize as we did not get the go-ahead. No international side had toured Pakistan following the attack on the Sri Lankan team in 2009, in any case.

When the BCCI refused to tour, the PCB lodged an official protest with the ICC and filed a complaint with the ICC's Dispute Resolution Forum (DRF), claiming compensation of ₹4.5 billion from the BCCI to cover up the loss of revenue. I agreed to help the BCCI's legal team in framing its replies to the charges and also appeared as one of the witnesses before the DRF, headed by Michael Beloff, in October 2018. The PCB lost the case and had to pay the BCCI 60 per cent of the legal costs incurred by the latter, apart from paying the ICC and its own legal team, of course. Thus, the PCB ended up draining its own coffers, instead of getting compensation from the BCCI.

9
AGM TALES

The AGM of the BCCI has been the biggest 'off-the-field' event in Indian cricket for decades. Every AGM was, and is, preceded by thorough planning and canny strategizing by those seeking to run Indian cricket. Traditionally, every AGM in which an election has been held, has featured unanticipated twists and turns, with the media going all out to shadow the protagonists and report the happenings.

In fact, we in the Board would joke that if a tender for telecast rights of the AGM were to be issued, the bidding for the same would be intensely competitive. Even seasoned politicians were wary of BCCI politics, with only 30 voters in the game and no clarity as to whom they would support.

Traditionally, there were some individuals who were fence-sitters and hence 'kingmakers'. They were able to bag plum posts in the various committees and also bag selection and managerial assignments for their supporters. A recurring feature of the AGMs was the presence of a team of officials and hangers-on from state associations, despite only one representative being permitted to attend, per association. The others would travel at the association's expense, of course, and they would lobby for positions.

When it comes to the BCCI's elections, one thing that has been noticeable over the years, is that friends turn foes (and vice versa) and the loyalties of people who are part of the same group, often shift. The Bindra-Dalmiya combination was going strong in the early 1990s, fighting the southern lobby, but a bitter rivalry developed between the two after 1996. Similarly, Rajbhai, who was a supporter of Mr Dalmiya's, switched over to the Pawar group in 2001. Mr Dalmiya masterminded Dr Muthiah's election in 1999, but the two were on opposite sides in 2001. Shashank Manohar and N. Srinivasan, who were on the same side from 2004 to 2013, were in rival camps during the 2015 elections. A few months later, Mr Srinivasan agreed to back Mr Pawar for the president's post after the untimely demise of Mr Dalmiya.

Fortunately for Indian cricket, the differences between the elected office-bearers who may have belonged to rival groups, have been known to take a back seat after the AGM.

Earlier, there was no fixed process for the elections in the Board and nominations for different posts were received on the floor of the house at the AGM. Every election would witness at least a couple of cases of more than one individual turning up and claiming to be the official representative of a member association. The chairman of the AGM (BCCI president) would then take a call on who was authorized to represent the association/s in question, after consulting the Board's lawyer. Invariably, those who professed their loyalty to the group of which the BCCI president himself was a part, would get the nod.

I started following BCCI elections in 1990, when Madhavrao Scindia was elected the president. Till then, he had represented Railways, which was a unit from the Central Zone, in the Board, but he contested the 1990 election as the representative of the HCA, which belonged to the North Zone. The representative of the Railways Sports Promotion Board (RSPB) was denied permission to attend the AGM. Attending in his place was Amrit Mathur, who produced a letter from the then Union railway minister, authorizing him to represent the RSPB although RSPB was an autonomous body and did not come under the ministry. The railway minister was none other than Scindia himself!

Something similar happened three years later, when Mr Bindra, who till then had represented the PCA from the North, contested the election as the representative of the Baroda Cricket Association, which belonged to the West Zone.

The first AGM that I participated in, as a representative of an affiliated unit, took place in 1997, at the Taj Coromandel in Chennai.

It was the Central Zone's turn to nominate the president that year. Rajbhai, who had been elected the president the previous year, was seeking to extend his term. His opponent was Dnyaneshwar Agashe, who was the president of the Maharashtra Cricket Association (West Zone), but was representing the Vidarbha Cricket Association (Central Zone) at the AGM. Agashe had lost the presidential election to Bindra in 1993, but equations had changed since and Bindra and Agashe were now on the same side.

The 1997 AGM, which was scheduled to be held in the last week of September, was preceded by reports that Mumbai had decided to support Agashe in the presidential election. It was also reported that Ravi Savant was to represent the MCA at the AGM and he had even attended the meeting called by the Bindra group to work out its strategy. However, there was a twist in the tale. A few days before the AGM, I received a call from Manohar Joshi, the MCA president and the chief minister of Maharashtra. He said that no less an individual than Lata Mangeshkar herself had requested him to support Rajbhai's candidature in the election and he had made a commitment to her to that effect. He also said that I should represent the MCA at the AGM, as Ravi Savant had already been seen to have aligned with the Bindra group. A Managing Committee meeting was hurriedly convened and it was decided that I would represent the MCA at the AGM and vote for Rajbhai.

It was at this AGM that I first met all the BCCI members, including Shashank Manohar, who was from Vidarbha, but was representing the Maharashtra Cricket Association.

Among those who turned up at Chennai's Taj Coromandel, the venue of the AGM, was an individual who claimed to be representing the Railways. I gathered that his brief was to support Agashe. But then, Mr Dalmiya, who was supporting Rajbhai, was always a couple of steps ahead of his rivals. A smartly attired individual arrived at the venue, 15 minutes before the start of the AGM, and the next thing we saw was the Railways' representative rushing towards the exit. Mr Bindra tried to stop him, only to get the reply, 'I cannot afford to lose my job!' The smartly attired individual who had turned up was M. Ananth, the zonal manager of South-Central Railways and the superior of the person who wanted to get away!

The AGM had to be adjourned, as the Bindra group raised some technical issues and claimed to have not got sufficient time to go through the minutes of the previous AGM. As mentioned in an earlier chapter, Mr Bindra never had the votes to back him. He relied on Mr Dalmiya for the same till they were together, but after their fallout, Mr Bindra had to think of other ways in which to make his presence felt. The elections too therefore got postponed.

For the elections which were held in November 1997, Mr Bindra got the Madras High Court to appoint a senior advocate as the observer, who would subsequently submit a report to the high court. The BCCI bosses failed to understand why an observer had been appointed and asked Ms Nalini Chidambaram, the senior advocate representing the Board at the time, to attend the AGM as well.

What followed was bizarre. The Bindra group wanted the observer to sit at the head of the table, while the Dalmiya group wanted him to sit on one side of the table. The arguments went on and on and finally, the gentleman was allotted a seat on one side as his job was only to observe!

The most important item on the agenda was the election of the office-bearers. Ranbir Singh Mahendra and I were appointed tellers, representing the Bindra and Dalmiya groups, respectively. Rajbhai won comprehensively and the Dalmiya group made a clean sweep.

Much to my delight, the issues which I had mentioned in my report after the Sri Lanka tour earlier that year—the need to appoint a professional coach, physiotherapist and trainer, and the adoption of a graded payment system—were discussed at the AGM. Of course, it took a while for the recommendations to be implemented, but at least a start had been made.

The 1999 AGM, which was held at the Rambagh Palace in Jaipur, was also a dramatic affair. It was the turn of the South Zone to nominate the president. The Hyderabad CA and Andhra CA aligned themselves with Mr Bindra and it was decided that Manohar Joshi, a vice president of the BCCI, the president of the MCA and by then, former chief minister of Maharashtra, would be their group's candidate. The Hyderabad Cricket Association then nominated Joshi as its representative for the AGM. Thus, the president of the MCA, which belonged to the West Zone, became a member of an association from the south! Mr Dalmiya, on the other hand, brought in Dr Muthiah, the president of the TNCA, as the presidential candidate of his group.

Four days before the AGM, Mr Joshi called me to his office in Mumbai. He was sitting with Pravin Barve, a prominent cricket administrator from the city, when I reached. Talk naturally veered towards the impending elections and I asked him how confident he was that he had the votes to win. He replied that Mr Bindra was working on the same. They were counting on the support of Maharashtra, Vidarbha, Saurashtra, Haryana, Madhya Pradesh and the Universities, all of whom were known to always stay together and vote for the same candidate. I expressed my doubts about these associations voting for him, for the simple reason that the MCA had not supported the presidential bid of Maharashtra's Agashe in 1993. In fact, we had not supported Agashe in 1997 as well.

However, Mr Joshi was unperturbed and said that he had spoken to Agashe and Mr Dalmiya as well. He then repeated what Mr Dalmiya had said to him: 'If you have 11 votes, then I will add six of mine to your tally.' When I heard this, I told Mr Joshi that he hadn't realized the point that Mr Dalmiya had made. Simply put, Mr Dalmiya had conveyed to him that he (Mr Joshi) did not have even 11 votes.

I advised Mr Joshi to pull out of the election, but he then spoke to Mr Bindra, who assured him of victory. Barve also felt the same way. Mr Joshi proceeded to take the morning flight to Jaipur, 24 hours before the AGM. I flew to Jaipur as the representative of the MCA, later that day.

My entry into the Rambagh Palace that evening coincided with a mass exit. The members of the Dalmiya group were on their way to P.M. Rungta's residence for dinner. Only four people, who were scheduled to attend the AGM the next day, were left in the hotel. They were Mr Bindra, A.N. Mate (Maharashtra's representative), B.B. Das (Odisha CA) and Mr Joshi himself. By then, he had seen the writing on the wall and realized that there was no substance in Mr Bindra's claims.

One of the sidelights of that 1999 AGM was Lalit Modi paying a 'donation' to the Himachal Pradesh Cricket Association (HPCA) to be its representative. Apparently, Lalit and his friend Harish Thawani, who headed Nimbus Communications, had gone from room to room to solicit support for Mr Joshi. Mr Kelkar, who was representing Vidarbha Cricket Association at the meeting, was so upset that he went to Mr Joshi's room and created a scene, claiming that two people had come to him and tried to bribe him into voting for the candidate of their choice. He even threatened to complain to the police. My friend Vijay Chougule, who was representing the Goa Cricket Association, was also approached by the duo and he too had a word with Mr Joshi about the same.

When I met Mr Joshi in his room, he was very upset. He told me that Madhavrao Scindia was not taking his calls and Shashank Manohar was not going to attend the AGM. It was obvious that the two individuals whom he had backed on, were not inclined to support him. He wanted to return to Mumbai without attending the AGM, but I advised him against it. The only way out was a face-saver.

I met Mr Dalmiya at around 11:00 p.m. that night. The point I made to him was that Mr Joshi, a vice president of the Board, a former chief minister and someone who was likely to become a central minister, was an individual of some stature and would be embarrassed if he were to suffer a heavy defeat the next day. Mr Dalmiya heard me out and said that he did not want to hurt Mr Joshi. He proposed that Mr Joshi become his group's candidate for the vice-presidentship of the Board from the West Zone. I suggested that he meet Mr Joshi the following morning, just before the AGM got underway, to discuss the way forward. He agreed and the two met the following morning.

Eventually, Mr Dalmiya's proposal was implemented. His group nominated Mr Joshi as the vice president from the West Zone and Dr Muthiah was elected president unopposed. Shashank told me later that his group had wanted Mr Joshi to contest, so that they could vote against him and he could be soundly defeated. The group had not forgiven the MCA for backing Mr Bindra in 1993 and Rajbhai in 1997. On the other hand, the Hyderabad Cricket Association and the Andhra Cricket Association were furious, Hyderabad more so because it had sacrificed its candidate for Mr Joshi.

Dr Muthiah, who completed two years as the BCCI president in 2001, wanted to contest for a third year, but this time around, he was up against Mr Dalmiya, with whom he had fallen out by then. Mr Dalmiya had completed his term as the ICC president in 2000 and now wanted to become the president of the BCCI. Ironically, Dalmiya and Shashank Manohar, who had been on the same side in 1999, were now rivals. Mr Pawar, who was in his first year in the BCCI, was expected to support Dr Muthiah. He was observing the goings-on keenly.

That AGM, which was held in Chennai, marked the 'debuts' of Rajeev Shukla, future vice president, and Anurag Thakur, future president. Madhavrao Scindia had deputed Ashok Kumat, a senior journalist, to represent the Madhya Pradesh Cricket Association (MPCA). The turnout at a dinner hosted by Dr Muthiah on the evening before the AGM, was impressive enough to convince many that he would win. However, they had reckoned without Mr Dalmiya's enterprise.

Mr Dalmiya was not very sure about the loyalties of the representative of the Assam Cricket Association. While this individual kept reiterating his support for him, Mr Dalmiya suspected that he had struck a deal with the other group. What happened next was incredible. Mr Dalmiya called Prafulla Kumar Mahanta, the then chief minister of Assam, and told him to fly to Chennai! Mahanta boarded a private jet on the morning of the AGM and made it in time. I was with Agashe in the lobby of the Taj Coromandel when Mahanta arrived with a posse of Black Cat commandos. Agashe was quite elated to see Mahanta and he said that Dr Muthiah's victory was now certain. I did not quite agree and reminded Agashe that no less a person than the chief minister of a state from the Northeast had flown all the way to Chennai at the behest of Mr Dalmiya. One did not have to be a genius to figure out who the chief minister would favour.

I never had any doubt that Mr Dalmiya would win and had told Mr Pawar the same, the previous evening itself. Having planned and executed successful campaigns for Mr Bindra, Rajbhai and Dr Muthiah in the years gone by, there was no way he was going to leave anything to chance when he was contesting himself. Before leaving for Chennai, I had written down the names of the associations, which according to me, would vote for Mr Dalmiya. I enclosed the sheet on which I had written the names in an envelope and handed it to C.S. Naik in the MCA. I told him to open the envelope only after the elections. He did and all the names tallied. Mr Dalmiya won by 17 votes to 13.

The AGM used to be a two-day affair at the time. Niranjan Shah and Jaywant Lele were pitted against each other for the secretary's post. Shah was Scindia's favourite and the latter had accordingly instructed Ashok Kumat to vote for Mr Dalmiya as the president, but not for Mr Lele as the secretary, despite his belonging to Mr Dalmiya's group. There was a 15-15 deadlock and Dr Muthiah, the chairman, exercised his casting vote in Shah's favour.

Just when the AGM was about to conclude, we got the tragic news that Madhavrao Scindia had died in an air crash.

It was the North Zone's turn to nominate a presidential candidate in 2004. Contrary to popular belief, Mr Pawar, who had by then become the rallying point for the anti-Dalmiya group in the Board, was reluctant to contest the election. In fact, he had assured Arun Jaitley, a member of Mr Dalmiya's group and the president of the DDCA, of his support, if he were to stand for the president's post. However, Mr Dalmiya proposed Ranbir Singh Mahendra of the HCA as his group's presidential candidate, and not Mr Jaitley. It was only then that Mr Pawar decided to contest. He represented the Jammu & Kashmir Cricket Association (JKCA) at that AGM.

With me on the flight to Kolkata, where the AGM was to be held, was Balasaheb Thorve of the Maharashtra Cricket Association. He had teamed up with Ajay Shirke to oust Agashe from the association and the matter was being heard in the Bombay High Court. The High Court had appointed B.G.

Deshmukh former chief secretary of the State of Maharashtra and M.N. Singh, former police commissioner of Mumbai, as the observers, to supervise the working of the Maharashtra CA. Thorve told me on the flight that Mr Deshmukh had sent a letter to the BCCI, stating that he had not approved Agashe's decision to attend the AGM as the representative of the Maharashtra CA.

I reached Taj Bengal, the venue of the AGM, and went to Mr Pawar's room where members of his group had assembled. Agashe too was there. I conveyed to the gathering what Thorve had told me, but Agashe claimed that there was nothing to worry and an order was expected from the Court.

Just before the AGM was to commence, Justice S. Mohan, the former SC judge (he was one of the judges who had delivered the landmark judgement in 1993 that the BCCI controlled the telecast rights), arrived at the Taj Bengal and handed over to Mr Dalmiya, who was in the Chair, an order of the Madras High Court, appointing him as an administrator to conduct the elections. Mr Dalmiya told Justice Mohan and the House that the Board's lawyers had appealed against the said order and the same had been vacated, but Justice Mohan insisted on seeing the order. Mr Dalmiya then adjourned the meeting till the order was received. Justice Mohan read the order and left.

Mr Dalmiya also had with him the letter written by the court appointed Observer of Maharashtra CA, wherein he had stated that Agashe had no locus standi to attend the AGM. He mentioned in the letter that Agashe had convened a Managing Committee meeting without their permission and got himself nominated as the association's representative. The letter was more than enough for Mr Dalmiya to keep Agashe and the Maharashtra Cricket Association out of the AGM.

Some attendees, whose support Mr Pawar had banked on, did a volte-face during the voting. Despite that, the election still went down to the wire. Mr Dalmiya, who already controlled the votes of the CAB and the National Cricket Club[28], also voted as the chairman of the meeting and then exercised his casting vote to get Mahendra elected. 'I had no chance as the bowler and the umpire were the same person,' Mr Pawar said later. For him, the defeat was a setback, considering that he had never lost an election in his life at any level. Of course, it would have been a different story, had a representative of the Maharashtra CA been allowed to vote.

The presidential election was followed by the one for the post of the secretary, in which Niranjan Shah was defeated by S.K. Nair of Mr Dalmiya's group. I had already served as the joint secretary for a year and was aware that members of Mr Dalmiya's group were far from happy with his decision to back me the previous year. In 2004, the members of his group prevailed upon him to declare Gautam Dasgupta as their candidate for the joint secretary's post. I was therefore surprised when Mr Jaitley, who belonged to Mr Dalmiya's group, called me over and told me to contest the election. Mr Pawar, whom he spoke to, concurred.

I contested, but lost 14-16. Shashank told me later that Mr Dalmiya would have been in a fix had there been a 15-15 deadlock and he may well have voted for me despite Dasgupta being his group's candidate.

Rajeev Shukla, a member of Mr Dalmiya's group, met me that evening and said that I ought to continue working as the executive secretary of the Board. I wasn't so sure, but then Mr Dalmiya called me himself and told me to forget what had happened in the election. I was touched when he said that the BCCI needed my services. I decided to carry on after speaking to Mr Pawar, who also felt that I should continue.

A reprisal from Mr Bindra was only to be expected after the landslide triumph of Mr Dalmiya and his team. It came

---

[28]The National Cricket Club, based in Kolkata, is a full member of the BCCI.

in the form of a judgement delivered by the Madras High Court, which appointed Justice Mohan, a retired SC judge, as the 'administrator' of the Board. The 'administrator' flew to Mumbai on a Friday evening and we were told that Mr Bindra was with him. Their plan was to reach the BCCI office at around 10:30 a.m. on Saturday and take charge.

I received a call from Mr Dalmiya early in the morning. He explained that if the administrator were to assume control, the case would drag on interminably in the courts, which in turn would be disastrous for Indian cricket.

When the administrator turned up at the Board's office with Mr Bindra and a large media contingent, eager to capture the 'takeover' for posterity, all they saw was a locked door. For them, it was an anticlimax, to say the least.

An upset Bindra called Mr Pawar, who then called me. I told him that I did not go to the BCCI office on Saturdays. I was the executive secretary-in-charge of the Board, not its employee. The BCCI staffer who had the keys of the office lived in Vasai, on the outskirts of Mumbai, and the staff had a holiday.

Mr Pawar was determined to make a mark at the AGM in September 2005, which was also to be held in Kolkata. He built his team in the months preceding the AGM and planned well for the showdown.

However, Mr Dalmiya was not going to yield without a fight. He moved the Calcutta High Court and got Justice Vikramjit Sen (Retd) appointed as an observer. But he was outmanoeuvred by Lalit Modi, who also moved the Calcutta High Court and had two more judges, Justice K.N. Singh (Retd) and Justice Madan Mohan Punchhi (Retd), appointed as observers. That made it three observers in all. Mr Ranbir Singh Mahendra called the meeting to order on the next day in the presence of the three observers and after an informal meeting of the representatives of the Pawar and Dalmiya groups, it was suggested that the AGM be adjourned. The chairman announced the same.

The adjourned AGM was then held in November 2005. The Honourable Supreme Court appointed Mr J.S. Krishnamoorthy, former Chief Election Commissioner of India, as election officer and gave him sole authority to take decisions regarding the eligibility of the voters and the process for the elections. This implied that the right of the chairman (Board president) to adjudicate on disputes, if any, regarding the official representatives of state associations, was withdrawn and only the election officer was authorized to take a call on the same. Minutes before Mr Krishnamoorthy called the meeting to order to explain the procedure for the elections, the representatives of the Hyderabad Cricket Association and Andhra Cricket Association disappeared from the room, only to be replaced by two others, both of whom were armed with authority letters. I learnt later that the 'replacements' were IAS officers from the state of Andhra Pradesh.

The 'Dalmiya Era' in Indian cricket ended on a bizarre note. Representatives of the two groups were seated on either side of the conference table when the election officer started counting the votes. Usually, the ballot box was shaken to ensure that the votes in it were mixed, but this time around, the ballot papers were drawn from the box and read out by the election officer's assistant in exactly the same order in which the representatives were seated! This ensured that everybody knew who had voted for whom.

Mr Pawar called on Mr Dalmiya at his residence, the day after the AGM, to put an end to the bitterness that had prevailed during the AGM and seek his support for the administration of the BCCI. I was told that Mr Dalmiya did not meet him.

Mr Pawar's election ushered in a phase of stability. The decision of his team to make the elections a triennial affair was significant, as it gave the office-bearers time and breathing space to plan, implement and execute, instead of having to focus on the next AGM within months of assuming office. The decision also meant that the elected office-bearers did not have to be under any obligation or pressure while appointing people on key committees, such as selection, finance and marketing. The BCCI also decided to put a proper election procedure in place. The names of the representatives of the associations were to be received two days before the AGM and candidates wishing to contest the elections were supposed to file their nominations, which were to be duly proposed and seconded also two days before.

Mr Pawar also introduced the practice of announcing the president-elect one year before the term of the incumbent president ended, so that the acrimony and group politics could be put on the back-burner. Thus, Shashank Manohar was declared the president-elect in 2007 and N. Srinivasan in 2010, a year before they took over as the president in 2008 and 2011, respectively. However, things were back to square one in 2015. Mr Srinivasan's term as the president was to end in September 2014, but the SC stepped in after the Board was hit hard by betting and fixing allegations in 2013.

The AGM was held in March 2015 and elections were held as per the directions of the Honourable Supreme Court. This time, the Pawar group took on the Srinivasan group. Ironically, both groups agreed to Mr Dalmiya becoming the president, and he was elected unopposed as a result. The three other elections were cliffhangers. Anurag Thakur from the Pawar group was elected the secretary, defeating Sanjay Patel by one vote. Anirudh Chaudhry from the Srinivasan group beat Rajeev Shukla of the Pawar group in the election for the treasurer. There was a tie between Amitabh Choudhary of the Srinivasan group and Chetan Desai of the Pawar group for the joint secretary's post. Shivlal Yadav, who was in the chair, then voted for Amitabh. The elections for the five vice presidents were also close encounters. Ironically, T.C. Mathew of the Kerala CA (South) was elected vice president of the West Zone and C.K. Khanna of the DDCA (North) was elected vice president of the Central Zone!

As per the BCCI constitution then, the vice presidents were not office-bearers and they looked after the interest of their respective zones.

Mr Dalmiya unfortunately passed away a few months after taking charge. The consensus within the Board was that Mr Pawar ought to take over. Mr Srinivasan was also in favour of his candidature, but Mr Jaitley pulled off a surprise by convincing Shashank Manohar to take up the post. Shashank agreed, much to the chagrin of Mr Pawar, who was upset that one of his confidants had switched sides. Shashank was unanimously elected as the president at a Special General Meeting (SGM) held in October 2015. A little over six months later, he quit to become the first independent chairman of the ICC. Anurag Thakur and Ajay Shirke were elected the BCCI president and secretary, respectively.

It is with a heavy heart that I have to admit that most of the members of the BCCI rarely raised any pertinent issues in the AGM and their primary interest was to get either themselves or their representatives nominated on the various committees and then wait for the treasurer to announce the subsidy amount that each full member of the Board would receive after the accounts were approved. Had all the members been proactive and spoken up, many of the crisis which the BCCI was confronted with, could have been avoided.

Narendra Modi, the honourable prime minister of India, attended the 2010 AGM, which was held at the Cricket Centre, as the representative of the Gujarat Cricket Association. He was the chief minister of the state at the time. By the time he settled into the meeting after the exchange of pleasantries, the approval of the accounts for 2009–10 came up for discussion. The annual accounts and the budget for 2010–11 were unanimously approved and the treasurer started reading out the quantum of subsidy payable to the member units.

I happened to be sitting next to Mr Modi. He turned to me and enquired as to why there was no discussion on the accounts or budget, which ran into thousands of crores. He had also noticed that the practice of calling in the auditors when the documents were approved, had not been followed. I took a deep breath and told him that the members of the Board's finance committee had vetted the accounts and budget and forwarded the same to the working committee with their observations. The working committee had then approved the accounts and budget and only then had the same been placed before the general body. I could sense that he was not fully satisfied with my explanation. He later observed that the members finished discussing most of the items on the agenda within 45 minutes and then deliberated for over an hour on issues related to Lalit Modi.

As per the recommendations of the Lodha Committee, all future elections of the BCCI will have to be conducted by a retired Election Commissioner of India, who will decide on the process as well as the matters related to the election, such as resolving disputes, if any, in the voters' list. This may well ensure that the BCCI elections become a largely peaceful affair, devoid of all the excitement and drama which had come to be associated with them. Hopefully, this will inspire all the members to devote more time to discussing and resolving issues which are critical to the well-being of Indian cricket.

10
A NEW LOOK

John Wright's decision to resign as the coach after the series against Pakistan in 2004–05 set in motion the search for his successor. Mr Dalmiya asked me to speak to some of the players and get an idea of who they felt ought to be approached for the role. However, most of the responses I got were cynical. They said that what they thought did not really matter, as the Board would only go by what the captain decided.

When prodded, some of the senior players said that they were keen on Tom Moody, the Australian all-rounder who had been a part of the World Cup-winning teams of 1987 and 1999. However, Sourav was keener on Greg Chappell, from whom he had sought technical advice prior to India's tour of Australia in 2003–04 and had even trained with him for a few days. The Indian captain had gone on to silence all those who had doubted his ability against quick bowling on lively tracks, with a brilliant 144 in the first Test of the series. His teammates then took a leaf from their skipper's book and excelled themselves in the matches that followed. India came close to winning the series, but eventually settled for a 1-1 draw and retained the Border–Gavaskar Trophy by virtue of having won the previous series against Australia. Sourav was grateful to Chappell for his inputs and thought very highly of him.

The Board invited both Chappell and Moody for interviews, along with Mohinder Amarnath, one of the architects of our 1983 World Cup win. Eventually, Chappell was appointed and

Moody went over to Sri Lanka. India's new coach impressed the panel with a detailed presentation on the pathway for Indian cricket, wherein he highlighted the country's potential to evolve into a cricketing powerhouse and the areas of concern that the BCCI needed to address and resolve if it wanted the Indian team to be the best in the world.

Chappell began his stint as the coach with a limited-overs tournament in Sri Lanka. Rahul captained the side in the absence of Sourav, who was serving a ban for India's persistently poor over-rate in ODIs. Sourav did join the squad in the latter half of the tournament, but Rahul continued to lead. Sourav was then named the captain for the tour of Zimbabwe, which was to follow.

A few days before the team was to depart for Zimbabwe, I was told by Mr Dalmiya of Chappell's demand that Ian Frazer, a long-time associate of his, be inducted into the team as the 'biomechanic expert'. Mr Gavaskar, who had been on the panel which had interviewed Chappell and the other candidates, was surprised when he got to know this. The issue of assistants had been discussed during the interview itself and Chappell had stated clearly that he would not require any. Then where did this demand come from?

However, Mr Dalmiya persuaded the office-bearers to appoint Frazer, probably because he did not want to rock the boat at the start of Chappell's stint. Just before the team flew to Zimbabwe, Frazer turned up at the Board's office and requested me to change the designation on his blazer from 'biomechanical expert' to 'assistant coach'. I refused.

The problems between Chappell and the senior members of the team began in Zimbabwe itself. While Chappell's cricketing stature and experience were never in doubt, his man-management skills left a lot to be desired. The differences between the senior players and Ian Frazer only added fuel to the fire. Chappell also committed the cardinal mistake of speaking to select journalists and providing them information pertaining to his fallout with Sourav and his conversations about senior players. By the time he realized that his ploy of taking a few journalists 'into confidence' and feeding them with stories had backfired, it was too late. His 'friends' in the media would gleefully pass on the information which they received from him, to others.

Chappell's email to Ranbir Singh Mahendra, the Board president, in which he castigated Sourav, among other things, hit the headlines after the team's return from Zimbabwe. The senior players believed that the root cause of the problems in Zimbabwe was Frazer more than Chappell himself. The Board swung into damage-control mode and summoned the captain and the coach to the Taj, Mumbai. A panel, which comprised the Board president, Mr Dalmiya and Mr Gavaskar, first met Sourav and Chappell separately and then jointly. They were told that they needed to sort their differences out. Not surprisingly, the lobby of the Taj was teeming with representatives of the print and electronic media. After the joint meeting was over, Mr Dalmiya suggested that a media conference be organized. We made arrangements for Mr Mahendra to address the media, but only 20-odd journalists turned up. The majority, including senior journalists from Kolkata, had congregated in Sourav's room, where another 'media conference' was being held simultaneously!

The BCCI chose to back Chappell and the selectors formally handed over the reins to Rahul Dravid in October 2005. Sourav found himself out of favour and out of the side under the new regime of the BCCI, which took charge in November that year. The Indian team under Rahul beat Sri Lanka comprehensively in an ODI series and then squared another ODI series against South Africa. The new captain was the toast of the nation, as was the new coach. It appeared that Indian cricket had moved on from Sourav, although he returned to the squad for the Test series against Sri Lanka and the subsequent tour of Pakistan, much to the displeasure of those who wanted him to be banished for good.

Sourav's right elbow, which he had injured in Zimbabwe, healed before the Test series against Sri Lanka. Dr Anant Joshi was to examine his medical report and intimate the Board accordingly. When the three of us met at the Taj Land's End in Mumbai, Sourav commented on the irony of the situation, in that the individual whom he had backed as coach was the one targeting him. It was sad to see Sourav, once a popular and successful captain, going through a tough phase.

Mr Pawar chaired a Working Committee meeting of the Board at the CCI, shortly after taking over as the BCCI president. I attended the meeting in my capacity as executive secretary-in-charge, just before flying to Pakistan for a reconnaissance trip ahead of India's tour of the country in early 2006. After the meeting, I handed Mr Pawar a note which Mr Gavaskar had asked me to pass on to him. Mr Pawar read the note and told me that Mr Gavaskar had requested him to do something about Frazer and the detrimental effect he was having on the team.

Mr Bindra, whom Mr Pawar consulted after reading the note, was a big supporter of Chappell's and he claimed that all was well. He also said that he had spoken to Rahul, Kiran More, the chairman of Selectors, as well as Sachin, and they had assured him that Frazer was doing a great job. Most importantly, Rahul, the captain, was happy with Frazer, Mr Bindra said.

Asking Sachin for his opinion did not make much sense of course, as he had missed the tour of Zimbabwe due to injury and hence did not have first-hand exposure to what had happened there. Anyway, Mr Bindra prevailed and Frazer continued to be a part of the team. The cracks were papered over by the success of the team in ODI series against Pakistan and England in the remainder of the 2005–06 season. In fact, the team created an ODI record by chasing a target successfully, 17 consecutive times.

However, our performances in the Tests against the same teams were not up to the mark. After two draws in Pakistan, we reduced the hosts to 39-6 on the first morning of the third Test at Karachi, with Irfan Pathan performing the hat-trick. However, the Pakistanis picked themselves up and won the game and with it, the series. In our next Test series against England at home, we were 1-0 up and firm favourites on the eve of the third and final encounter at the Wankhede Stadium. However, Rahul's 100th Test turned out to be a forgettable game, with England squaring the series. We made up for these lapses later in the year, by winning a Test series in the West Indies for the first time since 1971.

While Chappell and his supporters could cite the wins in the ODIs and the Test series win in the West Indies to claim that the Indian team had done well in his first 12 months as coach, they could not fall back on anything in the 2006–07 season, a nightmarish one for Indian cricket.

The ICC Champions Trophy, India's first home assignment of that season, would have been shifted to some other country, had it not been for the timely intervention of Prime Minister Dr Manmohan Singh. The ICC had revised some of its policies a few years previously and the board hosting the tournament had to sign an agreement that it would make 'best endeavours' to seek income-tax exemption on the earnings of the ICC from the event.

However, the Government of India was reluctant to comply with this request. Mr Dalmiya, after taking over as the BCCI president in 2001, had tried his best to convince the authorities to grant the exemption. He explained that India ran the risk of missing out on hosting international events if this was not done. However, the representatives of the National Democratic

Alliance (NDA) government, which was in power till 2004, as well as those of the United Progressive Alliance (UPA) government that succeeded it, did not budge. After failing to convince P. Chidambaram, the finance minister in the UPA government, Mr Dalmiya sought the help of G. Vinod, the then president of the Hyderabad Cricket Association, whose father G. Venkat Swamy, was a senior Congressman and close to the Gandhis. He organized a meeting between Mr Dalmiya and the prime minister. Mr Dalmiya was pleased to discover that Dr Singh was in favour of India hosting global sporting events and did not want the country to miss out on them. After being briefed by Mr Dalmiya, the prime minister spoke to Mr Chidambaram, who once again reiterated his opposition to what the BCCI was asking for. Finally, Dr Singh took the call himself and granted the exemption for ICC events.

A lot changed in the Board between 2003 and 2006. The dispensation which took over in November 2005 was not aware of the fact that India was due to host the Champions Trophy in 2006, until it received a reminder from Malcolm Speed, the CEO of the ICC. The Board started working on the event only in March 2006, when the tournament was six months away. Macky Dudhia, the ICC's tournament-in-charge, came to India, along with his team, to meet us. I was honoured to be asked to take charge as the tournament director, by Mr Pawar.

There were teething issues, of course. First, there was no staff at the BCCI to work on the tournament. Lalit Modi stepped in to help and he deputed his personal staff to assist me and even permitted the use of his office at Nirlon House at Worli in central Mumbai for the preparatory work.

A start was made by finalizing the venues of the tournament. The ICC had made it clear that the event had to be organized in not more than three or four venues, considering that its duration was only three weeks and as many as eight teams (10, counting the two which were eliminated in the qualifying round) were part of the main round. The travelling time of the teams had to be kept minimal and the TV broadcast crew and equipment had to be moved from venue to venue as quickly as possible. Trade-Wings, a pioneer in India's travel industry, was brought in to plan and coordinate the travel of the teams, officials and broadcast crews.

The ICC was to have full control over the branding at the venues, which had to be 'clean' and devoid of branding of any sort. This stipulation ruled out venues which had an ongoing association with sponsors. The Wankhede Stadium, which had a long-term association with the Tatas, after whom the northern end of the ground was named, missed out as a result. Rajbhai then offered the Brabourne Stadium. The catch was that the venue was not equipped with floodlights and did not have air-conditioned boxes, both of which were mandatory, as per the ICC's regulations. However, the CCI assured the ICC that these facilities would be created in time. The Brabourne Stadium was thus finalized, along with the Sardar Patel (Motera) Stadium at Ahmedabad, the PCA Stadium at Mohali and the Sawai Mansingh Stadium at Jaipur.

The CCI kept its word and incurred a lot of expenses in creating the required facilities. TV and radio commentary boxes were constructed at the top of the North Stand and corporate boxes came up in the West Stand. The floodlights also emerged, well before the first ball of the tournament was bowled. I guess what helped was that the CCI had no dearth of resources and enterprise. Like Rajbhai, many members of the club had dreamt of getting international cricket back to the Brabourne Stadium. The Champions Trophy gave them the opportunity to fulfil that dream and there was no way they were going to miss out.

The Sawai Mansingh Stadium had not hosted international matches for a while and quite a few shortcomings were identified there, a few months before the tournament. However,

Lalit Modi, who was heading the Rajasthan Cricket Association, was proactive and gave the stadium a new look in next to no time. His being on excellent terms with senior members of the state government also helped.

The match tickets for all the venues had to look the same. Hence, they had to be designed and printed centrally, which was something we in the BCCI were not used to. The tickets were printed at the security press at Manipal in Karnataka. Having them distributed to all the venues in time was a challenge, but we pulled it off.

Another issue was that the associations hosting the games were not used to the anti-corruption protocols of the ICC. Narhari Amin, the president of the Gujarat Cricket Association, which managed the Sardar Patel Stadium at Ahmedabad, was furious when he was denied a central accreditation that would grant him access to all the areas of the venue, including the players' dressing rooms. It had to be explained to him that everything was being done as per the guidelines of the ICC. If he had some urgent work in areas to which he did not have access, he could avail of a temporary pass from the Anti-Corruption Officer of the ICC. Even Mr Pawar, the BCCI president, had not been issued a central accreditation, he was informed.

Despite some delays, what helped a great deal was the clarity. The ICC adhered to its protocols, which were laid down clearly and expected us to do likewise. While the BCCI provided the venues, logistical support and security, the ICC handled the planning and execution and managed the TV rights, sponsors, media management and even the preparation of the wickets. It was a learning experience for me and all those who worked with me.

The tournament itself went off well, although India failed to qualify for the semi-finals. It rained on the day of the final between Australia and the West Indies at the Brabourne Stadium, but fortunately, not for long. Australia won, but their achievement was overshadowed by what happened at the presentation ceremony. Ramiz Raja, the former Pakistani captain, was conducting the post-match interviews for television and after speaking to Brian Lara, the West Indies captain, he invited Ricky Ponting, the winning captain, for a chat. Mr Pawar, who was to present the trophy to Ponting, was waiting on an adjacent platform. Even as the exchange between Raja and Ponting went on, one could sense that the Australian players, who were standing close by, were getting restless. All they wanted to do was get on the platform and pose with the trophy.

Finally, the interview ended and Ponting walked towards Mr Pawar, at which point his players made a beeline for the platform. Mr Pawar handed over the trophy to Ponting, but he found himself surrounded by the Australian players. Even as he tried to make his way out of the cluster, one of the Australian players pushed him off the platform. The incident was captured by the TV cameras and thus watched across the cricketing world. The Board wrote to Cricket Australia, condemning the incident and received an unconditional apology within 24 hours, including one from Damien Martyn, who had pushed Mr Pawar.

This wasn't the only 'pushing' controversy during the tournament. The liaison officer of the Pakistani team spilt the beans to the media about an incident in the team bus, wherein Bob Woolmer, the coach, was pushed by one of the players.

The Champions Trophy was preceded by the AGM of the Board at the CCI on 27 September 2006. I had completed three years as the executive secretary-in-charge by then and was proud of the fact that successive dispensations had shown faith in me. The AGM commenced as per schedule and the proceedings went off smoothly in the first half, which in itself was a welcome change from the acrimony which we had witnessed in the previous AGMs. Mr Pawar called me over when we broke for lunch. Shashank Manohar, who was the vice president of the Board from the Central Zone and tipped to take over the presidentship from Mr Pawar in 2008, was with him. They brought up the promise of giving the Board a 'professional' look, which they had made to the members of the Board at the time of taking over. 'We want you to become the Malcolm Speed of the BCCI,' Mr Pawar said to me in Marathi.

As had been the case in 2001 when Dr Muthiah had offered me the post of team manager, I wasn't sure. I told Mr Pawar and Shashank that I was due to retire in 2011 and had five years of my teaching career left. However, they would have none of it and insisted that I take up the responsibility. When I mentioned the 'uncertainty' in the Board, Mr Pawar told me to forget about 'BCCI politics'. He said that he was going to be in charge till 2008 and it had already been decided that Shashank would take over from him. Thus, there was nothing to worry about till 2011, at least. I requested for some time to think about the offer and went for lunch, where I met Mr Jaitley. When I mentioned the offer to him, he recommended that I take it up.

There was a surprise in store. Shortly after Mr Pawar started the post-lunch segment of the AGM, Lalit stood up and announced that the Board had decided to appoint me in an Executive position, following discussions between the president and office-bearers! The members unanimously approved the proposal and Mr Pawar and the other office-bearers were authorized to take a call on the designation and terms and conditions. To cut a long story short, I was not given any time to think.

The designation could not have been CEO, as the secretary of the Board was the Chief Executive, as per the then constitution of the Board. I was appointed the chief administrative officer and Mr Srinivasan himself addressed the media after the AGM, where my appointment was announced.

I was overwhelmed by a deluge of congratulatory messages and calls from former and current cricketers, fellow administrators, the media and followers of the game. The ball was now in my court and it was up to me to do my best and not let them down.

My stint as the chief administrative officer, which was to commence on 1 October 2006, was obviously a full-time one. I had already applied for six months' leave from my teaching duties after being appointed the TD for the Champions Trophy. Mr Pawar told me that the state government would issue an order to my college principal, stating that I had been deputed to the BCCI for a special assignment, till 2008. That would be extended later.

The president was simultaneously working on keeping another promise made by him and his team before the 2005 elections—that of creating a permanent HQ for the BCCI. For years, the address of whoever was the secretary of the Board would be considered the BCCI's address, with the office in Mumbai keeping track of the Board's correspondence and managing the appointments of officials. Mr Pawar understood the need for a single, permanent office, which would house professionals affiliated to different departments, all of whom would work together for Indian cricket. The senior office-bearers would operate from this office, whenever required. This had been discussed since the 1960s, but nothing had materialized. Till 2005–06, that is.

The MCA, which was also headed by Mr Pawar, was constructing a four-storeyed building between the Vinoo Mankad Gate and the Polly Umrigar Gate—the two main entrances of the Wankhede Stadium complex. Mr Pawar proposed that the MCA make two floors of the building available to the BCCI. A legal hurdle had to be cleared after the MCA's Managing Committee agreed to the proposal. The building was coming up on a plot of land which the state government had leased to the MCA and the latter therefore could not sublet it to a third party. Mr Pawar then spoke to Sushilkumar Shinde, the then chief minister of Maharashtra, and requested him to amend the pertinent clause. The lease agreement was amended to the effect that MCA was permitted to provide office space to the BCCI, its parent body.

Mr Pawar personally drove the process of completing the building and inaugurating the same, ahead of the Champions Trophy final. Godrej was roped in to design and furnish the office space.

The 'Cricket Centre' was inaugurated on 4 November 2006, a day before the Champions Trophy final. Mr Percy Sonn, the then president of the ICC, did the honours. The inauguration was followed by a function on the lawns of the Wankhede Stadium, where former captains of India, as well as present and past office-bearers of the Board were invited, along with representatives of the international cricket boards who had flown in to Mumbai for the Champions Trophy final and office-bearers of the state units. Ravi Shastri, a former captain of India himself, was the Master of Ceremonies. We also created an audio-visual, depicting landmark events in the history of Indian cricket. The former India captains and BCCI presidents were then felicitated.

In my welcome address, I drew the attention of the audience to remarks made by Malcolm Speed, the ICC CEO, in an interview to an Indian newspaper. He had been quoted as saying that while the BCCI had a lot of money, it lacked a professional set-up and silverware, in the form of trophies.[29] I told the audience that the professionalism of an organization had nothing to do with the number of people who worked for

---

[29]N. Ananthanarayanan, 'Performance, not money, counts', Rediff.com, 1 November 2006, https://www.rediff.com/cricket/report/speed/20061101.htm. Accessed on 26 November 2021.

it. It was all about how you ran and managed your activities. With a new office at our disposal and Mr Pawar at the helm, you would see changes in less than a couple of years, I emphasized. I was surprised when Sonn asked me for the text of my speech, as well as the issue of the newspaper which had carried Speed's interview.

This was also the period when the new regime was working towards isolating Mr Dalmiya and ending his sway over BCCI politics for good. He was accused of irregularities in the handling of the PILCOM/INDCOM account, which had been created for the 1996 World Cup. An enquiry was instituted against him and a Disciplinary Committee, comprising Mr Pawar, Shashank Manohar and Chirayu Amin, assigned to do the same. Mr Dalmiya refused to appear before this committee.

The members submitted their findings and recommendations in the form of a report and an SGM was convened at Jaipur in December 2006 to discuss the same. Mr Dalmiya did attend the meeting and explained his views to the House before the members passed a resolution by majority, pronouncing Mr Dalmiya guilty and declaring that he would not be allowed to hold any office in the Board or any of its state units.

This appeared more like an attempt engineered by Mr Bindra to settle scores with his old rival, who had tried to suspend him in 2001.

The resolution forced Mr Dalmiya to resign as the president of the CAB and he was out of action for a couple of years. However, he swung back into action by moving the Calcutta High Court and getting a stay on the decision taken at the SGM. We were then shocked to discover that the BCCI had not filed the amendments to its rules with the registrar of societies in Tamil Nadu for almost two decades.

The Calcutta High Court ordered criminal proceedings against the office-bearers of the Board and me, as I had filed the affidavits on behalf of the Board in which we had claimed that the amended rules have been filed with the Registrar of Societies, Tamil Nadu, at regular intervals. Mr Karunanidhi, the then chief minister of Tamil Nadu, came to our rescue and condoned the delay in filing the papers with the Registrar of Societies. The BCCI then challenged the decision of the Calcutta High Court in the Supreme Court, which stayed the order, much to our relief.

The BCCI then filed a first information report (FIR) against Mr Dalmiya at the Marine Drive Police Station in Mumbai for misappropriation of funds. I was totally in the dark about this move, till the TV channels showed Niranjan Shah, the secretary, and M.P. Pandove, the joint secretary, at the police station. This was probably the saddest day in the history of the BCCI. A civil suit for recovery of the money from Mr Dalmiya was also filed simultaneously in Mumbai. The Economic Offences Wing of the Mumbai Police started an investigation and summoned Mr Dalmiya to the police headquarters. Nothing much came out of this exercise and finally at the AGM in 2010, Shashank Manohar, the BCCI president, proposed that the civil suit, as well as the resolution passed at the SGM in 2006, be withdrawn. Mr Dalmiya then withdrew his case against the BCCI. I feel that the Board's attempts to target Mr Dalmiya backfired, as bigger problems came up in the process. The Income Tax authorities opened our returns from earlier years for scrutiny, based on the police complaint and the civil suit which had been filed against Mr Dalmiya.

These events took their toll on Mr Dalmiya's reputation and health. A man who relished challenges and never gave up, he was reappointed the president of the BCCI in June 2013 when Mr Srinivasan stepped aside. His health notwithstanding, Mr Dalmiya was elected unopposed as the president of the Board for the second time in March 2015.

During his second term as president, Mr Dalmiya proposed

that the BCCI appoint a Cricket Advisory Committee (CAC) to guide the BCCI on cricketing matters including the appointment of coaches and support staff for the national teams and the NCA. He requested Sachin Tendulkar, Sourav Ganguly and V.V.S. Laxman to be members of the CAC. I attended the first meeting, where these cricketers discussed the way forward at length and suggested a few names, the most prominent of them being that of Rahul Dravid's, as the coach of the India A and under-19 squads.

Unfortunately, Mr Dalmiya's health deteriorated after his re-election as the president and he passed away in September 2015.

11

TRANSITION

The contrast between the eminence of the BCCI in the cricketing world and the state of its old office in the North Stand of the Brabourne Stadium, was highlighted by Clayton Murzello, the national sports editor of *Mid-Day*, in a story in 2004, which won him an award from the Sports Journalists' Federation of India (SJFI). He wasn't the only one to have an issue with the rooms from which the Board functioned back then. John Wright, in his book *Indian Summers*, described the BCCI office as 'the greatest feat of camouflage since a sheep donned wolf's clothing'.[30] The BCCI had moved into the rooms in the North Stand of the Brabourne stadium in 1948. It was only in November 2006, with the inauguration of the Cricket Centre that the Board moved into an office befitting its stature. Clayton did another story in 2008, this time on the 'new' office.

All those who visited the Cricket Centre could not stop gushing about it. The first floor comprised a large conference hall, big enough to hold AGMs and other meetings of the Board. The area adjacent to it was earmarked for a museum. The second floor housed the new office of the Board. It had two conference rooms and spacious cabins for the Board president, secretary, treasurer, joint secretary and the chief adminstrative

---

[30] John Wright, *John Wright's Indian Summers*, Penguin India; Illustrated edition (2006).

officer. There was an extra cabin, meant to be used by a senior manager, and a smaller chamber just outside the president's room, for his personal assistant. The trophies won by the Indian team over the decades, including the World Cup in 1983 and the World Championship of Cricket Trophy in 1985, were displayed in a glass cabinet in the lobby of the second floor. The walls of both the first and second floors were embellished with framed images of our cricketing greats.

There was an unintended anomaly, in that most of the images on the walls were those of cricketers who had played post-1990. The reason for this was that the more recent the images, the easier it was to enlarge them, thanks to the technological improvements in the quality of analogue photographic film and the subsequent transition to the digital format. Older images tended to pixilate when blown up. The preponderance of post-1990 images triggered a reaction from Mr Gavaskar when he first visited the Cricket Centre. After he had looked around, he turned to me and quipped, 'Even we played some cricket, you know!'

The IPL office was subsequently created on the fourth floor of the Cricket Centre. The third floor housed the office of the MCA.

The new office did not change the fortunes of the Indian team, which had struggled in the Champions Trophy. The players flew to South Africa, where they were soundly beaten in the ODIs. They then staged an incredible comeback in the first Test at Johannesburg, winning by 123 runs, but lost the next two games and in the process, the series. Spirits were low, to say the least, and there was reliable information to the effect that the differences between the coach and senior players were out in the open.

We hosted the West Indies and Sri Lanka in back-to-back ODI series in the lead-up to the ICC CWC 2007, which was to be played in the West Indies. On my visit to Nagpur, where the first game against the West Indies was to be played, I received a message that some of the players wanted to see me after the game. I met seven or eight of them in the dressing room, where they told me that there was a trust deficit between them and the coach, which did not augur well for the team's prospects in the Caribbean. The latest of many conflicts had been triggered by the manner in which the coach had told Sachin that he would not open and bat at number four instead. I was told that Sachin's view had not been sought and he had been curtly informed about the change.

I informed the office-bearers about the unrest in the team, but they were not very responsive. A few days later, I went to Baroda for the fourth and final ODI against the West Indies, where I spent most of the evening before the game, trying to cool Sachin down. He was furious after being told by the coach to bat in the middle order 'in the interest of the team'. Sachin kept asking me whether he had ever done anything that was not in the interest of the team, at any point in his career. He said that he was ready to bat at any number, but was disappointed that his commitment to the team was being questioned. The next day, he batted at number four and scored an unbeaten century.

It did not delight me one bit to be proved right in my assessment that our World Cup campaign would be a forgettable one. We crashed out at the league stage itself, after losing to Bangladesh and then Sri Lanka. Pakistan's campaign was as disastrous, as they too exited the tournament after losing to the West Indies and Ireland. With two of the tournament's biggest draws out of the picture, spectator turnouts at the venues went down and tour operators faced massive losses, with fans from the subcontinent, who were to fly to the Caribbean for the second stage of the competition, cancelling their visits. The West Indies Cricket Board (WICB) also erred by pricing the tickets too high and putting off the locals in the process. The ICC had invited officials of all the participating teams for the semi-finals and final and I accompanied Niranjan Shah, the Board secretary, to the Caribbean. On more than one occasion on that trip, we were confronted by angry Indian fans, who demanded an explanation for the team's abject performance.

The aftermath of our first-round exit was shocking. Families of the players received death threats, mock funeral processions of the players were organized and their effigies burnt. Even Sachin, the darling of the nation, was not spared. Policemen had to be posted outside the apartment in which he lived. We feared the worst when the players returned to India. 'Fans' had gathered outside the Mumbai airport, armed with banners and placards denouncing the team. In a discussion with the police and airport officials in the terminal building, it was decided to take all the members of the team who were disembarking in Mumbai, out through Gate No. 8, which was used by owners of private jets. I remember Ajit Tendulkar, who had come to receive his younger brother, not being happy with this plan. He insisted that we use the main exit, but we did not want to take a chance as the situation outside was volatile and tempers were running high. The members of the team who were to catch connecting flights to other cities were driven to the domestic terminal from within the airport complex.

It was a terrible time for the Board, for it was battling the criticism of the cricket fans on one side and simultaneously coming to terms with the announcement of the 'rebel' Indian Cricket League (ICL) by the Zee group. Several first-class cricketers from India—both contemporary and former, players from overseas, and stalwarts such as Kapil Dev had joined the league, whose objective was to stage One-Day and Twenty20 games 'parallel' to those organized by the BCCI, across the country. The BCCI took immediate steps to ban all the players and officials involved in the ICL, in accordance with its rules and regulations. This led to a flurry of court cases, which went on for a long time.

An attempt was also made to conduct an autopsy of the catastrophe in the Caribbean. The office-bearers met Rahul Dravid, the captain, Greg Chappell, the coach and Sanjay Jagdale, the manager, separately at the Cricket Centre and sought their explanation. What I gathered from these meetings was that some of the office-bearers and senior members of the Board were keen that Chappell carry on as the coach. During that phase, comments critical of Chappell and attributed to Sachin and Yuvraj, appeared in the papers.[31] I had to perform the unpleasant duty of sending show-cause notices to both the players, asking them to explain their alleged comments.

A couple of days after the comments appeared, Chappell resigned. It was a sad end to a stint that had promised much when it had started, only to fizzle out. The former Australia captain did have his shortcomings as far as his handling of the senior players was concerned, but the fact is that he was excellent with the junior players. Many of the players he backed, went on to serve India with distinction for several seasons.

One slide in the presentation that Chappell had made to the office-bearers of the Board after the World Cup debacle stands out in my memory. 'The modern-day game is based on talent, strength, power, fitness, risk/reward, confidence, running between wickets and brilliant fielding. Discipline and team ethos are essential and non-negotiable. If the Indian team is to compete, the BCCI needs to address these issues,' it read.

I feel that the Indian team of 2021 ticks most of the boxes that Chappell had identified. We all had our views when a benchmark for fitness was set for the present set of players as an essential criterion for their selection, but the fact is that it

---

[31]'Tendulkar, Yuvraj reply to show cause notice,' Rediff.com, 14 April 2007, https://www.rediff.com/wc2007/2007/apr/14show.htm. Accessed on 26 November 2021.

has worked for the team. I am sure Chappell will be happy that the points raised by him were taken seriously in due course. They enabled the Indian team to top the ICC rankings, after all.

A few days after he returned to Australia, Chappell called me to check if the Board had taken a call on the possibility of his being involved with the NCA. Apparently, a senior official had spoken to him on the same. However, there had been no such discussion and I had to reply in the negative.

The office-bearers also met former India captains to understand from them what had gone wrong in the World Cup and what steps needed to be taken to get Indian cricket back on track. The captains made a few suggestions, such as increasing the emphasis on the training of cricketing skills, ensuring the participation of international players in domestic tournaments, not allowing the international players to do commercial shoots at least one week before the start of a series and during a series and instituting a committee which would advise on the scheduling of series and tournaments.

There were changes in the support staff for the tour of Bangladesh, which followed. Ravi Shastri was appointed the cricket manager and Venkatesh Prasad and Robin Singh came on board as the bowling and fielding coach, respectively. We did well on that tour, winning both the ODI and Test series. Consequently, the players were happier and a lot more relaxed than what they had been at the beginning of the year, as they prepared for their next assignment—a tour of Ireland and England.

Shastri's reluctance to continue as the cricket manager after the Bangladesh series meant that we had to look for a successor to Chappell. Two former captains who were involved in the search were Mr Gavaskar and Shastri himself. Shastri was keen on Dav Whatmore, who was coaching Bangladesh at the time, but Mr Gavaskar was not. The BCCI eventually advertised for the post and shortlisted two applicants: Graham

Ford, the former coach of South Africa and John Emburey, the former England captain. Both were invited to Bengaluru in the first week of June, to be interviewed by a panel comprising Mr Gavaskar, Shastri and the office-bearers of the Board. While Ford attended in person, Emburey was interviewed on Skype. The panel favoured Ford, who too was pleased to accept the job. The media accosted him for a reaction when he was leaving the hotel for the airport. I think the prospect of constantly being under the spotlight unnerved him. The very next day, he informed the Board that he had discussed the assignment with his family and decided to turn it down.

With the tour of Ireland and England only days away, we had no option but to look for another stop-gap candidate. Mr Pawar suggested that we check with one of the all-time greats. Chandrakant 'Chandu' Borde, the former India Test cricketer, captain, selector and manager, was surprised to receive a call from us, but he agreed to take up the role of the cricket manager. Sections of the media sniggered at the decision and highlighted Borde's being on the wrong side of 70. However, we did not expect him to run the nets and give the players catching practice. We wanted someone whom the players could look up to, be a calming influence in the dressing room and share his tactical nous with the captain and senior players.

The boys played some great cricket in the weeks that followed. Borde's sagely presence, coupled with the hard work put in by Prasad and Robin and the other members of the support staff, contributed in no small measure to our victory in the Test series, our first in England since 1986. It was an achievement which enabled the nation to move on from the World Cup fiasco.

By then, people had started mentioning the number of overs in order to differentiate the ICC CWC 2007 from its younger sibling, whose inaugural edition was to be hosted by South Africa in September. The Board took a while to warm up to Twenty20 and the inaugural edition of the inter-state T20 tournament for the Syed Mushtaq Ali Trophy, was played in the 2006–07 season. Prior to the ICC World T20 2007, as it was christened, India had played only one T20 International, on the tour of South Africa in 2006–07. Our international and domestic players were thus not very familiar with the format. The BCCI was in any case reluctant to participate in the ICC World T20 2007 and agreed to send a team only in exchange for getting extra time to prepare its bid for the hosting rights of the ICC CWC 2011.

The national selection committee, which was being chaired by Dilip Vengsarkar, was to meet at the Cricket Centre on 7 July 2007, to pick 30 probables for the ICC World T20 2007. The final squad of 15 was to be picked exactly a month later. Unusually and ironically in the light of what was to follow, there wasn't much speculation or curiosity among the fans and the media, regarding the selection of the probables for the tournament. The focus was on the tour of England, with the Test series scheduled to begin a couple of weeks later.

A day before the selectors met, I received a call from Rahul. He told me that he had spoken to Sachin and Sourav, his predecessors, and both had concurred with his view that Twenty20 was a 'young man's game'. He accordingly requested me to inform the selectors that the three of them would not be available for the ICC World T20. I told him that it would be better if he informed Dilip directly and connected the two just before the meeting commenced the next day. Dilip and his colleagues proceeded to pick 30 probables, sans the trio.

Later, the chairman told me that he had received a call from Sourav, who said that he was in fact available for selection and the information conveyed to him was incorrect. By then of course, it was too late to change anything, as the probables had been announced.

I was scheduled to fly to England for the first two Tests,

which were to be played at Lord's and Nottingham, respectively. We came close to losing at Lord's, but managed to force a draw. Zaheer Khan then made the Nottingham Test his own, bowling us to a seven-wicket victory.

The team was ecstatic, as was the nation, but the captain did not seem to be as thrilled as I thought he would be. I had known Rahul for over a decade, and while he was never an extrovert, I had never seen him as preoccupied as he was on that tour. I got the feeling that a few members of the team, who had been treated poorly by Chappell, were upset with him for not standing up for them. They believed that Rahul, as the captain, had abetted some of the controversial decisions taken by the former coach and selectors. That was probably weighing on his mind. Matters came to a head during the Nottingham Test when Times Now, a news channel, ran a story about Sourav calling Dilip after the selection of the probables and denying that he wanted to skip the ICC World T20. Rahul confronted the Times Now journalist who had done the story, in the lobby of the hotel in Nottingham. I was there and had never seen him so furious. He accused the journalist of questioning his integrity.

This was also the game in which S. Sreesanth 'elbowed' Michael Vaughan, the England captain, while returning to his bowling mark. I happened to be sitting with Ranjan Madugalle, the ICC referee, when this happened. It wasn't the first time Sreesanth had done something like this on a cricket field. Madugalle acted promptly and summoned the captain, manager and offender for a hearing at the end of the day's play. Rahul was not impressed and rebuked Sreesanth for what he had done. He made the point that aggression was best displayed by taking wickets and not by elbowing an opponent. I am not sure whether Sreesanth, who had been involved in a similar incident on the tour of South Africa, got the message. He was reprimanded and penalized by the referee.

Another story which hit the headlines during the third Test at the Oval more or less convinced Rahul that he was being subjected to some sort of a witch-hunt. He did not enforce the follow-on in that game, contending that his bowlers were tired. However, a statement by Zaheer was then taken out of context and highlighted, as if to show that the bowlers were in fact not tired.

The players who had been picked for the ICC World T20 2007, flew directly to South Africa after the end of the England tour. Rahul was among those who returned to India. The Board had by that time started the groundwork for the Indian Premier League (IPL), our answer to the 'rebel' ICL. A launch had been planned at the Taj Palace in Delhi. Rahul, Sachin, Anil and Sourav were to attend, along with Glenn McGrath and Stephen Fleming—two of the many foreign players who had already confirmed their participation in the league.

Rahul told me at the launch that he wanted to talk to Mr Pawar in private. I informed the president, who then invited Rahul to his room. Rahul came downstairs after a few minutes and met me in the lobby. He told me that he had a flight to catch and left immediately, not staying back for the official dinner. I thought that was quite strange, as he hadn't given me any indication of leaving early till then. I then received a call from Mr Pawar. I went up to his room and learnt that Rahul had submitted his resignation as the captain. Mr Pawar told me to keep it to myself for the moment. I had in a way expected it, after what I had seen in England. The resignation was announced on the eve of India's first game in the ICC World T20.

When asked by Mr Pawar who he thought should succeed him, Rahul recommended Mahendra Singh Dhoni, who was already leading the team in the ICC World T20 in South Africa. Dilip Vengsarkar and his co-selectors had already identified the wicketkeeper-batsman from Ranchi as captaincy material in the shorter versions. Mr Pawar then posed the same question to Sachin, who had been Rahul's deputy in England, when we were having dinner later that evening. Sachin repeated what Rahul had said. Thus, Dhoni had his credentials endorsed by two legends, both of whom felt that the Board needed to look ahead in the interest of Indian cricket.

Dhoni, who was already the T20 captain, was then appointed the ODI captain. The Test captaincy was entrusted to Anil Kumble, who had retired from the shorter variety but was still going strong in the traditional version. The way he conducted himself and handled the players on the tour of Australia in 2007–08, I was one of many who were left wondering why he hadn't led India earlier, especially given the fact that he had served as deputy to Sachin, more than a decade previously.

What happened between Rahul's resignation and Anil's appointment as Test captain is history. Dhoni's team won the ICC World T20 2007 and a nation of over a billion fell in love with the Twenty20 format. Although Shahid Afridi was declared the 'Player of the Tournament', there were many who believed that Yuvraj Singh deserved that honour. He pretty much set up the triumph with his explosive batting. The pièce de résistance were, of course, his six sixes in an over off Stuart Broad in the game against England. The BCCI president announced a prize money of $3 million for the team, which was over and above the prize money presented by the ICC. The Board also approved a special award of $1 million to Yuvraj, which was announced by Lalit Modi. Lalit had also promised Yuvraj a Mercedes car. I don't know whether Yuvraj got it.

Mr Pawar had flown to Johannesburg to watch the final between India and Pakistan, along with a few other officials. He called me after the game and talked about organizing a welcome for the team in Mumbai. He envisaged a drive from the airport to the Cricket Centre, followed by a public felicitation at the Wankhede Stadium. The catch was that the Indian team was scheduled to land in Mumbai on the morning of 26 September, the day after Anant Chaturdashi, which marks the end of the Ganesh festival. The Mumbai Police were known to work around the clock on the last day of Ganeshotsav, on which thousands of idols of the Lord are immersed in the sea, and the celebrations spill over into the next day.

It was therefore unreasonable and even unfair to expect the police to hit the streets for us even as the immersions were folding up. However, a way had to be found. I met R.R. Patil, the then home minister of Maharashtra, who convened a meeting with the Police Commissioner of Mumbai, who agreed to help us out. We could not thank him and his police force enough.

Memories of the welcome accorded to Ajit Wadekar's team on its return from England in 1971 were rekindled, on what was an unforgettable day. Even rain did not dent the enthusiasm of the Mumbaikars, who lined the streets and cheered the players as they passed by in an open double-decker bus. It was as if the entire population of Mumbai, including Lata Mangeshkar herself, who cheered for the team from the balcony of her apartment on Peddar Road, had taken time out to welcome the heroes. The crowds ensured that the bus took seven hours to travel a distance of 23 km! The players were an exhausted lot by the time they reached the Wankhede. There, they were felicitated by Mr Pawar and Mr R.R Patil in front of a capacity crowd.

The World Cup winners then spent a day in New Delhi, where they met the prime minister and president of India at their respective residences and were felicitated.

The victory in the ICC World T20 2007 was the perfect launchpad for the IPL, which became a blockbuster in its very first season in 2008.

12
STABILITY

The Test series win in England, the launch of the IPL and the victory in the ICC World T20 happened within a few weeks of each other and coincided with the start of a phase of stability for the Board. While the decision to have the elections once in three years undoubtedly helped keep things stable, what also did was the recruitment of professionals. They had a massive impact on the functioning of the Board.

The BCCI had a handful of full-time employees at the time of the shift to the Cricket Centre. Marvine D'Souza was the stenographer, Dalpat Vadolikar handled the office correspondence and scheduling of domestic tournaments, Vikas Pandit coordinated with the officials who were posted for international and domestic events and Mohini Deshpande handled the accounts. J.K. Sheth and B. Laxman were engaged on contracts. There were also two office assistants, in Sitaram Tambe, who had been in service since 1969, and Sunil Telgi. Dalpat's father Govind had also been an employee of the Board, as baggage-master. He had handled the baggage and equipment of teams touring India, for decades. He used to live in the old BCCI Office.

After the shift to the Cricket Centre, Tata Consultancy Services (TCS) was engaged to study the working of the Board, propose a secretarial structure and help with the head-hunting. It was decided that the Board would make the final selection from the three candidates shortlisted for every designation by TCS. In its report, TCS recommended the creation of departments to manage Cricket Operations, Game Development, Media and Corporate Affairs, Administration, Finance and Legal issues. Each department was to be headed by a manager, who would report to the CAO. The managers would be supported by assistant managers.

The first 'manager' to join the Board was Suru Nayak, the former Test cricketer from Mumbai. He had won many admirers with his diligence and dedication in the administrative department of the CCI, where he was employed at the time. We had him in mind as the Cricket Operations manager from the very beginning. Hence, we did not advertise for the post, but sought the advice of Rajbhai, the CCI president and Suru's boss at the time. Rajbhai was delighted that the Board, of which the CCI was a member, had evinced interest in an employee of his club, and gave us the go-ahead to approach Suru.

Suru was very methodical and did an exceptional job. He endeared himself to all the people he worked and corresponded with, including representatives of the affiliated units and the management of the ICC and international boards. He handled domestic and international cricket operations and single-handedly managed the requirements of the Indian team, which included travel, accommodation, clothing and obtaining visas for tours. In later years, he was one of the individuals responsible for the successful conduct of the ICC CWC 2011, on which he worked as the TD (India). He had managed the ICC Champions Trophy matches played at the Brabourne Stadium in 2006 and was hence familiar with the ICC's protocols. When the ICC Women's World Cup was held in India in 2013, Suru was the obvious choice for the role of TD, a responsibility he discharged with much aplomb.

It was a tough assignment, with the Shiv Sena having threatened to disrupt the tournament if the Pakistani team played in Mumbai. This resulted in all the group matches which were scheduled to be played in Mumbai, being shifted to Cuttack, thanks to Mr Naveen Patnaik, the chief minister of Odisha, who assured the BCCI that he would take care of everything, including security. Although India failed to make it to the knockout stage, the tournament was well organized and Suru and his team did a great job.

Devendra Prabhudesai came on board as the manager (Media Relations and Corporate Affairs) in January 2008. I had observed him at work during his stint at Mr Gavaskar's Professional Management Group and felt that he would be the ideal candidate for the role. Before his appointment was approved by the senior office-bearers, I spoke to Mr Gavaskar, who said that the Board had chosen wisely. The decks were thus cleared for Devendra's appointment.

The other managers came through TCS. Dinesh Menon came in to handle administration. K.V.P. Rao, who was selected as the manager (Game Development), could not join as there was an issue with his voluntary retirement at his then workplace, and Stanley Saldanha, who had been shortlisted for the role, was appointed instead. The Board did not appoint a full-time legal department as it was felt that a legal firm could be hired for the time being.

Mr Pawar wanted all the departments to function under the same roof. However, Finance proved to be the exception to the rule. It continued to function from the incumbent treasurer's office till 2015, when Shashank, in his second term as the president, got it shifted permanently to the Cricket Centre.

I was given a free hand to pick the assistant managers. Individuals who were based in Mumbai and had played competitive cricket or were associated with some form of cricket administration, were approached. Among those who fulfilled at least one of these criteria were Anant Datar, Alvin Gaekwad, Sumeet Mallapurkar and Amit Siddheshwar. Nilesh Dhulap joined the accounts department and Devendra Bhuvad was appointed as the IT-in-charge. They were thrilled to get an opportunity to work in the Cricket Board.

Hemang Amin's primary responsibility when he joined the BCCI in 2010 was to scrutinize the expenses of IPL 2010. He displayed his organizational skills in later years and played a key role in the successful conduct of the IPL. He is presently the COO of the IPL and also the Board's acting CEO.

The BCCI also set up a media centre on the fourth floor of the Cricket Centre. Gaurav Saxena, another competent individual who specializes in multitasking, was in charge. He went on to look after Cricket Operations in later years and is the go-to man for all issues concerning international teams.

Dr Vece Paes, the former Olympian, took charge as the anti-doping consultant in 2010, with Dr Abhijit Salvi joining as his assistant. They also handled the age-verification programme of the BCCI for junior age-group tournaments. Mr Ravi Savani joined as the head of the BCCI's Anti-Corruption Unit in 2013. While Dr Paes framed the Board's Anti-Doping Code, Mr Savani was responsible for framing the Board's Anti-Corruption Code.

Even as the managers were being assembled, we launched initiatives, most of which turned out to be significant in the long run. Our objective, as spelt out by me to the managers, was to complement the efforts that the players were putting in on the field. It was important to work towards enhancing the quality and productivity of the entire spectrum, from the players, who were at the forefront, to all those who worked behind the scenes.

Umpiring was an area of concern. Although India had become the global hub of the sport by then, Indian umpires were lagging behind their counterparts in other countries in efficacy as well as consistency. I did some research and presented some facts to the senior office-bearers. From 1997 to 2002, the BCCI had given international exposure to as many as 21 umpires, but had sacrificed quality for quantity in the process. Honestly, many of those assignments had been doled out, with most of those umpires not officiating in more than a couple of international matches. We lost out on genuine talent as a result. Of the state associations, only MCA, TNCA and KSCA were conducting regular coaching programmes for umpires. Consequently, candidates of these associations would clear the Board's umpiring exams with ease, but those belonging to other associations would struggle.

Nothing had been done to educate the umpires and upgrade their knowledge. The Board did try to encourage former cricketers to take up umpiring and a few even qualified, but they did not stick to the job for long.

The indifference to umpires wasn't restricted to the BCCI alone. In fact, Cricket Australia (CA) was the only international body to have grasped the importance of conducting educational courses for umpires. Following discussions with Mr Srinivasan, who was then the treasurer of the Board, I proposed that we seek CA's help to improve the standard of umpiring in India. CA's response was positive, and our only precondition was that Simon Taufel, then one of the world's top umpires, play an active role in the endeavour. We were pleased to hear that Taufel was more than willing to be a part of the CA team led by Ross Taylor and we entered into a three-year agreement with CA for umpire education.

This arrangement, apart from training the umpires on the BCCI panel, also comprised an umpire educator programme, wherein workshops were conducted for a select group of about 15 senior umpires. This workshop was followed by an individual assessment process and the candidates were graded. This enabled us to create a panel of umpire educators, who visited the state units to help candidates prepare for the Board's umpiring examinations. Simon made several trips to India in the years that followed and the umpires were thrilled to be 'coached' by someone of his stature. Simon was responsible in setting up a training programme for the match referees too.

We also initiated an umpires' assessment project in 2008. The Chennai-based SportsMechanics, whose senior representatives S. Ramakrishnan and Dhananjay had been part of the support staff of the Indian team as video analysts, was appointed to create a software to analyse footage of Ranji Trophy matches. In the first year of the project, SportsMechanics assigned Ranji games to video analysts from their team. The analysts would film the matches ball-by-ball, with two cameras installed at either end. Decisions given by the umpires in every match, including no-balls and wide balls, were then tagged for assessment by the umpire assessment committee. Every umpire was then given a DVD featuring the tagged decisions and both teams were given DVDs of the entire match.

S. Venkataraghavan, the former India captain and international umpire, was appointed the director of the umpires' assessment committee, which also comprised V.K. Ramaswamy and A.V. Jayaprakash, former international umpires both. The triumvirate assessed the performance of the umpires by watching videos of the tagged decisions. This practice ensured that the gradation of the umpires was not done in a haphazard manner, but was based on solid facts. We also instituted an 'Elite' panel of umpires for domestic matches, which was modelled on the ICC's panel for international games. Promotions and relegations were made every year on the basis of the ratings awarded by the members of the umpires' assessment committee.

Another milestone on the umpiring front was the institution of an annual umpires' exchange programme. We first tied up with Cricket Australia and then got into similar agreements with the England Cricket Board (ECB) and Cricket South Africa (CSA). Umpires from India thus got an opportunity to officiate in domestic matches played in these countries and umpires from these countries came over to India to stand in select Ranji and Duleep Trophy games. The experience that the shortlisted umpires—Indian and foreign—gained by officiating in matches played in hitherto unfamiliar settings, was invaluable. It was an arrangement that benefited all the parties involved.

The umpires' assessment project served us well till 2014. That Mr Srinivasan's innings in the Board ended the same year following the intervention of the SC, was by no means coincidental. He was someone who had backed the project to the hilt, as the treasurer, secretary and then the president of the Board. In his absence, the project ran out of steam and came to a standstill. However, we did manage to conduct special training sessions for the members of the 'Elite' umpires' panel, to enhance their third-umpire skills, especially when it came to the use of the Decision Review System (DRS). This was possible because of the support of Dev Shriyan and the BCCI's in-house TV production team.

We also replicated the ICC's 'match referee' model in domestic cricket. A code of conduct for domestic matches was put in place, which comprised rules for the players, match officials and also administrators. Every state association was asked to recommend two former cricketers as referees. The nominees underwent a training course, followed by an assessment. The ones who cleared this stage were inducted into the BCCI's panel. We unearthed some fine talent in the form of individuals who knew their job and were excellent man managers. Some of the referees who were discovered through this initiative went on to officiate in the IPL and were even appointed for ACC matches. Later, the BCCI also formed a panel of qualified female match referees.

Stanley Saldanha, who was a proactive game development manager, suggested in 2009 that we introduce a course for video analysts. He felt that these courses would enable us to create a pan-India panel of qualified video analysts. The office-bearers liked the idea and we had a panel ready in less than two years. The Board invested heavily in the exercise, purchasing state-of-the-art equipment such as video cameras, DVRs and other accessories required for live recording of matches. Every state unit was given two sets of the equipment, to be used during domestic games. We thus started covering each and every domestic game with as many as four cameras. This enabled the Board to archive footage of all its domestic matches.

Stanley also conceptualized an online scoring project. Scoring used to be done manually at the time, with refresher courses for scorers being conducted annually. A vendor was engaged and we started organizing workshops to educate scorers and encourage them to adopt the online format. Within a year, every BCCI game was being covered by an online scorer in addition to a manual scorer.

The BCCI relaunched its website with a provision for ball-by-ball coverage of all the domestic matches online. Later, score cards of all the matches of the Ranji Trophy, right from the first game in 1934 were made available on the website.

K.V.P. Rao, who replaced Stanley in 2010, carried on the good work. He was associated with the umpire development programme and also did a stint at the NCA, where he was based for a while.

We also tried to create a pool of statisticians to help the state units to compile and update data on a regular basis and organized workshops with the help of seasoned statisticians such as Sudhir Vaidya, Dinar Gupte and Ramesh Parab. However, this venture was not as successful as we had imagined it would be.

Audits were conducted at all the international and domestic venues in the country. India-made as well as imported super-soppers, grass-cutters, mowers and rollers, were procured centrally and then distributed to the international venues and subsequently domestic venues. Daljit Singh, a curator par excellence, played a crucial role in the acquisition of the equipment, along with his fellow curators Venkat Sunderam, Kasturirangan, Vishwanathan and Dhiraj Parsana. They did all the groundwork, contacting vendors and getting the rates, and we then discussed the same with the office-bearers and got their approval. Daljit and his colleagues also designed an educational course for curators. Based on his proposal, we started a certificate course for curators, which accorded equal importance to theoretical and practical aspects.

This was followed by a Level 1 course for curators, which included theory and practicals. Classes were conducted by experts from the industry and educational institutes, apart from the BCCI's curators. This exercise helped create a pool of curators, the members of which were then deputed to different centres for domestic games.

We also started sending two curators to Australia every year, to enable them to learn techniques of ground and pitch preparation in unfamiliar conditions. This added a new dimension to our education programme. Every curator who was a part of this venture gained a lot in terms of knowledge and experience. Today, India has a group of well-qualified curators such as Ashish Bhowmick and Taposh Chatterjee, to name just two, who are ready to take over from the likes of Daljit Singh.

We managed to initiate and conduct all these activities only because Mr Pawar and his team of office-bearers wanted to make a difference to Indian cricket. The team which took over in 2008, with Shashank Manohar as the president, N. Srinivasan as the secretary, M.P. Pandove as the treasurer and Sanjay Jagdale as the joint secretary, was as committed. Getting funds sanctioned for these initiatives was never an issue. All the office-bearers asked for was an assurance that the initiatives would be planned and executed in a professional manner.

While they were amenable to initiatives which they believed would benefit Indian cricket, the office-bearers of the time were not at all enamoured of the media and were in fact rather indifferent to it. A long-standing weakness of the Board is that it has never kept the media informed of all the good things that it has been doing for the betterment of the game. Devendra Prabhudesai and I did what we could to change the attitude of the office-bearers with regard to the media and attempted to streamline the Board's media management. A media database was created, so that the fourth estate could be apprised of news and developments related to the Board, in a more formal and structured manner.

Devendra was also involved in the process of drafting appropriate media accreditation guidelines for both international series and the IPL, along with Sports Law experts and Sundar Raman, the COO of the IPL.

An initiative close to my heart was *Within the Boundary and Beyond*, the Board's 16-page quarterly newsletter, through which we aimed to highlight the off-the-field activities of the Board, especially workshops and training programmes for umpires, video analysts and curators, in addition to happenings in international and domestic cricket. The newsletter also featured stories on the state associations and their activities. The inaugural issue was brought out in February 2008 and it made an immediate impact. Copies of the newsletter were printed and dispatched to former and current cricketers and officials, affiliated units, international cricket boards, the ICC and members of the media. The feedback, which came in from across the length and breadth of the cricketing world, was encouraging.

Within the Boundary and Beyond was painstakingly written and compiled by Devendra, who also worked on brochures, which we brought out on the eve of home series against visiting teams, as well as commemorative volumes. 'From Learners to Leaders,' a volume which commemorated the Platinum Jubilee of Test cricket in India, was released in 2008. It comprised articles by 20 of India's 31 Test captains at the time, from Dattajirao

Gaekwad, who led the side in England in 1959, to Dhoni, the incumbent. The other commemorative volume Devendra worked on was one that commemorated the Platinum Jubilee of the Ranji Trophy in 2009. He also compiled a volume to commemorate the World Cup win in 2011.

The office-bearers approved our proposal to recognize the top performers in international and domestic cricket annually. The inaugural BCCI Awards ceremony was organized in December 2007, on the eve of the Indian team's departure to Australia. This annual celebration of excellence in Indian cricket was long overdue, and it gained in popularity and prestige as the years went by. Every ceremony, starting from the first one, was attended by members of the cricketing fraternity and the media, to cheer for all those who had excelled at the international, domestic, senior and junior levels in a 12-month period from 1 October to 30 September of the following year.

Professional Management Group did a fine job as the event manager. The BCCI staff handled the logistics and coordination, with Devendra actively involved in the entire process, from the conceptualization of the ceremony to even its execution as the Master of Ceremonies.

The biggest award of the ceremony was the Col. C.K. Nayudu Lifetime Achievement Award, which the Board had instituted in 1993, his birth centenary year. This award has been given to some of the biggest names in Indian cricket since. Only once has a non-cricketer received the award. This was K.N. Prabhu, the distinguished former sports editor of *The Times of India*, who was felicitated in the late 1990s.

The annual award for the Indian cricketer of the year was aptly named for the great Polly Umrigar and is awarded to the most outstanding performer at the international level. The awards for the top performers at the domestic and junior levels were named after former Board administrators such as M.A.

Chidambaram and Madhavrao Scindia. The Lala Amarnath[32] Awards were instituted for the top all-rounders in the Ranji Trophy and domestic limited-overs competitions. The awardees received impressive and distinctive trophies, along with cash prizes.

The regular awards apart, special presentations were also made at the BCCI Awards ceremonies. After Dilip Sardesai's untimely demise in 2007, Mr Pawar instituted an award in his name for India's best performer in Test series against the West Indies, as a tribute to his splendid and series-defining batsmanship on India's tour of the Caribbean in 1971. At the BCCI Awards ceremony in November 2012, Mr Srinivasan and Mr Jagdale, who were then the Board president and secretary, respectively, decided to recognize and reward seven individuals posthumously for their services to Indian cricket: Vijay Merchant, Vinoo Mankad, Ghulam Ahmed, Dattu Phadkar, Vijay Manjrekar, M.L. Jaisimha and Dilip Sardesai. They had missed out on the Col. C.K. Nayudu Lifetime Achievement Award as it had been presented only to living individuals since its inception. The next-of-kin of these departed stalwarts were invited and felicitated on their behalf. Mr Jaisimha and Mr Sardesai were represented by their spouses and the others by their children. This practice of honouring cricketers posthumously was continued in subsequent awards functions as well.

In June 2008, the Board celebrated the silver jubilee of the 1983 World Cup win, that had changed Indian cricket forever. Kapil's Devils were felicitated at the Taj Palace in Delhi, in front of an audience which comprised former India captains and senior members of the Union government. Every member of that team—the 14 players and P.R. Man Singh, the manager— received a cheque for ₹25 lakh. Mr Salve, who had headed

---

[32]Independent India's first Test captain, Lala Amarnath was also the first recipient of the Col. C.K. Nayudu Lifetime Achievement Award in 1993.

the Board when history was made on 25 June 1983, brought the house down with his address, in which he light-heartedly reprimanded Kapil Dev and the other players for 'bullying' him on the balcony of Lord's on that unforgettable evening and demanding a handsome financial reward for what they had accomplished. Mr Salve reminded the gathering that the Board was not financially well off in those days. Back then, he had promised the players ₹1 lakh each, only to realize that the Board did not have the requisite funds. He then requested Lata Mangeshkar to sing at a music concert in Delhi, so that funds could be raised for the players from its proceeds. Being a cricket fan, she graciously agreed.

The Board gave special permission for an exhibition match between an Indian XI and a Sri Lankan XI at the Wankhede Stadium to raise funds for the great lady's Deenanath Mangeshkar Hospital project in Pune, in 2005. I was the joint convener of that game. It was the Board's way of repaying what it owed to the living legend. She remains an ardent supporter of Indian cricket and is entitled to complimentary tickets for every international match played anywhere in India.

A venture that Devendra and I initiated but could not complete, was the process of recording exhaustive interviews with India's former captains for posterity. It took off smoothly, with the likes of M.A.K. Pataudi, Gundappa Viswanath, Anil Kumble, Nariman Contractor and Dilip Vengsarkar being interviewed in the first few months. However, the priorities of the Board kept changing and we could not take the project to its logical conclusion. We also started bringing out a calendar, which was a big hit. From 2008 to 2014, we spotlighted the top 12 cricketers of every decade, from the 1940s to the 2010s, in the calendar. The 2015 calendar was dedicated to our best Test and limited-overs teams over the years. The demand for the calendar was huge and not everybody who wanted one could lay his hands on one.

Devendra and I also convinced the office-bearers to felicitate our heroes when they were in the process of bidding farewell. Anil Kumble and Sourav Ganguly were honoured at a function held in the clubhouse of the new Vidarbha Cricket Association Stadium at Nagpur, during the fourth and final Test of the 2008–09 series against Australia. Anil had retired at the end of the previous Test in Delhi and Sourav was to quit after the Nagpur Test. Sachin Tendulkar and V.V.S. Laxman were also felicitated at the same function for completing 12,000 runs in Tests and playing a hundred Tests, respectively. Earlier that year, Anil was felicitated for taking 600 Test wickets.

We organized a farewell for Rahul after he announced his retirement in March 2012. VVS Laxman, who also retired a few months later, was felicitated at the BCCI Awards ceremony that year. While Sachin did get a proper send-off in what was his 200th and last Test at the Wankhede Stadium in November 2013, I think the BCCI can do much better in terms of acknowledging the contribution of our cricketers who excelled at the sport and did the country proud.

The annual Mansoor Ali Khan Pataudi Memorial Lecture, in the honour of the former India captain, was Mr Srinivasan's brainchild. The inaugural lecture was delivered by Mr Gavaskar in 2013. He was followed by Anil Kumble, V.V.S. Laxman, Rahul Dravid, Farokh Engineer, Kevin Pietersen and Virender Sehwag in later years. The Pataudi Lecture was a standalone event for the first four years, but the Committee of Administrators, which took charge of the Board in 2017, decided to merge it with the BCCI Awards ceremony.

Mr Pawar had a lot on his mind when he became the president in 2005. He stated his desire of spending a substantial chunk of the money that the Board was making through TV rights, on the well-being of luminaries of yesteryears. The medical benevolent fund was enhanced to ₹5 lakh per individual. The monthly pension scheme, which the Board had introduced in 2004 as a part of its platinum jubilee celebrations, was also revised. Former Test and ODI players apart, cricketers who had played more than 25 first-class matches were brought under the aegis of the scheme, along with former Test and ODI umpires.

The annual outgoing of the Board in terms of pension increased to around ₹20 crore, with nearly 800 cricketers being covered by the revised scheme, but that did not deter Mr Pawar and his colleagues. The most significant decision with regard to the pension scheme was to extend it to widows of retired Test cricketers and umpires for their respective lifetimes. We received a touching letter from Ms Rekha Manjrekar, the wife of Vijay Manjrekar, the former Test batsman, shortly after the extension. 'Although my children are taking care of me, to get a pension which my husband would have got, for my lifetime, makes me feel good and independent,' she wrote.

Mr Pawar also replicated what international boards across the world had done, with regard to women's cricket. The Women's Cricket Association of India (WCAI), which ran women's cricket in the country, had done a fine job over the years, despite the lack of funds and infrastructure. I had interacted with members of the body both at the WCAI and their Mumbai team, and observed their struggle from close quarters. Women's cricket would always figure in the agenda of the AGMs of the Board, but it was never taken seriously. Some members voiced their opposition even when Mr Pawar advocated that the Board take over women's cricket. They suggested that some money be given to the WCAI to run its own affairs. However, the president put his foot down. The WCAI was expecting a merger with the BCCI, but that did not happen. The BCCI chalked out a domestic and international calendar for the ladies and went ahead with its plans, even as the WCAI continued to function and conduct cricketing activities.

It was a landmark decision. Shubhangi Kulkarni and Rani Noora, two former lady cricketers, were invited to a working committee meeting of the Board in 2006 and the process of absorption initiated. All the facilities and perks which were being provided to male cricketers, were gradually extended to female cricketers. Contracts for current cricketers and pensions for retired cricketers were introduced after a few years. If women's cricket in India is in the pink of health in 2022, it is only because of what Mr Pawar did in 2006.

Another important decision implemented by the Board before Mr Pawar completed his three-year term was to appoint national selectors for men and women on annual contracts, thus making them responsible and accountable to the Board. One of the stipulations for a selector's post was that the individual in question could not be a part of the managing committee of any state unit.

The Board's 'stable' phase coincided with an eventful but successful phase for the Indian team in at least two of the three formats. Our consistency in Test cricket at home and overseas in the 2000s enabled us to top the ICC's Test Rankings for the very first time, in December 2009. This happened one year after a seamless transfer of the Test captaincy. Anil Kumble was succeeded by M.S. Dhoni, who was already leading the team in the two limited-overs formats. Dhoni insisted that Anil, who had retired after the Delhi Test against Australia, be with the team for the final Test at Nagpur.

At the presentation ceremony following the game, which India won to take the series 2-0, Dhoni requested his predecessor to accompany him to receive the Border–Gavaskar Trophy from the two legends after whom the trophy was named. It was a fantastic gesture by the new captain.

That four-Test series against Australia was followed by a two-Test engagement against England in December 2008. Ahmedabad was to host the first Test and Mumbai the second. With the Wankhede Stadium undergoing renovation for the ICC CWC 2011, the Mumbai Test was assigned to the

Brabourne Stadium, which had last hosted a Test match in 1973. The game was scheduled to commence on 19 December 2008, almost exactly 75 years after the conclusion of the first Test on Indian soil, which was also played against England, at the Bombay Gymkhana from 15 December to 18 December 1933. We had planned to combine the BCCI Awards ceremony for 2007–08 with a celebration of the Platinum Jubilee of Test cricket in India on the lawns of the Bombay Gymkhana, on the eve of the Mumbai Test. However, that was not to be.

India and England were playing the fifth ODI of a seven-match series in Cuttack, when Mumbai was attacked by Pakistani terrorists. The last two ODIs were called off as a result and there was a question mark on the Tests. Frankly, cricket was not on anybody's mind after the tragedy. Eventually, both Boards decided to go ahead with the Tests, but at alternate venues, and the matches were shifted to Chennai and Mohali, respectively. The Platinum Jubilee celebrations were called off as a mark of respect to the martyrs of 26/11.

The inaugural edition of the Champions League, which was to be played before the start of the Test series against England, was also cancelled. The teams which were to participate in the tournament were scheduled to arrive in Mumbai and check in at the Taj Mahal Hotel on 28 November, two days after it was attacked.

The BCCI, in its own way, extended financial support to the families of the brave hearts from the NSG, Mumbai Police and Home Guards, who laid down their lives while fighting the terrorists. I personally visited most of the families in Mumbai and presented the cheques. The total amount distributed was ₹2.2 crore.

Our search for a permanent coach after Chappell's exit in mid-2007, ended in early 2008. Following discussions with Mr Pawar, Mr Gavaskar got in touch with Gary Kirsten, the former South African opener. What followed was an 'operation' that would have done a spy agency proud. Only a handful of people in the Board were in the know of Kirsten's trip to Delhi to meet the Board president. He was received at the airport and driven to Mr Pawar's residence. There, he was made to camp in a room. Waiting in another room were Mr Gavaskar, Ravi Shastri and Niranjan Shah, the Board secretary. While both Mr Gavaskar and Ravi knew who was in the adjacent room, Niranjan did not. The two former India captains took turns to visit the other room and talk to Kirsten. Mr Pawar was held up in a Cabinet meeting and he arrived at around 10.30 p.m., after which he met Kirsten.

Kirsten's appointment was confirmed from early 2008 till the end of the ICC CWC 2011, and he then left as stealthily as he had arrived. By the time the media got to know what had happened, he was already on the plane, on his way back to South Africa.

Gary proved himself in the months to come. He was a good man manager and was ably supported by Paddy Upton, who joined the team as mental conditioning coach. Gary had a successful tenure, which culminated with the World Cup triumph in 2011.

The BCCI then appointed Duncan Fletcher as the head coach of the Indian team for a three-year period, with Sanjay Bangar and Bharat Arun as the batting and bowling coaches, respectively. Ravi Shastri was brought in as team director on the tour of England in 2014, and he stayed with the side till 2016, when Anil Kumble took over as head coach. One year later, Shastri was back, this time as head coach. His stint ended in November 2021, with the ICC Men's T20 World Cup[33] in the UAE. Rahul Dravid, his successor, has been named head coach for a period of two years.

---

[33] The ICC World T20 (men) has been rechristened the ICC Men's T20 World Cup.

India's tour of Sri Lanka, 1997: (Sitting from left): The author (manager), Mohammed Azharuddin, Sachin Tendulkar (captain), Anil Kumble (vice-captain) and Madan Lal (coach).
(Standing from left): Nilesh Kulkarni, Venkatesh Prasad, Abey Kuruvilla, Debashis Mohanty, Ali Irani (physio), Rahul Dravid, Noel David, Ajay Jadeja, Navjot Sidhu, Syed Saba Karim, Robin Singh and Sourav Ganguly.

Independence Day celebrations at the Indian High Commission in Colombo, 15 August 1997.

Skipper and manager: The author with Sachin Tendulkar, Sri Lanka tour, 1997.

Khel bhi jeeto aur dil bhi (Win the game and hearts too): Members of the Indian team with Shri Atal Behari Vajpayee, the Honourable Prime Minister of India, on the eve of India's tour of Pakistan, 2003–04.

India's tour of Pakistan, 2003–04: The manager and captain with the prime minister.

The first ODI at Karachi, Pakistan tour, 2003–04: (From left): Amrit Mathur, Arun Jaitley, Jagmohan Dalmiya, Shaharyar Khan (Chairman, Pakistan Cricket Board), Pawan Munjal (Managing Director, Hero MotoCorp) and the author.

The first ODI at Karachi, 2003–04: Among the spectators was Imran Khan (seated third from left), former captain of the Pakistan cricket team and the incumbent prime minister of Pakistan.

The Indian cricket team on the Pakistani side of the Wagah Border, 2003–04.

Winners of the Test Series in Pakistan, 2003–04.

At work in the Cricket Centre, Mumbai.

ICC Cricket World Cup 2011: The trophy unveiling: (from left) The host tournament director with Mr Sharad Pawar, President, ICC and Haroon Lorgat, CEO, ICC.

The ICC CWC 2011 countdown board at the Cricket Centre, Mumbai.

ICC Cricket World Cup, 2011: The author at a promotional event organized by Star Sports, the official broadcaster, with (from left) Kapil Dev (World Cup-winning captain, 1983), Manu Sawhney (Managing Director, ESPN Star Sports), Sir Vivian Richards (World Cup winner, 1975 and 1979), Imran Khan (World Cup-winning captain, 1992), Arjuna Ranatunga (World Cup winner, 1996) and Alan Wilkins (media personality).

Host Tournament Director, ICC Cricket World Cup 2011.

Wankhede Stadium, 2 April 2011: Sachin Tendulkar congratulates Yuvraj Singh, the Player of the ICC CWC 2011.

With Sachin Tendulkar, to whom the World Cup win was dedicated, by his teammates.

The author with Dr Manmohan Singh, the former prime minister of India.

The author with the only captain to have the ICC Cricket World Cup, ICC World Twenty20 and ICC Champions Trophy titles under his belt.

The author with Sunil Gavaskar and Ravi Shastri.

October 2007: The Indian team celebrating the author's birthday in the dressing room.

The author delivers a vote of thanks at the BCCI's felicitation of Anil Kumble in Chennai in March 2008.

With Mr Sharad Pawar, Shashank Manohar and Varsha Manohar at the BCCI Awards ceremony in May 2011.

With Sanjay Jagdale.

Legends at the Wankhede Stadium: Allan Border and Sunil Gavaskar (standing fourth and fifth from left respectively) with the Border–Gavaskar Trophy and office-bearers of the Mumbai Cricket Association at the presentation ceremony, at the end of the 2004–05 series between India and Australia.

MCA officials at the Golden Jubilee celebrations of the Dr H.D. Kanga League, the most competitive inter-club tournament in the world, 1997.
(From left): The author, Ronnie Mendonca (Commissioner of Police, Mumbai), Ravi Savant, Ajit Wadekar, Manohar Joshi, Rashid Kudrolli, Avi Sule and Ramesh Kosambia.

The author with (from left) Arun Jaitley, Anurag Thakur, C.K. Khanna and I.S. Bindra at a working committee meeting of the Board in the early 2000s.

The author with (from left) I.S. Bindra, Sharad Pawar and Raj Singh Dungarpur.

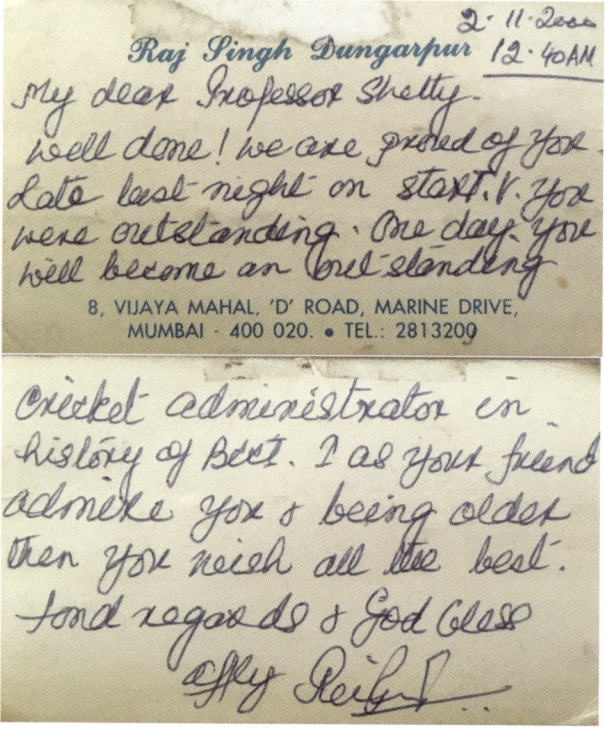

Letter of appreciation from Raj Singh Dungarpur.

The Chief Administrative Officer and his team: The BCCI staff at the Cricket Centre, 2012.

The annual BCCI Awards Ceremony on 21 November 2012: The author with N. Srinivasan (President, BCCI) and Sachin Tendulkar.

The highlight of the annual BCCI Awards Ceremony in January 2014 was the presence of India's two World Cup-winning captains. Kapil Dev and M.S. Dhoni exchanged the trophies that they had won in 1983 and 2011, respectively.

The author

November 2014: The author with Virat Kohli, on the eve of the Indian team's tour of Australia. Kohli became India's 32nd Test captain in the first Test of the series.

The author with Chandrakant Borde, former India captain and J.Y. Lele, former secretary, BCCI.

With Rahul Dravid, now the head coach of the Indian cricket team, and Ravichandran Ashwin.

The author with Lalit Modi (extreme left), Shashank Manohar and Niranjan Shah (back to the camera).

With the stalwarts: (From left): The author, Niranjan Shah, Sharad Pawar and N. Srinivasan.

Sharing a light moment with Sunil Gavaskar and Niranjan Shah.

With Anil Kumble and the man who succeeded him as India's Test captain, M.S. Dhoni.

A caricature of the author by Satish Acharya, the renowned cartoonist.

With Shri Narendra Modi, Prime Minister of India.

13
THE IPL STORY

One of Mr Pawar's 'teammates' when he won the BCCI elections in 2005 was Lalit Kumar Modi, who had been knocking hard on the doors of the Board for more than a decade.

Lalit first got in touch with the Board in 1996. Modi Entertainment Networks (MEN), his company, was at that time the franchise rights-holder in India for Fashion TV and ESPN, the newly launched sports TV channel. The World Cup had been played earlier that year, for which most of the leading venues in the country, such as the Wankhede Stadium, M.A. Chidambaram Stadium, M. Chinnaswamy Stadium and the PCA Stadium at Mohali had been embellished with floodlights. Although India did not make it to the final, the tournament was a success and Lalit wanted the Board to capitalize on the same. He proposed a 50-overs-a-side inter-city league to be played under floodlights, featuring teams representing the six metros—Mumbai, Delhi, Chennai, Kolkata, Bengaluru and Hyderabad—as well as Mohali.

In 1995, the BCCI had launched the Challenger Trophy, in which the top 36 cricketers in the country were divided into three teams, namely India Seniors, India A and India B. The inter-city league, as envisaged by Lalit, was obviously different. Not only would it feature the top India players of the time, but also players from overseas. Every playing XI in the league was to comprise two foreign players, as per his plan.

Lalit had also thought of 'catchment areas' for each of the teams to recruit its players from. For instance, players from the states of Maharashtra, Gujarat and of course, the separate cricketing entity that was Mumbai, would be eligible to be represent Mumbai in the inter-city league.

The state associations which were proposed as the hosts of the matches were definitely interested in the concept. The league was certain to attract huge crowds and in-stadia sponsorships, and thus boost the coffers of the host associations. To give the example of the Mumbai Cricket Association, a lot of money had been spent on the installation of floodlights in time for the 1996 World Cup, but the association itself did not know when it would host a day-night game next. An annual tournament like the inter-city league guaranteed financial security to the MCA and the other host associations.

However, Mr Dalmiya wasn't very keen on the idea, and he prevailed upon the members of the Board to shoot it down. Lalit was aggrieved because he believed that most of the associations were on his side. He bore Mr Dalmiya a grudge since then.

If you can't beat them, join them. Lalit probably had this dictum at the back of his mind when he started trying to find a foothold in the Board after his idea was turned down.

He paid a 'donation' of ₹25 lakh to the HPCA to be nominated as its representative at the 1999 AGM. This was the AGM at which Mr Dalmiya backed Dr Muthiah's candidature for the post of president. Mr Bindra, who was backing Mr Manohar Joshi for the post, took Lalit under his wing. Mr Joshi subsequently withdrew and Dr Muthiah was elected unopposed[34]. Lalit did not have any role to play in the AGM of 2001, in which Mr Dalmiya defeated Dr Muthiah in the presidential election. Mr Dalmiya went on to complete his three-year term, of course. When Mr Pawar contested against

---

[34]*As narrated in chapter no. 9.

Ranbir Singh Mahendra in the AGM of 2004, both Lalit and Kishore Rungta claimed to represent Rajasthan Cricket Association (RCA). Mr Dalmiya, who was in the Chair, ruled in favour of Rungta and Lalit had to sit out.

Lalit was determined to storm the RCA, which had been controlled by the Rungtas for decades. This was never going to be easy and Lalit failed at his first attempt. His fortunes turned in 2003, when Vasundhara Raje Scindia was elected the chief minister of the state. At that time, each of the 32 districts of the state had a vote in the RCA elections and there were 66 individual voters as well. Lalit pulled off a coup on the eve of the RCA elections in 2005 by getting the state government to pass the Rajasthan Sports Act, which deprived the 66 individuals of their voting rights. He then contested for the president's post and defeated Kishore Rungta by one vote. He was elected as the vice president from the Central Zone at the AGM of the BCCI later that year and given charge of the marketing committee.

The vice-presidency of the BCCI gave Lalit the opportunity and a platform to resurrect the inter-city cricket league. Twenty20 had arrived by then and he decided to adopt that format. The Indian Premier League (IPL) was thus conceived.

He elicited extreme reactions in the members of the Board. There were some who could not stop praising him and there were others who remained deeply suspicious of him and his motives. Of course, there was no way anybody could ignore him. There is also no doubt that some of his contributions were hugely significant.

For instance, no one who was either part of the BCCI or connected to it in some way had ever thought of registering its logo. It was Lalit who got this done. He took the lead in organizing a two-day workshop in Delhi on the 'Branding of the BCCI'. The workshop, conducted by professionals who had done similar exercises with the International Olympic Association and Football League, was an eye-opener for all those of us who attended it.

As the chairman of the marketing committee, Lalit utilized his knowledge and experience to create multiple opportunities to maximize the revenue for the Board by putting out tenders for an apparel sponsor, a media rights holder, a team sponsor and a series sponsor. He wanted the Board to sell the in-stadia advertisement rights for all the venues centrally, but this did not happen because the state units objected. I personally thought that this was a good suggestion and it would have in fact helped the state units earn more through international matches.[35]

Later, Lalit also issued tenders for a BCCI Cricket Rating sponsor, a BCCI Awards sponsor and a sponsor for the formal clothing of the national teams. These three bids were even finalized and awarded but not implemented. They are still in arbitration.

The BCCI got Nike on board as the apparel partner of the Indian team for a period of five years, following a transparent tender process. Lalit also negotiated the merchandising rights with Nike, which resulted in 'official' Team India jerseys being sold and becoming a familiar sight at India games all over the world. In his eagerness to secure a better merchandising rights deal, Lalit ended up allowing Nike to sell individual player jerseys bearing their names. This prompted Adidas, one of Nike's competitors and a brand endorsed by Sachin, to file a case against Nike with the Competition Commission of India, in which the BCCI too was made a party. Sachin apart, some other senior players also complained to the president about their names appearing on jerseys without their permission. They made the point that the players' retainership contract between the Board and them mentioned that a separate

---

[35] Anurag Thakur introduced associate sponsors for matches of bilateral international series played in India, in 2016.

agreement needed to be made for marketing players' rights.

The tussle between ESPN and Zee for the TV rights, which began in 2004, went on for two years. Television rights were offered series-by-series during this period, with Doordarshan being the biggest benefactor. Lalit took the monetization of the TV rights to another level. His contention was that the payment of telecast rights ought to be decided on the basis of the relative significance of the series. He argued that the series against Australia, England and Pakistan, for instance, ought to yield more money to the Board than series against teams such as Sri Lanka or New Zealand. In 2006, Nimbus won the TV rights for four years for a record $612 million, which was equivalent to about ₹2,500 crore.

However, the government brought in a law in 2007, making it compulsory for the rights-holder to share the clean feed of a sporting event of national importance with Prasar Bharati, Doordarshan's parent organization. Fifty per cent of the revenue generated by DD from advertisements, was to be shared with the rights-holder, as per this new law. Nimbus took up this matter with the Board, as it now stood to lose a substantial amount of money which it would have made otherwise. The Board considered the plea and the payment terms were renegotiated by a committee headed by Mr Jaitley.

Lalit also presented a plan to organize bilateral limited-overs series and tournaments featuring the Indian team at neutral venues, which would yield revenue through the marketing of media rights, in-stadia rights and event sponsorship rights. Hitherto, the BCCI had permitted series and tournaments at neutral venues in countries such as the United Arab Emirates (UAE), Kenya, Singapore and Canada, but in all those events, it was the organizers who laughed all the way to the bank and the Board had to settle for a mere participation fee. Lalit's plan was accepted and the Board issued tenders for media rights for matches at neutral venues. Zee won this bid and the first such series was organized in Abu Dhabi in 2006, with India playing Pakistan in two ODIs. A tri-series involving India, Australia and the West Indies was held in Kuala Lumpur later that year. Zee backed out at the last minute from an ODI series against South Africa, which was scheduled in Ireland in 2007, and Nimbus was asked to fill in. Zee then filed a suit against the Board and it was subsequently decided to not continue with the neutral venue tournaments.

His detractors accused Lalit of looking 'too far ahead,' but what he did for posterity cannot be forgotten. He played a pivotal role in the appointment of Prime Focus Technologies (PFT) to digitize over 12,000 hours of cricket content in the Board's archives on the fourth floor of the Cricket Centre, in 2010. The BCCI had ball-by-ball footage of every international match played and several domestic matches played on Indian soil, since 1993. Almost 1,500 to 2,000 hours of new content would be added to the archives every year and plans to acquire footage of matches played by the Indian team overseas and in ICC events, were also in place. The content was originally on DigiBeta tapes, which tended to deteriorate over time. Strangely, no one in the Board had thought of monetizing the footage or even using it for educational purposes at the NCA.

PFT's role was to acquire, digitize and archive the content. Every match was catalogued at two levels: match (venue, teams playing the game, etc.) and ball-by-ball (delivery of the ball, batsman on strike, bowler, audience reaction, etc.). The BCCI has since been able to generate revenue from the sale of its video content and the images which it owns, to external parties. I have no doubt that the revenue generated through the sale of images and video content has enabled the Board to recover the astronomical cost of installing the archives unit at the Cricket Centre, by now.

Lalit also did a lot of good work at the RCA. The Sawai Mansingh Stadium at Jaipur was upgraded and a state-of-the-art cricket academy, equipped with indoor and outdoor practice facilities and a residential complex, created. He had roped in IBM to design the software at the academy.

I enjoyed a good working relationship with Lalit, whether it was while organizing the Champions Trophy in 2006, the first T20 International on Indian soil against Australia at the Brabourne Stadium in 2007, or for that matter, the initial stages of the IPL when the staff was yet to be recruited. As chairman of the umpires committee, he extended his full support to the initiatives undertaken by us.

So, where did he go wrong?

I think Lalit's biggest undoing was that he forgot that he was part of a team which had been elected democratically. He would not have encountered the difficulties which he did, had he functioned as part of a 'system', but that approach did not appeal to him. He often took decisions without consulting his colleagues and forgot that as the vice president, he did not have the same rights as those of the president, secretary, treasurer or joint secretary, all of whom were ultimately answerable to the Board. He took it for granted that as the chairman of IPL, he alone could take decisions regarding the league, which was his creation.

Mr Pawar, who was the Board president when the IPL was launched and staged successfully for the first time, went out of his way to support Lalit. But even he at times found it difficult to comprehend what was going on in his vice president's mind. On most occasions, the president and secretary were not aware of what Lalit was doing. He was officially the 'chairman' of the IPL Governing Council, but preferred to use the designation 'Commissioner', which he had coined himself. Having sensed that he may not enjoy the same kind of support from future office-bearers, Lalit started doing everything he could to try and extend his tenure as chairman.

Lalit also got into trouble because he was perceived to be

arrogant in dealing with members of the Board and even with eminent members of the public. There were some incidents during the IPL which angered those who were at the receiving end of his temper.

The final of the first IPL season in 2008 was to be played at the D.Y. Patil Stadium in Navi Mumbai. I was shocked to be told by Dr Vijay Patil[36] that his father, who owned the stadium, was denied a seat in the front row of the VIP enclosure and told to sit at the back. I had a word about this with Mr Pawar before the game began and he invited Dr D.Y. Patil and his wife to sit next to him in the front row. During a game at Delhi in 2010, the owner of one of the country's biggest media houses was asked to vacate the seat he was occupying in the first row of the VIP stand, as some VIP guests of Lalit's had to be accommodated. Members of the national selection committee were not amused when they were told to vacate their seats during a game at the Brabourne Stadium in the same season.

Lalit was seen to be very close to Harish Thawani of Nimbus, but relations soured between them in 2009, when Lalit hired James Rego and Dev Shriyan, Nimbus employees both, to handle BCCI's TV Production. Thawani even took up the matter with the Board president and secretary, but neither could do anything.

There was a lot of talk in early 2009 about the possibility of the second season of the IPL clashing with the General Elections in India. We in the Board knew that the only way forward was to consult the central government itself. We were in touch with senior government officials and were waiting for an opportune time to meet them and discuss what could be done. One evening, I received a call from the then home secretary, who told me that the Election Commission was planning to announce the schedule of the elections in the

---

[36]He is presently the president of the MCA.

coming week and advised that the BCCI should not announce the IPL schedule before that. I requested him to speak to Mr Srinivasan, the Board secretary, and also spoke to the secretary myself. The other office-bearers were also informed accordingly.

However, Lalit still went ahead and announced the IPL schedule before the dates of the elections were announced. Why he did that, despite being advised to the contrary, no one knew. When he did that, we knew what was coming. Mr Chidambaram, the home minister, was furious. His stand was that the elections were far more important than a cricket tournament and security arrangements, which were controlled by the Election Commission for the duration of the elections, could not be guaranteed for the matches. Mr Pawar tried to intervene, but to no avail. The chief ministers of Maharashtra and Andhra Pradesh initially offered to help out, but withdrew under pressure from the home ministry. The BCCI was then left with no choice but shift the IPL to either England or South Africa, and after considering all the factors, including the weather and the telecast timings, it was felt that South Africa was a better choice. The franchises were taken into confidence before the official announcement was made.

The South African government and the cricketing establishment in the country went out of its way to help us. IMG, the tournament manager, did a splendid job of shifting the tournament at short notice. Lalit and his team spared no effort to make the second season of the league successful. The IPL also gave a fillip to the economy of South Africa. Ironically, the Board found itself in a soup the following year, when it was slapped with charges of violating the Foreign Exchange Management Act (FEMA) by the Enforcement Directorate.

That he had incurred the wrath of no less an individual than the home minister of the country, made no difference to Lalit. His way of working remained the same. After the conclusion of the 2009 season of the IPL, the TV rights contract with

Sony was terminated due to alleged lapses on the part of the network. The office-bearers of the Board were informed about the same through an email. Sony went to court to stay the termination, but Lalit and the legal team convinced the court that the BCCI-IPL had already signed a fresh agreement with World Sport Group (WSG), which was based in Mauritius. Sony eventually got the rights back, but not directly. They agreed to pay the BCCI around ₹8,500 crore, which was more than twice the amount they had committed to paying the Board directly when they were awarded the rights in 2008. However, they were to also earn additional advertisement revenue for the 'strategic timeouts', two per innings.

When this happened, Lalit was congratulated for increasing the Board's revenue. Everybody was happy. The catch in this deal, which came to light later, was the 'facilitation fee' of around ₹425 crore that Sony had to pay WSG (Mauritius), over and above what they were paying the BCCI.

These issues notwithstanding, there were some people who were still inclined to give Lalit the benefit of the doubt, considering what he had accomplished in the form of the IPL. But then, they could not do so forever. In early 2010, a month or so before the start of the third season of the league, the Governing Council discussed the addition of two teams to the league in the fourth season in 2011 and called for tenders. Given that the IPL was a tournament of the BCCI's, the Cricket Centre ought to have been involved in this process. However, this wasn't the case. The tender and bid documents were submitted at the office, which Lalit had set up at Hotel Four Seasons at Worli, in central Mumbai. When Shashank, who had succeeded Mr Pawar as the Board president in 2008, called me to check on the status of the bids, I told him that the BCCI office was not involved in the process.

In the days that followed, Shashank received calls from individuals and groups, all of whom claimed that the bidding process was flawed. An eligibility clause, as per which the net worth of a bidder had to be at least ₹1 billion, appeared to have been arbitrarily added to the document.

Shashank then decided to take matters in his own hands. The documents were to be opened at Hotel Four Seasons at Mumbai, in the presence of the IPL GC and bidders. The two bidders turned up on D-Day with their respective teams. One of the bidders had even got film stars along. They were in for a shock. When the meeting, which had been called to open and announce the bids, got underway, Shashank announced that he was cancelling the bids. He ended the meeting in five minutes flat and left.

When asked about the addition of the clause pertaining to the net worth of ₹1 billion, Lalit said that he had discussed the same with the office-bearers, but he could not substantiate his claim. IMG's legal team, when confronted, claimed that the addition had been made as per Lalit's instructions. The documents of the two bidders were with Lalit. He then claimed that he had returned them to the bidders after the BCCI president had cancelled the bids.

A re-tendering was announced and Sahara and Rendezvous Sports World ended up winning the bids for the Pune and Kochi franchises, respectively, on 23 March 2010. Lalit was not happy with this development and he started taking on Rendezvous Sports World on social media. One of the individuals he targeted was Shashi Tharoor, the minister of state for External Affairs in the central government. Lalit accused Tharoor of misusing his office to acquire shares in the Kochi franchise and the issue snowballed, resulting in the minister's resignation from the Union Cabinet.

A backlash was only to be expected. In mid-April 2010, the ICC's marketing team came to Mumbai to finalize a partner for the ICC CWC 2011. Of all the agencies which had bid for the marketing rights of the tournament, six had been shortlisted and asked to make presentations before the ICC team at the Cricket Centre. The exercise was to last three days, with two of the shortlisted agencies showcasing their credentials on each day, in the conference hall of the Cricket Centre. As the TD, I was in the Chair and my deputies from India, Sri Lanka and Bangladesh were also present, along with the members of the ICC's marketing team.

On the second day, when the presentations were on, I received a message that a team of officers from the Directorate of Revenue Intelligence (DRI) had reached the IPL office on the fourth floor to conduct a 'raid'. I immediately contacted the president and secretary of the Board, both of whom advised me to cooperate with the officers.

I rushed upstairs to meet the officers. I also received a call from the chief commissioner of the DRI, who advised me to tell his men what I knew. He assured me that I would not be 'harassed'. The officers then settled in the conference room of the IPL office and told me to take the seat opposite them. They then started 'interrogating' me. It did not seem to have crossed their mind that I was least likely to have any idea of alleged financial irregularities in the IPL. I told them that the IPL season was on and the entire IPL secretariat was operating from Four Seasons in Worli. They conveyed the same to their superiors and within no time, teams from the DRI reached Four Seasons as well as Lalit's office at Nirlon House.

I responded to the questions as best as I could. The point I made was that my involvement with the IPL had not gone beyond issuing tenders and collecting the bid documents. I had attended meetings of the Governing Council in my capacity as the CAO of the Board, but had no role to play in the planning and conduct of the league whatsoever. In fact, there was not a single sheet of paper related to the IPL in what was supposed to be the IPL office! The officers had come prepared to copy the hard disks of the desktops, but even there, they found nothing.

What the officers strangely did not get along was a laptop or recorder. Three senior officers were asking me questions, and a fourth—their junior—was writing down the questions which I was being asked, and my answers, in a notebook, in longhand. I found that odd. As was only to be expected, both his seniors and I were too fast for him, and he would invariably ask us to repeat what we had said. This happened several times during the 'interrogation'. At one point, one of the senior officers received a call from a colleague of theirs. It turned out that he was downstairs and wanted to join them, but was finding it difficult to enter the building because of the mediapersons, who had rushed to the Cricket Centre after hearing about the 'raid' and had blocked the entrance for all practical purposes. The junior officer, who was writing down the questions asked by his seniors, as well as my answers, was ordered to go downstairs, wade his way through the sea of humanity and escort the senior officer upstairs. The interrogation was thus halted. It resumed some 10 minutes later, after the junior officer did what he was told.

The interrogation had to be paused again a little later, because the junior officer received a call. That call was followed by another, and then another. You did not have to be a genius to figure out what had happened. He had been caught on camera by the representatives of the news channels outside the Cricket Centre, and footage of his escorting his senior colleague into the Cricket Centre was being flashed on television. I noticed the junior officer blushing while talking to all the callers, who had called him after seeing him on screen! He then started looking for the remote of the TV set in the conference room, as he wanted to see what his friends and relatives had seen. The remote was found and he then frantically surfed the channels, until he saw himself on the screen and beamed. Yes, even the interrogation had its share of lighter moments!

The DRI officers then ordered dinner, for which they picked

up the tab. By the time they recorded the details and finished the 'panchnama', it was close to 2.00 a.m. The BCCI staffers who stayed back with me that evening were Devendra Prabhudesai, Devendra Bhuvad and Nilesh Dhulap.

The next few days were eventful. Shashank spent over a week at the Cricket Centre, scrutinizing every document related to the IPL and questioning the members of Lalit's team. Lalit was absent. He tried to outsmart the office-bearers by informing them on 25 April 2010, just a few hours before the start of the IPL final, that he would preside over an IPL Governing Council meeting at the Cricket Centre, the following morning. By then, the office-bearers, led by the Board president, had decided to suspend Lalit. They chose to skip the final, which was to be played between Mumbai Indians and Chennai Super Kings at the D.Y. Patil Stadium at Navi Mumbai, that evening. The suspension was to be announced only after the conclusion of the game.

I returned to the Cricket Centre at around 9:00 p.m. that day. With me were Devendra Prabhudesai, our manager (Media Relations and Corporate Affairs), Devendra Bhuvad, who handled IT, and a couple of members of Mr Srinivasan's team. We had with us, the soft copy of the letter of suspension of Lalit and a media release announcing the suspension, both of which had been drafted by the Board president himself. We watched the final on television and then waited for the presentation ceremony to conclude. The moment the IPL trophy was presented to Dhoni, the winning captain, we sent the mail to Lalit, who was still on the dais. The media release was sent out a little later.

Shashank addressed an extraordinary media conference the next day. At least 150 mediapersons, including reporters, photographers and camerapersons, somehow created space for themselves in the Conference Hall of the Cricket Centre, which had been designed for a gathering of less than half that number.

Nevertheless, we managed, and the media conference went on for nearly 45 minutes, with Shashank making the Board's position clear on Lalit's suspension. Shashank subsequently instructed Lalit to hand over all the original papers relating to the IPL, minutes of the IPL Governing Council meetings and bid documents to me at the Cricket Centre. Mehmood Abdi, his lawyer, created a media event out of the handover, coming as he did with over 40 cartons of papers related to the IPL.

Lalit flew abroad after the IPL final. At the AGM in September 2010, a Disciplinary Committee, comprising Arun Jaitley, Chirayu Amin and Jyotiraditya Scindia was set up to investigate the charges levelled against him. Lalit tried his level best to stall the disciplinary proceedings by moving the courts. The Disciplinary Committee, after having several meetings and even giving Lalit an opportunity to respond to the charges (he was represented by his lawyers), pronounced Lalit guilty on most of the charges. The Board, in an SGM in September 2013, took cognizance of the findings of the Disciplinary Committee and expelled Lalit for life. He was banned from holding any position in the BCCI and any of its affiliated units.

Lalit did not make enemies in India alone. He had a running battle with Giles Clarke, the then chairman of the England and Wales Cricket Board. When Lalit proposed the Champions League in 2008, he ensured that only CA and CSA were made a part of the Champions League structure and not the ECB. The BCCI was to get 50 per cent, CA 30 per cent and CSA 20 per cent of the profits from the tournament. Clarke even lodged an official complaint with the BCCI, alleging that Lalit was interfering with ECB matters and had held meetings with county representatives in Mumbai, proposing a plan to start a T20 league in England on the lines of the IPL, without keeping the ECB in the loop.

Lalit's stint in the Board ended in 2010, but his brainchild was here to stay. The IPL has only gone from strength to strength since, thus proving that no one is indispensable and the institution is always greater than the individual. The success of the IPL has a lot to do with the fact that it is a property of the BCCI.

14

IN A 'LEAGUE' OF ITS OWN

Lalit put forth the proposal for a T20 inter-city league after being elected the vice president in Mr Pawar's team. The discussions on the league gained momentum in 2007, the year in which the inaugural ICC World T20 was to be played. The members of the Board endorsed the proposal and the ball was set to roll for what we know today as the Indian Premier League (IPL), undoubtedly one of the most popular and cash-rich franchise-based sports leagues in the world.

I attended a two-day workshop with Lalit and Mr Bindra at Singapore in August 2007, where the proposal for the league took final shape. Andrew Wildblood and his colleagues at the IMG made a presentation to a gathering that also comprised the CEOs of the England, Australian and South African cricket boards. The presentation covered the salient features of the league, some of which were as follows:

- The franchise-based T20 league was to be hosted and fully owned by the BCCI and would feature international players from the other member boards of the ICC.
- Bids for ownership of the teams would be invited from interested parties and each franchisee would pay the BCCI an annual fee for the first 10 years, based on the bid price.
- A pool of the Indian and foreign players would be made

available to the team owners, so that they could plan the composition of their respective squads.
- The team owners would get a chance to pick the players of their choice through a transparent player auction. Each team had to spend a fixed amount of money for the same.
- The league would be telecast live worldwide through a broadcast partner, who would also be selected through a transparent bidding process.
- There would be eight teams to start off with and the league would be played in a round-robin format on a home-and-away basis, with each team playing 14 games, followed by semi-finals and a final to decide the winner.

The IMG presentation also projected the prospective income streams for the BCCI and the team owners. The representatives of the ECB, CA and CSA liked what they were told and agreed to make their players available for the league. The BCCI then sought the approval of the ICC for the league. The ICC deemed the proposed league a domestic tournament of the BCCI, after which all the Full Members made their players available. They said that the players keen on participating in the IPL would have to seek an NOC from their respective Boards.

On our return to India, Lalit briefed Mr Pawar and the other office-bearers of the plans and sought their approval to appoint IMG as the agency to organize the league. The IPL was thus launched on 13 September 2007 by Mr Pawar and Ray Mali, the president of the ICC, in the presence of prominent cricketers from India and overseas. The BCCI constituted a Governing Council to run the affairs of the IPL with Lalit as its chairman (He later re-designated himself as the chairman and commissioner, IPL). The success of the Indian team in the ICC World T20 2007, which was played in South Africa, augured well for the IPL. Thanks to that triumph, India embraced the T20 format and the stage was thus set for the inaugural season of the IPL.

In the weeks following the victory in South Africa, Lalit got down to the business of finalizing the process of issuing the franchise bids, confirming the availability of foreign players for the auction, drafting agreements which were to be signed with the contracted players from India and inviting tenders for the broadcast rights. This apart, he was also working on the title sponsorship and associate sponsorships of the IPL. Tenders were floated for ownership of the eight teams, each of which was to represent a city. It was mandatory that each of the cities had a venue that had hosted international matches. The Board selected Mumbai, Delhi, Kolkata, Chennai, Bengaluru, Hyderabad, Jaipur and Mohali. A base price of $50 million was set for the ownership of a team.

The bids were to be opened on 24 January 2008. The crash of financial markets across the world in December 2007 had left some of us worried, but Lalit was determined to pull things through. He personally spoke to a number of corporate honchos and explained the business model of the IPL to them. I remember him telling me that if at all there were any queries from the media on the number of tender documents that had been picked up, we should paint a positive picture and mention the names of prominent corporate and international football and baseball clubs, which had expressed interest.

Despite this, there were only nine bidders who fulfilled all the prerequisites mentioned in the tender document, on the cut-off date for the submission of bids, which was 23 January 2008. Two more bids were received on the day of the auction, which was held at the Cricket Centre in the presence of the representatives of all the eligible bidders.

Lalit began the proceedings by informing the representatives about the two bids which had been received after the scheduled closure and asked them if they could be considered as well. The eligible bidders did not agree to this and only the nine bids which had been submitted before the cut-off date were opened, as a result. Based on the highest bid offered for each venue, the eight franchise owners were decided and their names announced.

Interestingly, while the BCCI had kept a base price of $50 million per team, the final figures for the eight teams worked out to around $720 million for 10 years, with the highest bid being for the Mumbai team ($112 million) and the lowest for the Jaipur side ($67 million). The teams were subsequently christened Mumbai Indians, Delhi Daredevils, Kolkata Knight Riders, Chennai Super Kings, Royal Challengers Bangalore, Deccan Chargers (Hyderabad), Rajasthan Royals (Jaipur) and Kings XI Punjab (Mohali), respectively.

The next tender invitation was for the broadcast rights and Sony, who had teamed up with WSG (India), bagged the India rights. WSG secured the world telecast rights, as well as the internet rights. The BCCI was to make an average of $100 million per year in the first decade of the league.

The modalities of the players' auction, an unprecedented event in cricket history that was to be held on 24 February 2008, were being worked out simultaneously. Players from India and overseas sent across their agreements, confirming their participation and base price in the auction. The foreign players submitted the NOCs of their respective boards.

Each team owner had the option of nominating an 'icon player' before the auction. As per the rules, a franchise was to pay its icon player 15 per cent more than what it was paying its most expensive buy at the auction. Mumbai Indians nominated Sachin Tendulkar, Royal Challengers Bangalore picked Rahul Dravid, Kolkata Knight Riders named Sourav Ganguly, Delhi Daredevils went with Virender Sehwag and Kings XI chose Yuvraj Singh. Chennai Super Kings, Deccan Chargers and Rajasthan Royals decided against naming an icon player. The BCCI also decided to allot one member of the national under-19 squad to each of the eight teams, in the wake of the boys' victory in the ICC Under-19 World Cup in 2008 under Virat Kohli's captaincy.

The player auction, which was telecast live on Sony TV, was watched by millions across the world. M.S. Dhoni emerged as the highest-paid Indian player and Australia's Andrew Symonds, the highest-paid foreign player. They were bought by Chennai Super Kings and Deccan Chargers, respectively.

IMG, who had conceptualized the league and framed its rules and regulations, had drafted various tender documents. The organization's legal team scrutinized the bid documents for the teams and broadcast partner, before they were opened. Lalit engaged IMG to conduct the IPL at a fee of 10 per cent of the revenue accrued to the BCCI each year. At that time, no one in the Board had the faintest idea of what the Board was likely to make from the IPL. The 10 per cent fee to IMG thus came across as astronomical when the office-bearers of the Board added up the revenue earned from the franchise fees and broadcast rights.

This led to the first clash between Lalit and Mr Srinivasan, who was the treasurer of the Board at the time. Mr Srinivasan argued that he was only protecting the rights of the Board, and 10 per cent was a huge amount. IMG's fees were then re-negotiated and revised for the remaining period of 10 years, starting with the third season in 2010.

The IPL got underway with a spectacular opening ceremony at the M. Chinnaswamy Stadium in Bengaluru, followed by the first game between Royal Challengers Bangalore, the home team, and Kolkata Knight Riders. The former was owned by Vijay Mallya, the 'King of Good Times', and the latter was co-owned by megastar Shah Rukh Khan.

New Zealand's Brendon McCullum, who was representing Kolkata Knight Riders, got the IPL off a flying start with an electrifying 158 in the opening game. The excitement in the stands was complemented perfectly by the TV viewership ratings. It would not be wrong to say that the IPL captured the imagination of the public in that very first game, played on 18 April 2008. Nothing much has changed since. In fact, things have only got better.

What also worked in the IPL's favour was that it coincided with the summer vacations. Youngsters and their elders could not wait for the daily dose of cricket to unfold on their TV screens, every evening. The IPL even impacted the viewership of 'prime-time' TV programmes and even the release of films in theatres!

For all his optimism, I am sure that even Lalit himself had not expected the IPL to take off the way it did. The franchise owners were obviously thrilled and the Board, overwhelmed. The end of the first season was as sensational as its beginning. The final between Rajasthan Royals and Chennai Super Kings went down to the wire, with the Shane Warne-led Rajasthan Royals beating Dhoni's Chennai Super Kings by three wickets, off the final ball.

The popularity of the IPL grew every passing year and its brand value kept rocketing. It was ranked among the top five sporting events in the world in next to no time. Of course, there have been problems and hiccups over the years, but the IPL has withstood all that and continues to hold fort as an extraordinary entertainer. Television and internet viewership have both grown manifold, irrespective of whether the league has been played in India or overseas, as was the case in 2009, 2014 (partly), 2020 and 2021 (partly). The impact of the ever-increasing viewership on TV and the internet was evident in 2017, when BCCI tendered the broadcast rights for a five-year period.

Whatever his critics might say or claim, Lalit's contribution to the success of the IPL simply cannot be overlooked or downplayed. He was the one who worked tirelessly to ensure that it was launched as planned and it combined cricket, entertainment and glamour to become the best franchise-based sports league in the world.

The BCCI safeguarded the interests of the IPL by taking some key decisions, such as prohibiting Indian players who were a part of the league from participating in any other T20 league in the world, paying the foreign boards 10 per cent of the fees earned by their players and starting the Champions League, in which the top four teams of the IPL could participate alongside the winners of the domestic T20 leagues conducted by other Full Members of the ICC.

The BCCI also managed to get the support of the ICC members to secure a window of eight weeks for the conduct of the IPL, which guaranteed the availability of top international players for their respective franchises for at least a substantial portion of the league, if not in entirety. The league adhered to the anti-doping and anti-corruption codes for international cricket and the world TV and internet rights were marketed and sold by the Board to ensure that the IPL was viewed in most of the cricket-playing nations.

The team owners who had made huge investments in the IPL and were struggling in the initial years were happy after the tenth season as they did not have to pay the franchise fees thereafter. From the eleventh year, they started receiving close to ₹200 crore annually, as their share of the IPL revenues. With the popularity of the league only increasing, their income pool increased substantially and they started making profits. The franchises also created a huge fan base, with the social media connecting the teams to the fans.

The IPL team, led by Sundar Raman (COO from 2008 to 2015) and later Hemang Amin, managed the league along with IMG, professionally and quite brilliantly, year after year. We in the BCCI could see the difference in the arrangements and conduct of an IPL game, as compared to a bilateral international game at the same venue.

The league took a huge leap in 2015, when the Board came up with the idea of creating Fan Parks in cities and towns which were not likely to host IPL matches. Local fans flocked to these Fan Parks to watch the matches on big screens and get a feel of the atmosphere in the stadia. This venture has been hugely successful. The IPL also launched a Fantasy League, inviting fans to play for free. The winners received gifts in the form of autographed team jerseys.

The IPL has been contributing huge amounts to the government treasury each year, in the form of income tax and goods and services tax (GST), apart from creating jobs for thousands, every season.

The league was also a pioneer, in that it inspired other sports to start their own leagues. In the previous decade, we have seen the advent of the Indian Super League, Pro Kabaddi League, Hockey India League and Premier Badminton League, to name just a few. The IPL also motivated other countries to institute their own cricketing leagues, such as the Big Bash League in Australia, the Caribbean Premier League, the Pakistan Super League and so on.

The sailing hasn't been smooth, of course. The IPL has witnessed its share of controversies over the years. Some of them are as follows:

2008

Serial blasts in Jaipur threatened to disrupt the league, but Lalit used his contacts and resources to ensure that it went on. Harbhajan Singh was suspended for the major part of the season after he slapped S. Sreesanth at the end of a game between Mumbai Indians and Kings XI Punjab. Mohammed Asif (Delhi Daredevils) became the first player in the IPL to test positive in a dope test.

2009

The IPL was shifted to South Africa due to the General elections in India. The season was a success, but the Enforcement Directorate charged the Board for FEMA violations.

2010

The IPL terminated the broadcast rights of Sony for alleged violations of the contract. Sony eventually regained the broadcast rights after agreeing to pay the IPL around ₹8,500 crore for nine years (till 2017). This amount was more than double of the 2008 deal, which had been signed for the same period.

Ravindra Jadeja was penalized for privately negotiating monetary deals with a franchise, despite being contracted to another.

The much-hyped bidding process for additional two teams was cancelled by Shashank Manohar, the BCCI president.

Fresh tenders were issued with a base price of $225 million. The Sahara group and Rendezvous Sports World became the franchises for Pune and Kochi, respectively. The new franchises were to contribute around $470 million over a decade, as opposed to the $720 million which was to be contributed by the original eight franchises during the same period. The new teams were confronted with a number of issues, including their commercial viability, and they were eventually terminated. This triggered legal battles, which ended up in arbitration, the final outcome of which is still awaited.

A bomb blast outside the Chinnaswamy Stadium during a playoff game forced the organizers to shift the final to the D.Y. Patil Stadium at Navi Mumbai at short notice.

Lalit himself was suspended from the BCCI for several alleged irregularities in the IPL deals. He left the country.

The office of the IPL at the Cricket Centre was raided by

the DRI. The Enforcement Directorate started enquiries into the working of the IPL, starting with the franchise bids, broadcast rights bids and alleged irregularities committed during the 2009 season in South Africa.

2012

Shah Rukh, the co-owner of Kolkata Knight Riders, clashed with Security staff and officials of the MCA after a game at the Wankhede Stadium.

There were unconfirmed reports of unsavoury incidents during post-match parties.

A news channel did a sting operation on some cricketers, who openly talked of fixing local games. The Board instituted an enquiry and penalized the players in question.

2013

The Delhi Police arrested three members of the Rajasthan Royals team for alleged match-fixing and spot-fixing. Charges of betting were slapped on Gurunath Meiyappan and Raj Kundra. The Anti-Corruption Unit of the BCCI was established and it was decided that every IPL team would be accompanied by an integrity officer and security officer 24/7, in addition to every match being overseen jointly by members of the ICC's and BCCI's anti-corruption units.

2014

The SC ruled that Mr Srinivasan could not continue as the president of the BCCI. Shivlal Yadav, the senior-most of the five vice presidents of the Board at the time, was asked to take over as the president of the Board. The SC also appointed Mr Gavaskar as the interim president to supervise the execution of IPL 2014. In the days that followed, Mr Gavaskar brought on board Deepak Parekh, the chairman of HDFC Bank, as his special advisor.

The 2014 season of the IPL coincided with the General Elections in India, but this time around, the BCCI and IMG worked out the dates in such a way that the first 20 matches were played at Abu Dhabi, Sharjah and Dubai in the UAE and the remaining 40 games were played in India.

A co-owner of a franchise lodged a police complaint against another. Preity Zinta of Kings XI Punjab accused Ness Wadia of abusing and molesting her during a game at the Wankhede Stadium. This kept us in the BCCI busy as the police wanted to view the footage of the entire match to substantiate the claims made by her.

2015

Chennai Super Kings and Rajasthan Royals were suspended for two years, as per the recommendations of the Justice Lodha Committee.

2016

The seasons of 2016 and 2017 featured two new teams: Rising Pune Supergiant and Gujarat Lions, which were based in Pune and Rajkot, respectively. Players from the two suspended sides were made available to these teams.

2018

Chennai Super Kings and Rajasthan Royals were reinstated. The former came back with a bang and won its third title, beating SunRisers Hyderabad in the final.

2019

Although there were General Elections in India, the IPL got the support of the government and the entire tournament was played in India.

2020

There was a huge question mark on whether the IPL would be played in the first year of the COVID-19 pandemic. The league was eventually conducted in the UAE from September to November. The matches were played sans spectators. Bio-bubbles were created at the venues and hotels where the teams were staying.

2021

The BCCI took the bold decision to host the IPL in India without spectators and at limited venues, with strict SOPs and biobubbles for the teams and officials. However, things went awry due to the second wave of COVID that hit India. The BCCI suspended the league midway after some players and officials tested positive. The season was eventually completed in the UAE in October.

The BCCI-IPL team, franchise owners, players, support staff, the official broadcaster and of course the UAE Cricket Board, deserve all the praise for their enterprise and commitment.

2022

The 2022 season will be bigger than its predecessors. The valuations of the existing teams had increased when two teams had been added back in 2010. Something similar is bound to happen this time around as well, with the BCCI announcing the addition of two new teams, representing Ahmedabad and Lucknow, on 25 October 2021. The teams were bought for a combined sum of ₹12,500 crore. The media rights of the IPL, which will come up for renewal in 2022 for the period 2023–27, will also rake in more money than in the previous five-year period, for sure.

The positives of the IPL need to be recognized and acknowledged. For starters, it has ensured quality cricket infrastructure at the match venues, with the state units and franchises working together to enhance the viewing experience at the stadia. The IPL also created new cricket fans, as was proved by the fact that the number of first-time female and children spectators at the venues have constituted over 30 per cent of the total number of spectators overall.

The IPL has had a direct impact on the future of Indian cricket. It has provided young cricketers a platform on which to express themselves and get noticed. There are innumerable stories of cricketers hailing from modest backgrounds, having attained superstardom through their exploits in the IPL. The league has given Indian cricketers the opportunity to play, interact with and observe cricketing stalwarts from across the world and in the process, imbibe their respective approaches to the game. The experience of playing in front of capacity crowds has enabled youngsters to eliminate the 'fear factor' and prepare themselves mentally to achieve their final objective—representing the country. The quality support staff attached to each team has facilitated a revolution in fielding and fitness standards.

The BCCI deserves all the accolades it has got for the IPL, and more.

15

INSTABILITY

The stability ushered in by Mr Pawar lasted more than half a decade and enabled the BCCI to consolidate its standing as the best-run and administered sports federation in the country and also the most influential cricket board in the world.

The annual pre-election acrimony in the Board vanished after 2005, as mentioned in an earlier chapter. The new dispensation ruled that the president and vice presidents would serve for a maximum of three years. It was also decided that the secretary, joint secretary and treasurer could serve for a maximum of five years, but all of them would have to contest the elections after completing three years in office.

Before 2005, the Board granted ₹4 crore annually to every state association for infrastructure development. Mr Pawar increased this amount to ₹50 crore per association. The impact of this move was visible in the years that followed. The Board's advice to all the associations was to create one arena of international standard and simultaneously develop venues for domestic and junior-level matches. These grounds were to be equipped with basic facilities such as dressing rooms, a broadcast room, rigs for TV cameras and rooms for the umpires and referee. Blueprints for international and domestic venues were prepared and shared with the associations. The outcome was the creation of magnificent stadia in cities such as Rajkot, Ranchi, Visakhapatnam, Pune, Dharamshala, Guwahati and Nagpur, to name just a few. State-of-the-art academies, embellished with indoor and outdoor training facilities as well as gymnasiums, also came up across the country. Traditional venues such as the Wankhede Stadium, M.A. Chidambaram Stadium and Eden Gardens were refurbished during the same period. Stadia with private participation came up in Trivandrum, Dehradun and Lucknow. Talking about stadia, the new Narendra Modi stadium, which was built recently by the Gujarat Cricket Association on the site of the old Sardar Patel stadium at Motera in Ahmedabad, is now the largest stadium (in terms of seating capacity) in the world.

The development of infrastructure was complemented by the Board's decision to invest in the concept of the 'A' team. More matches and series were organized, at home and away, for the India 'A' side, with an aim to give all the players who were on the fringes of national selection, greater exposure and opportunities to hone their skills against quality opposition in diverse conditions. The under-19 players, too, started getting greater international exposure.

If, in 2022, some people are saying—and justifiably so—that India has enough talent to be able to field two teams at the international level, then the steps taken by the Board in the late 2000s and early 2010s to unearth talent and create an environment conducive to the optimal development of that talent, deserve to be credited.

Women's cricket, which Mr Pawar had brought under the ambit of the Board in 2006, took a couple of years to take off. Yes, some individuals took that long to shed their indifference to women's cricket. The state units opened their doors to lady cricketers and some quality players were discovered over the next few years, many of whom are still going strong with the Indian team. The India 'A' concept was introduced for the lady cricketers as well in 2017 and tours of countries such as England and Australia were organized to give exposure to youngsters.

It was a pleasure to work with individuals who cared deeply about the game. Mr Srinivasan, who had served as the treasurer and secretary of the Board before becoming its president in 2011, was an outstanding and proactive administrator. He and Sanjay Jagdale, who was elected the secretary in 2011, worked well in tandem, as did Shashank and Mr Srinivasan as the president and secretary, respectively, from 2008 to 2011. Sanjay, who had represented Madhya Pradesh in the Ranji Trophy and served as junior and senior national selector in the early 2000s, is a gem of a person who cares deeply for the sport. M.M. Jagdale, his father, had also been a national selector and served on the panel in the historic season of 1970–71, when Ajit Wadekar was appointed captain of India and the team went on to create history in the West Indies and England.

Shortly after the AGM in 2012, Mr Srinivasan called me for a meeting and told me that he wanted to redesignate me as the general manager (Admin and Game Development), as I had been involved in all the developmental activities of the Board for a long time. He also spoke about appointing general managers for Cricket Operations and Finance, in line with the recommendations made by TCS, a few years earlier.

I had no issues with my new designation. Any change was welcome, as long as it benefited the Board in the long run. However, what certainly did not make sense to me and members of the BCCI staff, was an 'unofficial' decision to blur the line between the BCCI and the IPL.

From 2008 to 2012, the BCCI and the IPL had functioned separately, but under the same umbrella. In contrast to the BCCI's staff on the second floor, which comprised over 20 members, the IPL team, which was based on the fourth floor, was skeletal. A bigger team was not needed for the IPL, with IMG having been entrusted the task of running the league. The IPL team was headed by Sundar Raman, the COO.

Sundar apart, members of the TV Production team headed

by James Rego, which handled the international and domestic cricket broadcasts, the BCCI website team headed by Gaurav Saxena and the Operations team managed by Hemang Amin, operated from the fourth floor. Devendra Prabhudesai, who handled Media Relations for both the BCCI and the IPL, was stationed on the second floor. This had worked very well.

What could have most certainly been avoided, was the attempt to get the BCCI and IPL teams to work together, which was initiated in the days following the 2012 AGM. There was simply no need to tinker with the systems created by the BCCI staff, all of which had ensured a smooth and harmonious day-to-day functioning. It was also easier to hold individuals accountable for their actions when the two teams were functioning separately. However, the 'merger' caused confusion, overlapping and uncertainty, all of which the Board could have done without. What added to the ambiguity was that nothing was official. The BCCI and IPL teams continued to be separate entities on paper, but the reality was different.

There was another aspect that made this 'merger' rather queer. If at all, the BCCI and IPL teams had to work together, then the BCCI ought to have called the shots. The IPL was a subcommittee of the BCCI, after all. However, exactly the opposite happened. The impression outsiders and even some members of the BCCI staff got was that the skeletal IPL staff had been given a free hand to intrude into the working of the BCCI.

The annual BCCI Awards function was a case in point. Members of the BCCI staff, who had managed and executed the first five ceremonies, from 2007 to 2011, could not understand why the IPL team was trying to get involved in the execution of the sixth awards ceremony in 2012. This only led to confusion and bitterness on the second floor of the Cricket Centre, which we could have done without.

The year 2013 was a nightmare. It all began in May, when

the Delhi Police arrested three cricketers of the Rajasthan Royals team for alleged spot-fixing during the IPL. There was a national uproar and the BCCI suspended the players in question. Even as the Delhi Police was conducting its enquiry, we asked Ravi Sawani, the head of our Anti-Corruption Unit, to do likewise and submit a report to the Disciplinary Committee of the Board. A week or so later, Gurunath Meiyappan, the son-in-law of the Board president, was arrested on charges of betting, along with Vindu Dara Singh, the son of Dara Singh, the legendary wrestler and actor. The Delhi Police also accused Raj Kundra, one of the co-owners of Rajasthan Royals, of betting during the IPL.

That India Cements had advised the IPL to accredit Meiyyapan as 'Team Principal' of Chennai Super Kings, was leaked to the media. The media trial that followed declared Mr Srinivasan as the 'main accused'. That there was no evidence against him did not matter. The term 'cricket enthusiast', which was used by India Cements to describe Meiyappan's association with the Chennai Super Kings franchise, did not go down well at all.

While Ravi Sawani was investigating the alleged involvement of players in match-fixing/spot-fixing, the Board appointed a committee to delve into the betting issue involving Meiyappan and Kundra, in accordance with the rules of the IPL. This committee comprised two retired judges of the Madras high court and Sanjay Jagdale, the Board secretary. However, both Sanjay and Ajay Shirke, the treasurer of the Board, resigned from their respective posts. They expressed their disappointment at the turn of events and declared that they did not want to be associated with the controversy. It was then decided that the two judges could carry on, inquire into the allegations and submit a report.

Those were dreadful days for the Board. Sections of the media claimed that the entire Board was at fault and even dragged the cricketers into the affair. The Indian team was to leave for England for the Champions Trophy, a couple of days after the IPL final. At the pre-departure media briefing in Mumbai, Dhoni, the captain, was heckled when he refused to take questions related to the fixing controversy. He had obviously been briefed to speak only about the upcoming tournament. Footage of the heckling was splashed across all the channels and we copped tremendous flak, not only from the media but also the public, which was believing everything that the media was reporting. The credibility of the Board had sunk to an all-time low.

At the Emergent Working Committee meeting, which was held in Chennai on 2 June 2013, the senior members, including Shashank, opined that Mr Srinivasan should resign and return after the judges had submitted their report and the issue was resolved. However, the president would have none of it. He argued that there were no charges against him and his resigning would be interpreted as an admission of guilt.

I think this was the point when the BCCI became a divided house, all over again.

Eventually, a compromise, suggested by Mr Arun Jaitley, was reached. Mr Srinivasan 'stepped aside' and Mr Dalmiya took charge as the president. This arrangement was to last till the judges submitted their report. At the working committee meeting that followed, Mr Dalmiya announced that Sanjay Patel and Ravi Savant would fill the vacancies created by the resignations of Sanjay Jagdale (secretary) and Ajay Shirke (treasurer), respectively, till the AGM in September 2013. Sanjay Patel continued as secretary even after the AGM, while Ravi Savant was replaced as treasurer by Anirudh Chaudhry.

Even as all this was happening, sections of the media were crying themselves hoarse, with one channel taking the lead. Its anchor was reporting the Board's meetings as if he was covering the proceedings live, with claims of having first-hand information and all that. This person even called for the lynching of the BCCI members who agreed to Mr Srinivasan stepping aside instead of making him resign!

Mr Srinivasan did return as the president later in 2013, after the two judges submitted their report, but then Aditya Verma, who was representing the Bihar Cricket Association, filed a writ petition against the BCCI in the Bombay High Court. The high court ruled that the constitution of the two-member committee was illegal as it was not in accordance with the IPL rules. The BCCI appealed against the decision in the SC, at which point Verma also moved the SC. That the apex court of the land was getting involved in the working of the BCCI, was an ominous sign.

One thing which was becoming clearer by the day was that Verma was fighting on behalf of someone who was trying to settle scores with Mr Srinivasan. I learnt later that Mr Subramanian Swamy, Member of Parliament, had submitted an application to the SC, wherein he had questioned who was funding the case. Nothing came out of it. Mr Swamy was present in the court every single day when the SC heard the BCCI matter.

In March 2014, the Honourable Supreme Court reacted to the writ petition filed by Verma by appointing a committee headed by Mukul Mudgal, the former chief justice of Punjab and Haryana High Court, to look into the match-fixing/spot-fixing affair, the allegations of wrongdoings by Meiyappan and Kundra and the two IPL franchises: Chennai Super Kings and Rajasthan Royals. The other two members of the committee were L. Nageswara Rao, who is presently a judge in the SC and Nilay Dutta, a legal luminary from Assam. Apart from appointing the committee, the SC also announced that Mr Srinivasan could not continue as the president of the Board. Mr Gavaskar was appointed the interim BCCI president for the 2014 season of the IPL and Shivlal Yadav named the interim president for all the other activities of the Board.

It is important to note that the Justice Mudgal Committee went on to clear Mr Srinivasan of any wrongdoing. Incidentally, Aditya Verma, the complainant in the case, also declared in 2018 that he had nothing against Mr Srinivasan, who he said had served the game well. Verma, in fact, named a few BCCI officials who he said had instigated him.

2013 also witnessed the end of an age. I was informed by Mr Srinivasan that the Board had invited the West Indies for a two-Test series in November. The second Test would be the 200th and last of Sachin Ramesh Tendulkar's glorious career. The first Test was to be played in Kolkata and the Board had accepted his request of staging the second at the Wankhede Stadium, his home ground. I was assigned the job of coordinating the arrangements for what promised to be an unforgettable occasion.

The CAB planned meticulously for Sachin's 199th Test. An innovative thing they did was printing Sachin's image on masks and distributing them in the stands. India won the game in less than three days.

Sachin's 200th and last Test commenced on 14 November 2013. In what was an extraordinary coincidence, his first Test had begun exactly 24 years previously, against Pakistan at Karachi on 15 November 1989. The toss was preceded by a presentation ceremony. India Post had come up with the idea of releasing a stamp and first-day cover in Sachin's honour. Mr Kapil Sibal, the Honourable Minister for Communications and Milind Deora, the Minister of State, unveiled the same and presented it to Sachin. Sachin was also felicitated by the Board president and secretary. A special, gold-plated coin had been designed for the toss. Dhoni and Daren Sammy, the rival captains, were presented a coin each and the shirts of the Indian players had '200' embossed on them.

The BCCI was joined by the MCA in its bid to make Sachin's

last Test an unforgettable experience for the spectators, TV viewers and of course, the man himself. Sachin requested us to create a ramp at the entrance of the President Box of the Wankhede Stadium, so that his mother and Ramakant Achrekar sir, his guru, could be brought on wheelchairs to watch the game.

Sachin wanted to make a speech and I advised him that he could do so at the post-match presentation ceremony. As in Kolkata, India won in less than three days and the stage was set for a formal send-off. Chants of 'Sachin, Sachin,' which the cricketing world had heard for over two decades, reverberated across the Wankhede Stadium and beyond when Ravi Shastri, who was anchoring the post-match presentation ceremony, invited the maestro to speak.

Sachin spoke eloquently and passionately. He expressed his gratitude to all those who had guided and supported him on his cricketing journey. He thanked his family, his coach, the BCCI, the MCA, his colleagues in the Indian and Mumbai teams, members of the support staff, the media and of course, his fans. He then did a lap of the ground, surrounded by teammates and members of the security staff, but left all of them behind when he set out to do something very personal. He made his way to the pitch, all alone, touched it and folded his hands. A champion cricketer was paying his respects to the 22-yard strip of land that meant everything to him. Emotions ran high that afternoon. In the stands at the Wankhede, the media box, the ground and across the cricketing world, thousands wept as their favourite cricketer bid adieu.

Sachin was with his mother and members of the family in the President's Box of the Wankhede Stadium after the game, when I received a call from the PMO. Dr Manmohan Singh, the then prime minister, wanted to talk to Sachin and I passed on the message to him. I have to say that when the call from the PMO came, I sensed what was about to follow. It was quite obvious. The official announcement was made a couple of hours later. Sachin was to receive the Bharat Ratna, the highest civilian award of the Government of India. It was a richly deserved honour.

A couple of months before Sachin brought the curtains down on his career, Mr Srinivasan began the Board's AGM in 2013, which was held at the Park Sheraton in Chennai, by announcing the appointment of Dr M.V. Sridhar, former Hyderabad captain and an administrator in the Hyderabad Cricket Association, as the general manager (cricket operations) of the Board. This took many of us by surprise.

Till then, Suru Nayak had been the sole point of contact for international boards and the state associations. What he went through in the following months was terrible. Everything that he was working on was taken away from him and handed over to Dr Sridhar. Suru's sidelining was bizarre, to say the least, considering that he had been appointed the TD for the ICC Women's World Cup, which was hosted by India in early 2013. He had worked as the TD (India) for the ICC CWC 2011 as well. No one cared to clarify how and why someone who was good enough to be named the director of a global tournament, had become persona non grata within months of that event.

Suru's annual contract with the Board was to expire on 30 June 2014. In the last week of June, he received a mail from the email id of Shivlal Yadav, the interim president of the Board, informing him that his contract would not be renewed. I spoke to both Shivlal and Sanjay Patel, but neither could explain what had happened. This was no way to treat someone who had served the Board honestly and diligently. Suru's exit was an irreparable loss.

It was sad that politics had crept into the corridors of the second floor of the Cricket Centre. I had always told my colleagues to discharge their duties to the best of their abilities and steer clear of politics. However, the endeavour of the BCCI staff to abide by my instructions were not being complemented by other forces. Sundar Raman, the IPL COO, had started getting involved in the running of the BCCI office on the second floor, Dr Sridhar had come on board and the incumbent president had been told to stay away by the SC. It was a very difficult time. I remember Mr Dalmiya asking me, when I met him in Kolkata after his 'reinstatement' as the president in 2013, about Sundar Raman's role in the functioning of the Board and whether it was affecting me in any way.

Even more worryingly for the Board, the Honourable Supreme Court took cognizance of the report submitted by the Justice Mudgal Committee in November 2014 and constituted a Justice Lodha Committee in January 2015. It was headed by R.M. Lodha, former chief justice of the SC, and comprised Justice Ashok Bhan and Justice R. Raveendran both retired judges of the SC. The committee's brief was to decide the quantum of punishment to be awarded to Chennai Super Kings and Rajasthan Royals, probe the role of Sundar Raman, recommend reforms in the practice and procedures of the BCCI and also suggest amendments to the Memorandum of Association and rules and regulations. Justice Lodha and his colleagues met nearly 75 people, including administrators, cricketers, journalists and other individuals connected to the game in different capacities, over the next few months.

The Lodha Committee submitted the first part of its report in July 2015, in which it recommended action against Chennai Super Kings and Rajasthan Royals. The franchises were banned for two years as a result. However, the first part of the report did not shed any light on the sealed envelope that had been handed over to the Supreme Court by the Mudgal Committee, which contained the names of individuals that had cropped up during the enquiry by the Committee.

Copies of a questionnaire drawn up by the Lodha Committee were sent to the office-bearers and representatives of the affiliated units. Some of us were called to depose before the Committee in Mumbai. Sanjay Jagdale, Ajay Shirke and I appeared on the very first day and were asked many questions. The members wanted to know how the BCCI functioned. I answered their queries on the administrative structure of the Board and explained how the functioning of the Board was in accordance with its Constitution.

As was only to be expected, the committee wanted to know whether politicians were a detrimental influence on Indian cricket. This was in line with the populist view that politicians were abusing their powers to destroy Indian cricket. I told the committee that it was wrong to assume that politicians were ineffective administrators. I cited the examples of S.K. Wankhede, Manohar Joshi, Sharad Pawar, Arun Jaitley, Madhavrao Scindia and Anurag Thakur. The point I emphasized was that all these individuals had already reached a certain level in politics before getting into cricket administration. They were not going to gain anything extra by running cricket and all of them had contributed to the growth and development of the game and never interfered in its administration.

Incidentally, this was a time when a few state associations were feeling the heat from the authorities. The CBI was investigating the disappearance of ₹43 crore from the coffers of the JKCA. Earlier, the Lodha Committee had questioned me about the JKCA and I had admitted that there was an issue. The secretary and treasurer of the association were eventually implicated in the affair. Police enquiries into alleged malpractices were also being conducted in the Odisha Cricket Association, Assam Cricket Association, Kerala Cricket Association and Goa Cricket Association.

The Board had not been able to hold its AGM in 2014 due to the legal issues. The AGM and elections were eventually held on 2 March 2015, as per the instructions of the Honourable Supreme Court, in Chennai. Mr Dalmiya returned as the president and Anurag Thakur was elected the secretary. Unfortunately, Mr Dalmiya passed away in September 2015, after which Shashank was reappointed the president.

Shashank, who was summoned by the Lodha Committee after his reappointment, had an inkling of what was coming, even before the latter submitted the final part of its report. At the next AGM of the Board, which was held in November 2015, he implemented some of the points that the Committee had discussed with him, such as a third-party audit of accounts of the state associations, the insertion of a 'conflict of interest' clause in the Constitution and the Board president relinquishing his prerogative to exercise a casting vote in the event of a tie, as well as the right to approve national teams after they had been selected.

Deloitte and KPMG were appointed to scrutinize the audit reports of the state units of the previous three years. Their findings were meant to be confidential and were to be submitted directly to the president. They were to be kept in the custody of Cyril Amarchand Mangaldas, the solicitors of the Board. However, the reports of some of the state units were leaked and they reflected the misuse of the money; that the BCCI was paying its constituents annually, in the form of TV and IPL subsidy. It was a sorry state of affairs.

Shashank also implemented the conflict of interest rules and appointed an ombudsman.

He told me to take up additional charge of the 2016 season of the IPL. The probe against Sundar was still on and Shashank did not want him to continue. Sundar was told to leave and he did, but to be fair to him, the Lodha Committee gave him a clean chit in the final part of its report, which it submitted to the SC in January 2016. There was no evidence of wrongdoing by him.

Shashank also decided to appoint a CEO and a Chief Financial Officer (CFO), in accordance with what the Lodha

Committee had recommended. Niranjan Shah argued that the secretary of the Board was its CEO, as per its Constitution, but we went ahead nevertheless and sought the help of a headhunting agency. Representatives of Korn Ferry, the agency that was appointed, met Dr Sridhar and me, but we knew that it was only a formality.

Rahul Johri and Santosh Rangnekar came on board as the CEO and CFO, respectively and took charge on 1 June 2016.

The new CEO was to make a presentation on how he would go about augmenting the Board's revenue and improve the day-to-day administration, and the CFO was to outline how he would tackle pending tax issues and iron out accounting policies. To the best of my knowledge, these presentations never happened, as by then, Shashank himself had quit as the Board president and joined the ICC as its chairman. Anurag Thakur then took over as the president and Ajay Shirke, who had resigned as the treasurer in 2013, returned as the secretary.

The Lodha Committee report featured the views of its members on the BCCI itself, its constitution, the constitutions of the affiliated units, voting rights and other issues. I have to concede that the Board officials took everything very lightly. They were of the view that the Committee was only making some recommendations and the latter would not be binding on the Board. By the time the officials realized what was happening, it was too late. Ajay Shirke was one of those who felt that the Committee ought to be approached and spoken to. He even discussed the same with me, but I told him that I could not do anything without the permission of the Board president.

In February 2016, Aditya Verma filed an application in the Honourable Supreme Court, praying that the recommendations of the Lodha Committee be enforced upon the BCCI and the state units. The SC took up the matter and issued notices to officials of the Board. A majority of the state units, which were to be affected by the recommendations of the Lodha Committee, also filed applications in the SC. Thus, the SC started hearing the parties two to three days a week, with a galaxy of senior counsels representing the BCCI and state units. The 'BCCI matter' had become the most important legal issue in the country.

After several hearings, the SC passed an order on 18 July 2016, making it binding upon the Board and state units to implement the recommendations of the Lodha Committee. The senior counsels representing the Board and state units did everything they could to stall the order, but the SC was in no mood to hear their pleas.

However, even after five years of this judgement, there is still no finality to the matter as a number of issues have been raised by the BCCI and the state units before the SC.

In my humble opinion, the Lodha Committee did not take a holistic view of the functioning of the BCCI and the state units. I also felt that the members of the Committee failed to understand and acknowledge the fact that the BCCI was the best-run sports federation in the country and one of the best in the world.

While those who were invited to talk about the Board and its 'failings'were taken seriously, the Lodha Committee did not consider the practical difficulties of implementing the recommendations it came up with. The recommendation that all the affiliated units have a uniform Constitution, was an example. This was impossible, as some associations were registered as societies, others were registered as 'Section 25' companies and a few were registered with the Charity Commissioner.

Mr P.S. Narasimhan, who was appointed as amicus after Mr Gopal Subramanium relinquished the position, did understand the problems of the state units. He held meetings with the representatives and eventually allowed the associations certain concessions while framing their respective constitutions. I had also written to the amicus, explaining some of the issues that the state associations were likely to face. Incidentally, Mr Narasimhan is now a judge of the Honourable Supreme Court.

The Lodha Committee's recommendation of a three-member selection panel was another anomaly, which the SC corrected in October 2018 by reverting to a five-member panel. The committee's recommendation of withdrawing the voting rights of some of the full members was also unreasonable and the SC restored the voting rights of the Mumbai CA, Maharashtra CA, Vidharbha CA, Baroda CA, Gujarat CA and Saurashtra CA.

The 'conflict of interest' clause recommended by the Lodha Committee is another bone of contention. This clause will make it impossible for cricketers to take up positions in the state units or even the BCCI itself, as many of them get into coaching after retirement, by either joining an existing academy or starting their own. It is unlikely that they will give up their permanent source of income for a stint at either the BCCI or state units, the tenure of which will be fixed and reviewed every year.

Having worked in both the MCA and the BCCI, I can say that asking the state units to amend their rules and regulations in such a way that they mirrored those of the BCCI, was fundamentally wrong and not a workable option. The role and functions of the BCCI fundamentally differ from those of the state units. The Board plans international tours and domestic tournaments and decides on the schedule, playing conditions, rules and regulations and the appointment of match officials. The state units, on the other hand, run day-to-day cricketing activities and most of them conduct scores of matches to identify and nurture talent, and then give the youngsters a platform by selecting them in the senior or junior state teams. Indian cricket is what it is today, primarily because of the work put in by the state units.

The Lodha Committee also recommended that the BCCI set up an 'apex council' of nine members and the composition of the 'apex council' of the state associations mirror that of the Board's. Practically, the apex councils of the state units and Board cannot be identical for the simple reason that more manpower is needed to run cricketing activities on a day-to-day basis in the state units. The apex council of a state unit would have to comprise at least 15 members, including the five office-bearers. The state units would need to create committees to discharge different responsibilities, such as managing tournaments, player registration, and managing the umpires, grounds, to name just a few. The state units would also need to appoint a finance committee and a marketing committee. Even as far as the BCCI itself is concerned, an apex council alone cannot do everything, and therefore, it is necessary that some of the old committees of the Board's be revived. The Lodha Committee's recommendation that all the state units appoint a CEO is difficult to implement in practice, unless the terms are different from those applicable to a CEO of the BCCI. Also the eligibility criteria for the appointment of the selectors in state units has to amended suitably so that cricketers are available to be appointed.

I am not sure whether some of the changes which have been made in the Constitution of the Board, are in the best interests of Indian cricket. Earlier, an individual could become an office-bearer of the BCCI only if he was an office-bearer of a state unit or had attended at least two AGMs of the Board. This clause no longer exists. Consequently, just about anybody can step in and become an office-bearer of the Board. Is this right? Shouldn't an office-bearer have an idea of how the body that he wants to represent has functioned in the recent past? There can be no substitute for experience.

Thankfully, both Sourav Ganguly and Jay Shah, the current Board president and secretary, respectively, as also the other office-bearers, are no strangers to the BCCI and know how it functions. They have served as office-bearers of state units and had attended meetings of the Board before taking charge.

I do agree that some of the recommendations of the Lodha Committee, which called for enhancing the transparency of the Board and state units and making them more accountable for their actions, especially those pertaining to finance, made sense. The one to grant Full Member status to the North-eastern states, for instance, was pending for a long time. The Lodha Committee ensured the same. There is no doubt that the full membership will facilitate the development of the game in that part of the country. Another laudable recommendation was to bring differently abled cricketers within the gamut of the BCCI. This will definitely give these cricketers a boost. The move to display all the information pertaining to the issuance of tenders, payments made beyond a certain value, as well as information on the capacity of the stadia, rates of tickets and the distribution of tickets during international matches, is also welcome.

The Lodha Committee emphasized the need to appoint professionals and withdrew all powers of the elected representatives. Its contention was that unlike the elected members, the professionals could be held responsible and accountable. It is true that the volume of cricket activities has increased so much, even in the state units, that full-time professionals are definitely needed to run the operations.

Having said that, the administrative structure of the state units and BCCI should be such that the professionals, including the CEO, should report to the Secretary and apex council on all matters, for the simple reason that it is the elected office-bearers and apex council members who have to face the general body and not the professionals.

An attempt to completely overhaul a system which had existed and functioned effectively for decades, without trying to understand it in its entirety, was bound to face resistance. But having said that, I don't blame the Lodha Committee alone. While it is true that it chose to go by the versions of the people it interacted with, many of whom had an axe to grind with the Board, I wish the office-bearers of the Board had reached out to Justice Lodha and his colleagues before the report was submitted. We ought to have met the members of the Committee, explained our side of the story and promised corrective action. That did not happen.

16
MCA TALES

My association with what was earlier known as the BCA, began when I started representing Wilson College (one of the founder members of the BCA) at its AGM in 1975. In the years that followed, I served the MCA in different capacities, as a member of the Bombay University Cricket Tournament Committee from 1982 to 2006, as a member of the BCA Tournament Committee from 1986 to 1990, as a member of the Managing Committee from 1990 to 1994, as joint secretary from 1996 to 2005, as treasurer from 2005 to 2011 and as the vice president from 2011 to 2012. As a Managing Committee member and office-bearer, I always gave my best and ensured that any decision that I took in the discharge of my duties and responsibilities would always be fair and without any prejudice. I never ever compromised the interest of my association, which is something I am extremely proud of.

As the convener of the selection committees that picked the Mumbai teams for the BCCI's tournaments, I limited my participation to reporting on the fitness reports and availability of players, before the selectors discussed and finalized the composition of the team. In the junior selection committee meetings, I requested the selectors to ensure that justice was done to the youngsters and every deserving player got an opportunity to display his talent. It was a pleasure to work with junior selection committee chairpersons such as Hemu

Dalvi and Pravin Amre. When they headed the junior selection committee, they kept notes and recorded the reason why a player was picked or overlooked.

For a sports organization to function effectively and efficiently, it is essential to have a constitution, rules and regulations in place, and dedicated individuals to manage, direct and shape. Those who have run the BCA/MCA over the decades have been visionaries, for whom, the game was paramount. They accorded top priority to the creation and maintenance of a robust cricketing structure, whose components were grounds, coaches, umpires, scorers and ground staff, tournaments at the school and college levels and also for corporates, which could provide employment opportunities to the cricketers. The BCA was among the earliest associations to put a player registration process in place to ensure the smooth conduct of local tournaments.

I thoroughly enjoyed my role as an office-bearer of the MCA. Running local cricket was as satisfying as following the exploits of the senior Mumbai team in the BCCI's tournaments. My first season as an office-bearer in 1996–97 was an unforgettable one, as Mumbai won the Ranji Trophy and Irani Cup and the under-19 side won all the trophies on offer. Cricketers from Mumbai have been known to value their lion-crested caps and give their best on the field. It was a pleasure to work with the cricketers, selectors and coaches of Mumbai teams over the years. In fact, my experiences at the MCA merit a book by themselves. I will mention a few significant ones here.

In my years in the MCA, I worked with individuals such as V.B. Prabhudesai, R.D. Jukar, Bal Mahaddalkar, Ramesh Kosambia, Rashid Kudrolli and Bakul Desai. These administrators were the pillars of the association. They facilitated the development of club cricket and moulded generations of cricketers. They ran cricketing activities in the city passionately and played a huge role in the promotion of the sport in the suburbs. Their efforts were complemented by the owners of clubs, who ensured that the youngsters got plenty of opportunities to train and play. Some of the owners even brought home-cooked food for the players on match days. We were also blessed to be supported by volunteers who helped us organize local tournaments, as well as international matches. All this was at a time when there was no money in the game and people were happy to spend from their pockets.

One of my closest associates in the MCA was C.S. Naik, who I met for the first time in 1985 on a visit to the then BCA office. We bonded instantly and have enjoyed a friendship based on trust and respect ever since. He has given his best to the association over the years and it has pleased me to see him head the association's administration in the last few years, which has been challenging. Naik also used to assist Mr Madhav Mantri and Polly kaka when they were treasurer and executive secretary of the BCCI respectively.

My experience of interacting with the various stakeholders of the game—from the players to the groundsmen—as the organizing secretary of the Junior College Cricket Tournament and subsequently as a member of the tournament committee of the MCA, came in handy when I was first elected to the association's managing committee in 1990. Six years later, I was elected the joint secretary along with Kudrolli, a veteran administrator. He guided me at every step although we belonged to different 'groups'.

The BCA created the Garware Club House in the Wankhede Stadium complex. A few years later, some of the BCA's own people switched loyalties to the Garware Club House and members of the latter then started claiming independent status. This led to a prolonged legal battle and expenses running into lakhs of rupees. The war ended only in the new millennium, when Mr Pawar, in his capacity as the president of both the MCA and the Garware Club House, oversaw the signing of a memorandum of understanding (MOU) between the two bodies. Although the Garware Club House is an independent identity, the Bombay High Court ruled that its properties are vested with the MCA.

A highlight of my 'innings' at the MCA was the inception of the Mafatlal Bowling scheme in the early 1990s. The scheme, which aimed at unearthing bowling talent in the areas under the jurisidiction of the association, was coordinated by Makarand Waingankar, a journalist and my senior at Wilson College, who in later years, conceptualized the BCCI's TRDO system. The three-year commitment made by the Mafatlal family was one of the best things that happened to Mumbai cricket.

Frank Tyson, the former England fast bowler, was the chief coach and he was assisted by former Test cricketers such as Balwinder Sandhu and Kenia Jayantilal. Nariman Contractor, the former India captain, was also on board as advisor. Tyson introduced us to the concept of video analysis, a novelty at the time. The trainees, who were selected through a screening process, were mentored by Tyson and his colleagues, and the results were there for everybody to see. Abey Kuruvilla, one of the trainees, was straightaway drafted into Mumbai's playing XI for the 1990–91 Ranji Trophy final against Haryana. Most of Tyson's pupils went on to represent Mumbai for at least a decade, if not more, and a few, such as Abey Kuruvilla, Paras Mhambrey, Nilesh Kulkarni and Sairaj Bahutule, played for India. Sairaj was able to return to cricket after a serious car accident only because of the special interest that Tyson took in him. Tyson returned to Mumbai for a short camp in 2001, thanks to Waingankar, despite the managing committee's opposition. He also conducted a programme for coaches during this visit.

I first visited a police station in 1991, when the pitch at the Wankhede was dug up by a group of Shiv Sainiks[37], in

---

[37]Members of the Shiv Sena.

protest against an upcoming ODI against Pakistan, which had been allotted to the MCA. Ironically, the Shiv Sainiks who vandalized the pitch were led by Shishir Shinde, a friend of mine. I accompanied Bal Mahaddalkar to the police station to lodge a complaint. The match and series were later called off. The South Africans were invited to tour instead. The three-match ODI series that they played, proved to be serendipitous for the BCCI.[38]

The MCA will forever be indebted to Mr S.K. Wankhede, who was the president from 1963 to 1987, for shedding the association's dependence on the CCI. He was also the president of the BCCI for two years in the early 1980s. Mr Madhav Mantri, who was the president of the MCA when I was elected on the managing committee in 1990, was an astute administrator like his predecessor. I got into altercations with him on a couple of occasions, but he did not hold that against me and told me that he understood my point of view. Mr Manohar Joshi, who defeated Mr Mantri in the presidential election in 1992, was a keen follower of the game. He completed four terms as the president and always made it a point to tell people that contesting the MCA elections was more challenging than fighting the assembly elections. When he was the chief minister of Maharashtra from 1995 to 1999, we could meet him at 'Varsha', his official residence, without an appointment.

I remember calling him late in the night once when the West Indies team, which was on a tour of India, had landed in Mumbai without visas. The players had been held up at the airport as a result. Mr Joshi contacted the Union home minister and got the matter resolved. The immigration authorities allowed the West Indies team to leave the airport, after receiving an assurance from us that the documents in question would be submitted to them within the next 24 hours.

---

[38]As documented in chapter four.

We delivered what we had promised.

Mumbai was scheduled to host the third and final Test of a series against England in February 1993. The city witnessed riots in two spells, in December 1992 and January 1993, respectively. The Maharashtra government promised all help to the MCA in hosting the Test match and India went on to make a clean sweep of the series. A couple of weeks after the game concluded, Mumbai was rocked by serial blasts, perpetrated from across the border, in which hundreds of innocent people died and many more were injured. It was then that the central government urged Sharad Pawar, who was a union minister at the time, to rush to Maharashtra and take over as the Chief Minister. People of the state still remember how quickly he turned things around.

The MCA has always enjoyed a harmonious relationship with the Mumbai Police. The Mumbai Police hosts the Police Invitation Shield, one of the MCA's most popular tournaments, which is now in its 73rd year. The Police force goes out of its way to help the MCA during international and IPL games at the Wankhede Stadium. It also comprises quite a few cricketers, who represent its cricket team in inter-office tournaments. After the 1993 riots, the Mumbai Police used cricket as a means to propagate communal harmony by starting a 'Mohalla' cricket tournament, featuring teams from different areas of the city. The tournament was a huge success.

The MCA was scheduled to host the league match between India and Australia in the 1996 Cricket World Cup. Just two weeks before the game, one arm of the crane, which was being used to install the floodlights, tripped and fell on the outfield, damaging it as a result. Mr Joshi, who was then the chief minister of the state, came to the rescue. He got Larsen & Toubro to clear the ground and help Philips complete the installation of the floodlights. The Essar group was roped in to get the outfield back into shape, with Rashtriya Chemicals &

Fertilizers Ltd providing beds of grass. The damaged portion of the outfield was then relaid by Ramesh Naidu, who was incidentally a 'Wilsonian' like me. Nobody could make out the 'patchwork' on the day of the match. The game went off without a hitch. The floodlights apart, we had invested in a Mega Vision Video Screen, as part of the refurbishment of the Wankhede Stadium. However, we could not market it as planned. The MCA lost close to ₹5 crore on the Mega Vision Screen, as there were glitches in its functioning. It was dismantled and sold in scrap, a couple of years later.

The MCA hosted two ODIs against South Africa later that year, both of which India won under the captaincy of Sachin. The first of those games was the final of the triangular Titan Cup. During the game, I had to request the manager of the South African team to evict two Indians who were seated in the players' area, wearing the accreditations of South African players. There was no anti-corruption unit at the time. It transpired later that this was one of the games that Hansie Cronje, the then South African captain, claimed to have 'fixed'. In fact, Cronje was so upset that the game was not going as per plan that he vented his anger on Avi Sule, the local manager of the South African team, during the break between innings. He literally lifted Avi with his bare hands and threw him out of the dressing room. The South African captain's physical strength can only be imagined, given that Avi was well-built and hefty himself. We took up the matter with the match referee.

The second encounter was a benefit match, sanctioned by the BCCI to Mohinder Amarnath. He had been trying to find a venue for the game and the MCA helped him out. The partnership was beneficial for both parties. He got a decent amount from the proceeds and the association also gained.

This was the second official 'benefit' match that the MCA had hosted. When asked to pick a venue for the benefit game that was sanctioned to him by the Board in 1994, Dilip

Vengsarkar, a Mumbaikar, chose his home ground. The ODI against the West Indies was marred by rain, but India were declared winners on net run-rate. It was a day game, as the stadium did not have floodlights then.

The MCA hosted a special event in 1997. A painting of Sir Don Bradman's, depicting his famous walk to the middle, by Colin Dudley, was unveiled at Lord's, the Melbourne Cricket Ground and the Wankhede Stadium. This was done in partnership with the Wheelchair Sports Organisation. We invited Sir Don to attend the unveiling, but he expressed his inability to travel to India. His letter to me is one of my most prized possessions.

During a Test match against Sri Lanka in the same year, Rashid Kudrolli, C.S. Naik and I discovered that the agencies bidding for the in-stadia rights had formed a cartel and were harming our interests in getting a proper value. We took the managing committee into confidence and suggested that the tender process for the in-stadia rights be scrapped. It was a bold call to decide to sell the advertising boards ourselves, but we ended up making more money than what we would have earned from the agencies.

That Test was Sachin's first as the captain of India at his home ground. He was another individual who felt strongly about Mumbai cricket and was totally committed to its interests. Just before the 1999 World Cup, he requested Mark Mascarenhas, chief of WorldTel and his then manager, to help the MCA get a team sponsor, as that would benefit the cricketers. Mascarenhas spoke to Ravi Shastri and me and then sent a proposal, which I placed before the marketing committee of the association. Unfortunately, one of the members of the committee leaked the figure mentioned in the document. At the managing committee meeting that followed, we received another proposal from a 'pen' company, which was worth ₹1 lakh more than what WorldTel had offered. The committee decided to go ahead with the second proposal and Sachin and some of the players shot for a promotional advertisement as well. The company then got a little carried away and started using an individual image of Sachin's, instead of the team's, in its campaigns during the World Cup 1999. This was an unethical move and it led to legal hassles.

Sachin consented to wearing a shirt with its logo during a Ranji Trophy match after the World Cup, in the interest of the Mumbai team, despite the sponsor's unprofessionalism. When Mr Pawar became the MCA president, he helped us rope in National Egg Co-Ordination Committee (NECC) as the team sponsor. This relationship continues even today.

Mr Pawar defeated Mr Ajit Wadekar in the MCA elections in 2001. As the president, his objectives were to end the legal tussle with the Garware Club House (which was also headed by him), create and develop infrastructure for the game in the suburbs of the city, make the association financially stable instead of relying entirely on the funds allotted by the BCCI, set up a corpus to help the maidan clubs run their cricket activities and streamline the cricket administration by setting up a Cricket Improvement Committee (CIC). The CIC, he suggested, would comprise former cricketers, who would be authorized to take all decisions on cricketing matters, such as the appointment of selectors and coaches and the scheduling and conduct of local tournaments. It was a brilliant idea, as cricketing matters were best left to the cricketers themselves.

The MCA's commitment to cricket can be understood from the fact that the association has always cared for, assessed and realigned the local cricket structure at regular intervals. I was a witness to two such committees. The first was chaired by Polly kaka in the early 1980s and the other by Mr Gavaskar in the 1990s.

It was during Mr Pawar's tenure that the MCA started a monthly pension scheme for Mumbai cricketers who had played between one and 24 first-class matches and were therefore not covered by the BCCI's pension scheme, for which only those who had played at least 25 first-class games were eligible. He also donated a generous sum to institute scholarships for deserving boys and girls.

Mr Pawar delivered everything that he had promised and in 2008, the House unanimously approved the amendment of the rules to ensure that he continued as the president beyond the eight-year limit. After a two-year break from 2010 to 2012, when he was heading the ICC, Mr Pawar returned as the MCA president in 2013. He continued in office till January 2017, when he gave up the post in accordance with the SC order, which made it mandatory for state associations to implement the recommendations of the Lodha Committee.

He created two magnificent cricketing facilities in the suburbs. The first was in the Bandra Kurla Complex, which was appropriately christened the MCA Sharad Pawar Recreation Centre in 2013. The Recreation Centre houses an Indoor Cricket Academy with seven practice pitches, a gymnasium and of course, a floodlit cricket ground, which was lovingly created by Polly kaka in the mid-2000s. The other facility came up in the western suburb of Kandivali and was named the MCA Sachin Tendulkar Gymkhana. This plot of land was leased to the MCA by the Brihanmumbai Municipal Corporation (BMC). The MCA Sachin Tendulkar Gymkhana has better facilities than the one at BKC and it has hosted matches in the BCCI's age-group tournaments since, apart from local games. Both facilities were constructed on a 'Build-Operate' basis, as the MCA did not have the funds to create the same. The revenue earned through the club houses has helped the MCA look after its cricket without having to wait for funds from the BCCI. Mr Pawar also backed a cricket facility at Boisar, which was created by Bipin Patil and his team of the Palghar-Dahanu Taluka Sports Association.

Another facility within the jurisdiction of the MCA, came very close to becoming Mumbai's fourth venue to host an international match. This was the magnificent D.Y. Patil Stadium at Navi Mumbai, which had hosted the final of the first IPL season in 2008.[39] The MCA was allotted the seventh and final game of an ODI series against Australia in the 2009–10 season. With the Wankhede undergoing reconstruction for the ICC CWC 2011, we decided to stage the game at Navi Mumbai. Our preparations for the game received a boost when it was conveyed to us that the prime minister of Australia, who was on a visit to India, would attend the game. However, things got a bit complicated when a driver of Indian origin was found murdered in Australia, a week or so before the game. The news made headlines and the Shiv Sena threatened to demonstrate against the prime minister of Australia at the venue. The threat eventually did not materialize, as it rained heavily and the match was abandoned without a ball being bowled.

Mr Vilasrao Deshmukh was the MCA president from 2011 to 2012. As the vice president of the association from 2009 to 2011, he played a key role in the reconstruction of the Wankhede Stadium. It was only because of the leadership displayed by him and Mr Pawar that the venue could get ready in time for the World Cup. A decade previously, he had allotted land in the Bandra-Kurla Complex to the MCA, in his capacity as the chief minister of Maharashtra. He had promised the plot at a function held at the Wankhede Stadium to felicitate Sachin for completing 10,000 runs in ODIs, in May 2001.

Mr Wankhede, Mr Joshi, Mr Pawar and Mr Deshmukh may have been politicians, but they were also cricket-lovers. They never interfered with the working of the association and backed both the players and administrators to the hilt. They

---

[39]The venue also hosted the final of the third IPL season in 2010. It was one of the venues of the FIFA Under-17 World Cup, which was played in India in 2017.

were approachable and amenable to suggestions.

To Mr Pawar goes the credit for insisting and ensuring that Mumbai hosted the final of the ICC CWC 2011. We did look around for a bigger plot of land on which a new stadium could be constructed, but the land that was offered to us had already been encroached upon. The project would have been delayed and that was something we could not afford. It was then decided to give the Wankhede Stadium a new look.

Everything about the 'new' Wankhede Stadium was new, be it bucket seats, spectator facilities, player dressing rooms, media centre, floodlights, broadcast facilities and nearly 50 air-conditioned boxes. The bucket seats reduced the seating capacity from 45,000 to 32,000, but that was fine, as the spectators were assured of an unforgettable viewing experience. We were greatly indebted to Messrs. Larsen and Toubro, who completed the work in record time, in spite of innumerable hurdles, including a PIL, complaints from residents of the buildings in the neighbourhood, clearances from the government agencies and the heritage committee.

The MCA's managing committee, along with the infrastructure committee and finance committee did a great job, supervising the progress on a day-to-day basis. The help rendered by Shripad Halbe and Ashok Pradhan during the reconstruction and later when the World Cup matches were staged, was invaluable. Sudhir Naik, the curator, and his team, lived up to the challenge of preparing the pitch and outfield, despite the construction work going on around them. Abhay Patankar, a 'Wilsonian', helped us install a sand-based outfield which helps in making the ground dry quickly after a shower. We were racing against time and I am proud to say that the MCA won the race. The World Cup final was a huge success, thanks to all those who worked relentlessly behind the scenes, from the managing committee to the volunteers.

As stated in the first chapter, one of the mandatory

requirements of the ICC is stadia have to be 'clean', in that they are devoid of pre-existing advertisements, if any. This stipulation forced the MCA to forego matches of the Champions Trophy in 2006, as it had a long-term tie-up with the Tatas, due to which the northern end of the ground is called the Tata End. This time around, Mr Pawar spoke to Mr Ratan Tata, Chairman of the Tata Group, who readily agreed to waive off their naming rights for the duration of ICC CWC 2011 matches. It can be safely said that it was because of Mr Tata that the Wankhede Stadium was able to host matches of the World Cup, including the final.

Mr Mukesh Ambani, owner of the Mumbai Indians franchise, was as magnanimous. The MCA realized that we would have to take a loan of ₹50–60 crore to complete the reconstruction of the stadium. It then struck us that selling around 15 corporate boxes to interested parties for a decade or so for both bilateral and IPL matches, would be a better option through which to generate funds. Halbe and I briefed Mr Pawar accordingly and we then met Mr Ambani. We asked him if he could give up 15 of the 40 corporate boxes that Mumbai Indians were entitled to use during the IPL. He permitted us to do so for a period of 10 years.

Talking about the IPL, there was a major controversy during the 2012 season, when Shah Rukh Khan, after a game between Mumbai Indians and Kolkata Knight Riders, the team he owned, got into a fracas with the MCA security staff and the MCA officials. The fracas resulted in the MCA banning Shah Rukh from entering the Wankhede Stadium for five years.

I remember an initiative during this period, which had a lot of promise. New South Wales was to Australian cricket what Mumbai was to Indian cricket, in terms of supremacy in domestic cricket and representation of players in the national team. Dr Harinath, a member of CA and an official in the New South Wales cricket association, came up with the idea of the MCA and Cricket New South Wales tying up for reciprocal cricketing visits, as well as training and development programmes. We agreed and Mr Barry O'Farrell, the premier of New South Wales, came over to sign the MOU between the two associations. The Mumbai team also travelled to Sydney to play a few games. Sadly, the initiative did not move ahead, due to a lack of interest and follow up from our end.

A lot has been said and written about my equation with Ravi Savant, another individual who had a long innings in the MCA. My first encounter with him was in Madhav Mantri's chamber, at a time when both of us had independently filed complaints related to the conduct of the 1987 World Cup matches in Mumbai. Both Ravi and I were first elected on the MCA managing committee in 1990 and we got along well. Ravi, C.S. Naik and I devoted a lot of time and energy to the legal battle against Garware Club House, which Ravi had initiated on behalf of the association.

Things turned sour in 1997. Ravi was to represent the MCA at the AGM of the BCCI in August 1997, but Mr Manohar Joshi, the president, replaced him with me at the eleventh hour, with instructions to support Raj Singh Dungarpur in the presidential election and not his rival Dnyaneshwar Agashe, whom we had originally decided to support. Ravi took this personally and the differences between us grew with time.

Vilasrao Deshmukh's unexpected and unfortunate demise in 2012 left the association without a president. As per the rules, the post was to be filled up by a member of the managing committee till fresh elections were held the following year. Being the vice president at the time, I decided to contest. Ravi, who was the treasurer, filed his nomination against me and won. I then resigned from the MCA and focussed on my job at the BCCI.

In hindsight, I am thankful to Ravi for defeating me, as that enabled me to continue as the general manager of the

BCCI till 2018. Had I won, I would have had to resign from the BCCI and would have then held the caretaker president's position for not more than a year, with Mr Pawar set to return as the MCA president after the end of his term at the ICC in 2012.

My resignation from the MCA was followed by a suspension, which was done primarily to satisfy the ego of Mr Ravi Savant.

There was a background to the episode. In the good old days, when Test venues were limited, the BCCI had a rule that a state association hosting an international match should reserve 350 tickets for other associations from the same zone. This was followed for several years, even for ODIs. The associations which wanted to buy the tickets were required to make a request in writing to the host association and pay for the tickets in advance, two weeks before the game. At a Board meeting in 2002, I flagged the likely misuse of this quota of tickets, especially when it came to ODIs, based on my experience at the MCA. I was supported by most of the members of the Working Committee. The Board then decided to reduce the number of tickets to 150 per association from the same zone and 25 for others, on the condition that the payment would be made in advance by cheque and the tickets would be meant only for members of the association.

A decade later, India played Pakistan in a T20 International at Ahmedabad. It was brought to my notice that the MCA, which belonged to the same zone (West) as the Gujarat Cricket Association, had booked 150 tickets for the game and paid for the same in advance, although only two members of the MCA had asked for and paid for the tickets. One of the secretaries of the MCA had written to the GCA that the 150 tickets would be collected by a person, whose name and details were mentioned. This obviously raised suspicions as to who the actual beneficiary was.

I raised this issue in a letter to the MCA and sought a reply, which never came. I then raised the issue at the AGM in 2013 and demanded an inquiry. I pointed out that the MCA had received the payment for the tickets, months after the game, not from the GCA, as was being claimed, but from an individual.

The managing committee retaliated by suspending me for five years for making false allegations and bringing disrepute to the MCA and its office-bearers. The BCCI office-bearers stood behind me when I told them that I was taking the MCA to court for this unjust decision.

I was pleasantly surprised to receive messages of support from people from different walks of life, including the likes of Malcolm Speed, former CEO of the ICC, and James Sutherland, CEO of Cricket Australia.

I challenged the suspension in the City Civil Court with a defamation suit and claimed damages on the grounds of malafide action to hurt my image. My contention was that the rules did not permit the managing committee to take such a decision in the first place and it was only being done to harm my reputation. I was lucky to find a senior counsel in Mr E.P. Bharucha, who was suggested by a close friend of mine. Mr Bharucha had not appeared in the Civil Court for a long time, but he agreed to take up the matter as a special case on the request of my friend.

On the very first day of the hearing, the judge asked the MCA counsel if he would like to withdraw the suspension, as the plaintiff (I) was only a whistleblower and had provided all the details related to the case. However, the MCA counsel replied in the negative. After hearing the arguments of both parties for several days, the judge passed an interim order, staying my suspension.

The MCA appealed against this order in the Bombay High Court, regardless of the fact that the MCA was to lose lakhs of rupees by way of legal fees in the process. The appeal was rejected.

The BCCI subsequently decided to reduce the number of paid tickets to be given by the staging association for all international bilateral games, to 25 tickets to state associations in the same zone and 10 tickets to other state units.

I wasn't very happy about having to take my own association to court, but I had no choice. When Mr Pawar was re-elected the president in 2013, he advised me to withdraw the case (the defamation part was yet to be heard). He assured me that the association would withdraw the suspension letter. I respected him and the matter ended there.

The fact remains that my last few years in and around the MCA were not harmonious, but when I look at the overall picture, the moments of happiness far outnumber those of frustration. That is good enough, as far as I am concerned.

I enjoyed listening to stories of Bombay/Mumbai cricket from former cricketers. They would reminisce about their playing days, the long train journeys to the Ranji Trophy venues, the meagre match fees they earned, the never-say-die spirit they were endowed with and the camaraderie that existed between the players. All this made Mumbai cricket so special. Cricketers from the city took a lot of pride in representing Mumbai, respecting the association's logo and winning matches. Rajbhai used to always say, 'If Mumbai Cricket is strong, then Indian Cricket will be strong.'

I was fortunate to watch the Little Master, the Lord of Lords and the Master Blaster[40] in inter-collegiate and club tournaments, in their formative years. They went on to do their city and country proud. To have worked with these giants was an honour.

I must put on record, the support I enjoyed from the cricketers, past and present, in administering the game. I had the privilege of working with selectors such as Ajit Wadekar,

---

[40]Sunil Gavaskar, Dilip Vengsarkar and Sachin Tendulkar.

Ramakant Desai, Dilip Sardesai, Dilip Vengsarkar and Milind Rege, among others, over the years. I also got to work with coaches such as Balwinder Sandhu, Vijay Bhosle, Ashok Mankad, Karsan Ghavri, Lalchand Rajput, Chandu Pandit and Pravin Amre, among others. My association with Mumbai captains such as Sanjay Manjrekar, Sachin Tendulkar, Sameer Dighe, Amol Muzumdar, Paras Mhambrey, Sairaj Bahutule, Wasim Jaffer and Ajit Agarkar was memorable in every sense.

There is a lot to look forward to. Earlier, cricketing infrastructure was limited to the city, and cricketers from the far-off suburbs had to travel long distances to train and play. However, the suburbs also boast some excellent infrastructure today. This has reduced the travel time of the players considerably and enhanced their focus on the game and it is not surprising to see a number of players from the distant suburbs making it to the Mumbai Ranji Trophy squad. Nilesh Kulkarni, the former left-arm spinner, was a resident of the central suburb of Dombivali, as was Ajinkya Rahane, who led India to a historic series win in Australia in 2020–21. Shardul Thakur, one of India's heroes of that series, hails from the western suburb of Palghar. He was a product of the Palghar-Dahanu Taluka Cricket Association, which is a member of the MCA. There is every reason to be optimistic that many more cricketers will emerge from these areas in the years to come and do their city and country proud.

I owe my innings as a successful cricket administrator to the Mumbai (then Bombay) Cricket Association. But for the MCA, I would have retired as any other college teacher.

I will always remember the support that the club secretaries gave me during my tenure at the MCA. It was great working with my colleagues in the Managing Committees.

17
THE EXIT

My innings in the BCCI lasted nearly 22 years. From initially representing the MCA at meetings of the Board from 1996 and then as the joint secretary, executive secretary-in-charge, chief administrative officer and lastly, general manager (administration and game development), I discharged my designated duties to the best of my abilities and developed a rapport with the senior office-bearers, representatives of the state units, the various stakeholders of the Board and most importantly, the players, whom I got to work with. I will cherish the memories and friendships I made forever, not only in India but also in the ICC and its other Full Member Boards. I got an opportunity to visit all the Test-playing nations and study their cricket infrastructure. My association with the BCCI gave me an opportunity to meet three prime ministers, in Shri Atal Behari Vajpayee, Dr Manmohan Singh and Shri Narendra Modi, as well as Smt Pratibha Patil, who was the president of India from 2007 to 2012, apart from meeting the heads of states of other Asian Countries.

It rankles me that the Board did not try hard enough to avoid getting into a tight spot, after the events of 2013. It was a difficult time. Just when you would start thinking that things could not get any worse, they would.

It did not surprise me to hear from Ajay Shirke, who became the BCCI secretary in 2016, shortly after Rahul Johri's appointment as the CEO, that I was a marked man. Within days of his joining the Board, Johri worked out a plan with Dr Sridhar and one R.P. Shah, who was involved in the financial management of the Board, to 'revamp' the administrative structure of the Board.

One of the 'recommendations' of Johri's plan was that I was past my prime and ought to be told to go. When he apprised the secretary about the plan, he was reminded that he had just joined the Board and had no idea of my contribution and the work I had put in for the Board. He was advised to focus on his job and get a hang of things instead. It was obvious that he was uncomfortable with me around. As far as I was concerned, the only thing that mattered was to focus on the duties assigned to me.

After the SC's order on 18 July 2016, wherein it was made mandatory for the BCCI and state units to implement the Lodha Committee recommendations, the BCCI think tank in its wisdom sought legal opinion from eminent retired judges. One of them was Markandey Katju, a retired judge of the SC. He opted to present his opinion at a media event, where he was critical of the SC, especially the Chief Justice, in dealing with the BCCI matter. I have no doubt that his outburst only hardened the views of the SC against the BCCI.

We filed a review petition in the SC, which was summarily dismissed. This meant that that the BCCI had no choice but to abide by the order. Anurag and I were also pulled up for an affidavit that had been filed before the SC, which claimed that the BCCI had never sought any letter from the CEO of the ICC. The SC pointed out that Anurag had in fact written to Shashank, the ICC chairman and requested a letter from him, stating that the appointment of a representative of the Comptroller and Auditor General of India (CAG) on the apex council of the BCCI, amounted to government interference in the working of the Board. Anurag was reprimanded for lying on oath and was informed that he was liable for prosecution. The court ordered him to be present in court in person and file an affidavit tendering an unconditional apology, which he did. The matter was then treated as closed.

Managing and tackling cricketing aspects during this phase, when it sometimes appeared that the Board was focussed more on courts than the sport, was a relief. The Under-19 Asia Cup was scheduled to be held in Sri Lanka in December 2016. The team was selected on the basis of the age cut-off advised by the cricket operations department of the Board and the players were asked to report for a camp at the NCA in Bengaluru. I happened to check the eligibility rules for the tournament and to my shock, discovered that at least six of the selected players were ineligible. I apprised Anurag and Ajay Shirke, who instructed the junior selection committee to meet immediately. The six ineligible players were then replaced just 10 days before the tournament was to get underway. The president and secretary then asked me to take additional charge of junior cricket and women's cricket until further orders. I enjoyed both assignments. Our girls went all the way to the final of the ICC Women's World Cup in 2017, where they lost to England. The under-19 boys won the World Cup in New Zealand in 2018.

The stand-off between the Board and affiliated units on one hand and the SC on the other, persisted as the members of the Board did not agree to the appeal of the president and secretary to amend the constitution as per the recommendations of the Lodha Committee, at the AGM in 2016. There was another setback for the Board in January 2017, when the SC held Anurag and Ajay responsible for not implementing the recommendations of the Lodha Committee and relieved them of their positions. C.K. Khanna, the senior-most vice president at the time, and Amitabh Choudhary, the joint secretary, were elevated as acting president and acting secretary, respectively.

The SC also appointed a Committee of Administrators (COA) to run the BCCI and its activities. It was to be headed by Vinod Rai, the former CAG, and comprised Diana Edulji, the former India captain, Vikram Limaye, eminent banker, and Ramachandra Guha, author and cricket historian.

This arrangement added to the confusion in the Cricket Centre. Nobody knew who was calling the shots: the office-bearers or the COA. Ironically, the professionals, whose contribution to the Board over the years had been praised by the Lodha Committee, were the worst affected by the situation. The CEO and staff often found themselves stuck between the COA and the office-bearers. The office-bearers would call for meetings and the COA would refuse to approve those meetings.

Two incidents deserve to be recounted here. Rahul Johri, the CEO, convened a meeting of the junior and senior selection committees as per the advice of the legal team, although he was aware that Amitabh Choudhary, the acting secretary, had already sent out a notice for the meetings in his capacity as convener of the selection committees. Things got a bit ugly and led to a heated exchange of words. Johri felt threatened and had a bodyguard appointed. This bodyguard sat in the office and accompanied the CEO wherever he went. A few months after this happened, the CFO complained that he had been 'threatened' by Anirudh Chaudhry, the treasurer. Strangely, the CFO was then advised by both the CEO and COA, it seems, to file a complaint with the SC, which then instructed Anirudh to file his reply. These were nightmarish times for the professionals in the Board and the turmoil in the minds of those working under the CEO and CFO can only be imagined.

None of the committees of the Board was functional and some inexplicable decisions were taken, such as Vikram Limaye representing the Board at a meeting of the ICC in Dubai, where governance and the distribution of finances were two of the items on the agenda. Limaye may have been a banker, but the fact was that he had no knowledge as to what had transpired in the previous meetings of the ICC Board. Ideally, one of the office-bearers, who had been a part of the Board for years and was therefore aware of the Board's stance on the issues, as well as its equations with the ICC, ought to have attended.

Eventually, the SC had to step in again to adjudicate and decide the powers of the COA and those of the office-bearers. Not surprisingly, the COA gained precedence over the office-bearers, whose designations were reduced to mere titles. While C.K. Khanna was happy to enjoy the president's title, the acting secretary and treasurer did not seem to be on the same page. The reason for this was the distrust between the two, which the COA capitalized upon by playing the divide-and-rule card and heaping praise on the secretary at regular intervals initially. Later, the COA placed even the secretary on its radar, when it pleaded before the SC that the office-bearers be removed.

To emphasize the need to implement the 18 July 2016 order of the SC, the COA met members of the BCCI in two separate groups, instead of meeting all of them together. This did not go down well with the stakeholders, who realized that the COA was planning to create a rift among them. To add to the confusion was the role of Cyril Amarchand Mangaldas, the solicitor firm, which the Board had engaged when Shashank Manohar was the president, to argue its case in the SC. The firm had all along worked on building a case on the practical difficulties in implementing the Lodha Committee's recommendations, but it was now advising the COA on how to go about implementing the same recommendations! It was a mess.

The events leading up to the resignation of Anil Kumble as coach of the men's team after the ICC Champions Trophy final in June 2017 showcased the murkiness that had steadily crept into the corridors of the Cricket Centre. I happened to meet Virender Sehwag and Sachin Tendulkar at the Wankhede

Stadium, on the eve of an IPL game between Mumbai Indians and Kings XI Punjab, in the second week of May. Sachin and Viru were mentoring Mumbai Indians and Kings XI Punjab, respectively. I was taken aback when Viru informed me that Dr Sridhar had advised him to apply for the position of the coach of the Indian team. Anil's record as coach had been outstanding since his appointment the previous year and hence, what Viru said did not make sense. However, he is one of the most honest individuals I have known and hence there was no reason to not believe him.

I flew to Hyderabad a few days later for the IPL final. The game was preceded by a meeting of the COA at the ITC Kakatiya, where we were staying. Anil and Virat Kohli, who by then had become the all-format captain, were to make a presentation on the way forward for Indian cricket, at this meeting. Both Vinod Rai and Diana were attending, along with Johri. Anil was present physically, while Virat was to participate virtually.

After a characteristically comprehensive presentation by Anil, in which he focussed on a variety of aspects, such as the payment structure for the players and support staff, Rai informed the gathering that Virat would make his presentation later.

Rai then asked me what process had been followed by the Board to appoint a coach for the national team in 2016. I informed him that applications had been called for, after which some of the candidates had been shortlisted and interviewed by the Cricket Advisory Committee (CAC), which comprised Sachin Tendulkar, Sourav Ganguly and V.V.S. Laxman. What happened next was shocking. Rai said in front of the entire gathering, Anil included, that the same process would have to be repeated soon! Anil was stunned and so was I. The COA then told us to leave the room and Johri was told to stay back.

It was then that it all fell into place. I remembered my

conversation with Viru in May and told Anil about it. Surely, Dr Sridhar would not have told Viru to apply of his own volition. It was obvious that some people did not want Anil to continue as coach. The captain and coach did not appear to be on the same wavelength and it seemed that the captain had the upper hand.

The CAC members were keen on continuity and advised that the captain and coach sort their differences out. I learnt later about a meeting that took place in London before the final of the Champions Trophy, which we lost to Pakistan. This meeting was attended by Virat, Anil, Johri, Amitabh Chowdhary and Dr Sridhar. Apparently, Virat was not happy with Anil 'for not standing up for the players and creating a tense atmosphere in the dressing room', among other things. For someone who had been at the forefront of the discussions between the players and the Board on retainerships in the early 2000s, to be accused of not backing the players, was ironic. I was shocked to hear that none of the officials present at this meeting stepped in when Virat said what he did.

If a cricketing legend like Anil Kumble could be treated so shabbily, then what chance did employees of the Board have? On 30 December 2017, Johri told me to call the BCCI staff for a meeting in the Conference Hall, the following day. At this meeting, three employees of the Board—Sitaram Tambe, B. Laxman and Jayant Jhaveri—were informed that it was their last day in the office. The official reason given for the termination of their services was that all three were over 60 years of age. They were handed letters in front of their colleagues and told to go.

We were dumbfounded. These were individuals who had discharged their duties diligently. Tambe had served the BCCI for over 40 years. The very least they deserved was a notice period and a formal send-off. However, the COA and CEO did not have the inclination for such things, and so it was.

Had Johri had his way, I too may have been asked to go

that day. I learnt later that he had proposed at a meeting held at the NCA in Bengaluru earlier that month that I also be told to retire. However, he was overruled by the COA, who decided to let me continue for three more months.

An unfortunate tragedy had taken place a couple of months previously. The COA had charged Dr Sridhar on grounds of 'conflict of interest' and told him to resign. He passed away shortly after that.

Shortly after the ignominious exit of my colleagues, I received a letter from the COA, which stated that I would have to retire on 31 March 2018. The experiences of the past few months had mentally prepared me for anything, of course. I flew to New Zealand for the Under-19 World Cup, which we won comprehensively under the captaincy of Prithvi Shaw and mentorship of Rahul Dravid.

One quality of Rahul I must highlight here. After the World Cup win, the COA announced cash rewards for the players and support staff of the team. They announced ₹50 lakh to Rahul and ₹25 lakh each to Paras Mhambrey and Abhay Sharma. Rahul did not agree with the differential treatment and refused to accept the money stating that the head coach and the two assistant coaches had contributed equally and should be paid the same.

Amitabh Chowdhary, who was also on the trip, told me that he and the office-bearers were aware of the COA's letter to me. He said that the office-bearers would send me another letter, 'permitting' me to work beyond 31 March, as they were not in agreement with the COA's decision. I thanked Amitabh, with whom I had attended a lot of Board meetings, for his support, but said that I did not want to put myself in a potentially embarrassing position. Since its inception, the COA had asserted its supremacy whenever the office-bearers had proposed something. The same was bound to happen after the office-bearers would send me their letter. I did not want to be caught in the crossfire, not when I was retiring.

After my retirement, I was contacted by Shriniwas Rao, a journalist with *The Times of India*. He asked me if there had been any clarity in the lead-up to my exit. I told him the truth. There had been none. The functioning of the Board itself lacked clarity. Along with me, Neeraj Kumar, who had succeeded Ravi Sawani as the BCCI's Anti-Corruption Unit Head in 2016, was also told to retire on 31 March 2018, although he was to turn 60 only in July that year. Being a former top cop, he had been forthright in his views on how the BCCI was being run and was hence shunted out.

In 2015, when I was very much a part of the BCCI, the High Court of Rajasthan had assigned me the responsibility of running the cricketing affairs of the Rajasthan Cricket Association. Two similar assignments came my way after my retirement from the Board. Diana and Johri called me from a COA meeting in Delhi in June 2018 and requested me to become the convener of the Uttarakhand Cricket Association's Cricket Committee. Uttarakhand had just been granted full membership of the BCCI and its association needed guidance, on and off the field, as it took its first steps.

I took up the assignment, as it was an opportunity to help an association evolve. I had already visited Uttarakhand a number of times since 2001, when the new state was carved out of Uttar Pradesh and the association had first contacted the Board for affiliation. I was therefore familiar with the region and its cricket officials.

Another assignment came up down south. In February 2017, the Hyderabad High Court took note of the issues within the Hyderabad Cricket Association (HCA) and nominated me to conduct the Test match between India and Bangladesh, which was to be played in the city. I did so and then submitted a confidential report to the court after the match, highlighting the shortcomings of the HCA.

In August 2018, the Hyderabad High Court appointed me, along with two retired judges, on a Committee of Administrators to manage the HCA. Our brief was to look after the day-to-day working of the HCA, run the cricketing activities of the association and ensure the implementation of the Lodha Committee's recommendations. We did so and organized elections in 2019, after which we handed over charge to the newly elected body.

It was great to get the opportunity to help out the member associations of BCCI. I was also offered an advisory role by Zimbabwe Cricket in 2019. but I could not take up the assignment due to health-related reasons.

Looking back, I feel that my years in the Board, especially after being appointed chief administrative officer in 2006, were like a roller-coaster ride. There were debilitating lows and glorious highs.

As far as the lows were concerned, I have to mention the suspension and filing of the police complaint against Mr Dalmiya in 2006, our disastrous performance in the ICC CWC 2007, the DRI raid on the IPL office in April 2010 and the betting and match-fixing/spot-fixing controversy in the 2013 season of the IPL, which hurt us irrevocably. The stress we underwent in the wake of those incidents, is best forgotten.

The fallout of the 2010 and 2013 incidents meant appearing before agencies like the Enforcement Directorate, the CBI, the Finance Committee of Parliament and of course, the courts, to help our legal teams fight for the Board and sometimes even the state units, and protect their interests. Those appearances were frustrating. There were times when you felt that the whole world was ranged against you and nothing you would say would convince the authorities to change the belligerent posture which they had adopted with regard to the BCCI. I will always remember the day when I was called up by the SC to explain the distribution of funds to the state units and the rationale behind the same, which I conveyed quite convincingly, to the satisfaction of the Court. The Chief Justice then asked me to name the state associations which were being investigated by agencies like the Police, CBI and Enforcement Directorate, for alleged misuse of funds. That was a sickening moment, but I had no choice but to reply and state the facts. I was summoned to appear before both the Justice Mudgal Committee and the Justice Lodha Committee.

There were plenty of highs as well. The senior players ensured that the Board withstood the match-fixing controversy of 2000 and the game of cricket made an extraordinary comeback. Our victory in the inaugural ICC World T20 in 2007 enabled us to overcome the trauma of the disaster in the Caribbean earlier that year. The Test team topped the ICC's rating for the first time in December 2009 and was presented the Test Mace. We won the ICC CWC 2011 and the ICC Champions Trophy 2013. I was the manager of the team that created history in Pakistan in 2004, winning both the ODI and Test series. I had been involved to some extent in the creation of the NCA in 2000 and the launch of the IPL in 2008. I will always have fond memories of managing the ICC's events in India, such as the Champions Trophy in 2006 and the ICC CWC 2011. I was also involved in the ICC Women's World Cup in 2013 and ICC T20 World Cup in 2016 as an advisor.

It was a pleasure to work with veteran administrators such as Jagmohan Dalmiya, Raj Singh Dungarpur, Dr Muthiah, Sharad Pawar, Shashank Manohar and N. Srinivasan, to name just a few.

We had a great run from 2006 to 2013. The Cricket Centre would buzz with activity through the day. The senior managers, assistant managers, stenographers and office assistants took their responsibilities very seriously and did their best for Indian cricket. The senior office-bearers monitored the developments closely and encouraged us at every step.

The events that unfolded after 2013 were tragic. It was sad to see one of the best-run sports bodies in the world undergoing the kind of scrutiny that it was subjected to.

The primary brief of the COA, as spelt out by the SC, was to ensure that the SC's order, pertaining to the Lodha Committee's recommendations, was implemented by the BCCI and the state units. Did this happen? Did the COA achieve this in its two years in office? Your guess is as good as mine.

The irony is that while Anurag and Ajay Shirke were relieved of their posts for not implementing the recommendations of the Lodha Committee, the members of the COA were allowed to function for more than two years.

Eventually, it was another SC order in 2018, as per which, the Board and its affiliated units were ordered to revise their respective constitutions and register the same with the authorities within one month and hold fresh elections, which forced the changes, and not the COA.

Having said that, there are still around 15 state units, whose applications citing the various problems arising from the order of the SC, are still pending. The COA, through the BCCI CEO, filed the revised constitution of the Board with the Registrar of Societies in Chennai and conducted fresh elections in 2019. However, the current office-bearers of the Board have challenged the Lodha Committee's recommendation related to the 'cooling off' period between terms. Thus, things are far from settled, even today.

I will not hesitate to say that the COA could have done much better. The four members never gave the impression of working together as a team. Ramachandra Guha was vocal in his criticism of the way the Anil Kumble matter was handled, or for that matter, the issue of the Board not giving a commentary contract to Harsha Bhogle. Guha was the first to resign from the COA, followed by Vikram Limaye, who joined the National Stock Exchange.

Vinod Rai and Diana, the two surviving members, both loved the media, but they often contradicted each other in public. They made their disagreements public on several issues, such as the '#MeToo' complaint against Rahul Johri, the payment of a bonus to the CEO and the changes in the eligibility rules of domestic tournaments, which appeared to favour some associations and individuals.

Certain decisions of the COA were questionable, like the one to award the Col. C.K. Nayudu Lifetime Achievement Award posthumously (in spite of my bringing the anomaly to their notice), putting on hold the decision of the Sourav Ganguly-headed Technical Committee to play a Test against the West Indies at Rajkot under lights and the lack of transparency in some appointments.

At the same time, I would like to laud some of the COA's calls, like the one to present the Col. C.K. Nayudu Lifetime Achievement Award to domestic veterans Rajinder Goel and Padmakar Shivalkar, the appointment of a full-time manager of the Indian teams, paying a monthly gratis to lady cricketers who had represented the country in Tests and ODIs, instituting a Lifetime Achievement Award for lady cricketers, starting a Women's Challenger during the IPL with three teams including Indian and foreign players, and paying a bonus to the women's team for reaching the World Cup final in 2017. Fixing the match fee of first-class players at ₹35,000 per match day was also a great decision. The COA also implemented a couple of decisions taken by Anurag in 2016, such as transferring match fees directly into the bank accounts of players and match officials, and supporting differently abled cricketers.

The COA betrayed its lack of cricketing experience on more than one occasion. The recommendation of the Lodha Committee to give the north-eastern states full membership of the Board and voting rights had its merits, but the fact was that cricketing standards in that region had a long way to go before they could catch up with the rest of the country. The Lodha Committee had taken cognizance of the same and suggested that the Ranji Trophy feature one team comprising players from all the north-eastern states, for the first few years. The states could field individual teams in junior-level tournaments.

This recommendation was sound. The Northeast has produced several quality footballers, but cricket has lagged behind and will take a while to seep into the consciousness of the people there, most of whom are naturally fit and athletic. Infrastructure would have to be created and efforts undertaken to promote the sport at the grassroot level. This holds true for the entire region, including states such as Sikkim and Manipur, which gained affiliation to the Board way back in 1997, but have hardly progressed since. Two states which have done well since 2008 are Meghalaya and Nagaland, where local cricket has been nurtured and expanded.

I endorsed the Lodha Committee's suggestion in a meeting that had been convened to discuss the cricketing integration of the Northeast. I suggested that the north-eastern states could field individual teams in the BCCI's under-16, under-19 and under-23 tournaments and focus on creating a core group of players, all of whom would evolve over a period of four to five years. This would facilitate the smooth transition of the north-eastern states from the junior levels to the Ranji level, half a decade or so later.

However, the COA insisted that all the north-eastern states be allowed to play the Ranji Trophy as individual entities straightaway. It was obvious that this would lead to several one-sided matches, with the north-eastern state sides up against far more experienced teams, but this was not considered. That this would adversely affect the standard of cricket on display, was also not taken into account.

My principal had imparted an invaluable lesson when I was appointed the assistant warden at Wilson College in the 1970s.

He had emphasized the importance of being friendly with the residents of the hostel, but at the same time, maintaining a distance. I adopted the same principle with regard to the cricketers when I became an administrator, and most of the individuals I worked with at the BCCI also subscribed to the same. This ensured mutual respect between the two sides. I have to say, without getting into the specifics, that the members of the COA did not adhere to this principle. In fact, there were times when they behaved like fans rather than administrators, unnecessarily getting into nitty gritties involving individuals.

The silver lining for the Board during this dark period was the Indian cricket team itself. The players covered themselves in glory on the field and domestic cricket was also managed well. We did our best to ensure that nothing went awry. The performances of the cricketers—international and domestic—kept Indian cricket aloft and popular.

From 1928, when the BCCI was established, to 2021, there has not been a single complaint against the Board for financial mismanagement. I don't think the same can be said for several other sports bodies in the country. Credit needs to be given where it is due. Yes, the JKCA was one of the associations which was at fault, with ₹43 crore going missing in 2016, but one swallow does not make a summer. It was unfair to paint everybody with the same brush.

For most of the twentieth century, the BCCI was not the financial behemoth it is today. It is difficult to say where it would have been today, had its office-bearers not gone out of their way to run it at a time when finances were scarce. There were many instances of the incumbent president and secretary shelling out money from their own pockets to ensure that Indian cricket was not jeopardized. An administrator like P.M. Rungta used to make his house available for BCCI meetings. How many sports officials in the country and elsewhere have done something like that? A long-serving treasurer of the KSCA, I am told, owned a number of cinema halls in Bengaluru. Every time the Karnataka team travelled for matches, he would collect cash from his cinema halls and hand it to the team manager to take care of the expenses on the trip.

India would not have become the force that it has in world cricket, had the dedication of the players on the field not been complemented by the determination of those who worked behind the scenes. That the sport and those who played it, would always come first, was never in doubt and never questioned. Quality was always given precedence over quantity. The outcome of this approach, which was adopted way back in 1928, is there for everybody to see in the third decade of the new millennium.

Presently, Indian cricket is flourishing on the field, but enveloped in uncertainty off it. The SC order passed in 2016 has still not been fully implemented, and there is unlikely to be a change in the status quo, given the number of practical difficulties in adopting some of the recommendations of the Lodha Committee.

But then, this deadlock cannot last forever. Should there be no resolution, there is every possibility that the confusion off the field might adversely affect the action on it. This has not happened so far, but nothing can and should be taken for granted. The sooner there is clarity, the better it will be for Indian cricket and its stakeholders.

18

CHALLENGES

For me, the game always came first, followed by the cricketers and then, the administrators. As the joint secretary and later executive secretary-in-charge of the BCCI, I was able to observe the functioning of the Board and its member units from close quarters. The notes I made at that time ensured that I was mentally prepared for the responsibilities I would have to discharge and the challenges I would have to tackle, when I was appointed the CAO in 2006. I did my best and was lucky enough to be backed and trusted by the office-bearers of the Board, as well as the representatives of the state units I worked with.

Some of the challenges which presented themselves during my years in the Board, were as follows:

STATE UNITS

The BCCI is a member-driven body and the state units are primarily responsible for the development and promotion of the game in the areas under their respective jurisdictions. Till the time the BCCI started providing funds to them, most of the member associations had done quite well with whatever little help was extended by the Board, plus the resources they were able to raise on their own. The revenue stream of most of the state units consists of the BCCI's funds and the profits that are generated when they get their turn to host an international match. The revenue generated in the process helps the state units run their local cricketing activities and participate in BCCI tournaments.

It was only after 2006 that the Full Members started receiving substantial funds from the BCCI, in the form of TV subsidy and later IPL subsidy (2008 onwards). The state units utilized these funds and the increased one-time infrastructure subsidy of ₹50 crore to create new infrastructure or to refurbish whatever existed, and initiate welfare measures for retired cricketers who were not covered by the BCCI's schemes.

Ironically, the sudden receipt of huge amounts of money from the Board annually, created a problem for a few state units, because they neither had the administrative structure nor the plans to utilize the funds properly. These units failed to adhere to fiscal discipline, leading to alleged misuse of the funds, which was highlighted when the Board called for a third-party audit of accounts in 2015–16. The audit reports of the state units exposed the misuse of BCCI funds, which in some cases was so blatant that the BCCI cheque was not deposited in the official bank account of the association.

In some cases, members of the state units started drawing their 'share' of the funds. An official of a state unit kept more than hundred cheques of the gross revenue share of the Ranji Trophy players in his drawer for almost two years instead of distributing them to the latter. This sort of irresponsible behaviour rubbed off on the office staff of the state units, who also misused funds. The blame lies at the doorstep of the BCCI, which did not seek a report from the state units on how the funds were being utilized. I also wonder how the auditors of the state units missed out on the lapses.

Another issue with many of the state units was that they did not have a proper working office and a professional staff. This was reflected in the difficulties they encountered in administering the game, be it communicating with the

Board, filing player registrations or disbursing the match fees of players. There were instances of the list of the playing XI and reserves in matches not tallying with the official score sheet, leading to a delay in the release of the match fees of the players.

The cricketing infrastructure in the Full Member states, be it stadia or academies, have improved by leaps and bounds over the years, with the BCCI regularly conducting audits of the facilities and procuring the best of equipment centrally, for the maintenance of the grounds.

During my stint at the Board, the KSCA was way ahead of the others when it came to infrastructure. The KSCA built a ground and clubhouse in every district of the state. The earnings from the clubhouse were used to maintain the venues and run cricketing activities at the grassroots level, thus making every district self-reliant. The roof of the M. Chinnaswamy Stadium, the association's premier venue, was used to generate solar power, resulting in substantial saving on electricity bills. A sewage water treatment plant was installed in the stadium complex to provide water for the maintenance of the ground. The drainage system at the ground is good enough to ensure the resumption of a game within half an hour of the rain stopping. The facility at Alur is also outstanding. It comprises as many as three full-size grounds, equipped with the infrastructure to host first-class matches, and a separate training ground with practice pitches. The Saurashtra Cricket Association, which is headquartered in Rajkot (Gujarat), has also done a great job in terms of developing infrastructure.

Many of the member units would do well to pick up the best practices of their better-run counterparts such as the KSCA. This will enable them to execute their administrative operations better and organize local cricketing activities a lot more efficiently. Unfortunately, some of them have been obsessed with organizing T20 leagues and that too by outsourcing the same to a third party. The member units need to remember that we reached a point at which the SC had to step in because some of them displayed an utter disregard for accountability and transparency. The interests of the BCCI were compromised in the process, in addition to their own.

The BCCI needs to focus on the north-eastern states. The Board will have to invest at the grassroot level and appoint qualified coaches, support staff and even selectors from its pool, for the first few years at least. The states need more inter-school tournaments to ensure that more and more children take to the game. Incidentally, an impressive number of candidates who appeared for the examinations for umpires, coaches, scorers and video analysts from this region, did reasonably well.

THE NATIONAL CRICKET ACADEMY AND SPECIALIST ACADEMIES

I have written about the establishment of the NCA in an earlier chapter. The BCCI purchased 30 acres of land from the Government of Karnataka in 2008, to shift the academy from the M. Chinnaswamy Stadium complex, but the staff at the NCA felt that the location was inconvenient and too far away from Bengaluru's new airport. The plan was thus shelved. The Board then purchased another 50-acre plot on the outskirts of Bengaluru in 2017. However, there has been no development-related activity on the same for the last four years, although the COA, in its infinite wisdom, did appoint a 'general manager' (a person from the hospitality sector) for the NCA. This individual even visited Australia to study the facilities there and discussed the NCA project with the Indian players, who were touring the country at the time!

Things took a turn for the better when Rahul Dravid was handed the reins of the NCA. When he took over from Ravi Shastri as coach of the Indian team, he was succeeded at the

NCA by V.V.S. Laxman, his partner-in-history. With individuals like these calling the shots at the NCA, there is every reason to believe that the creation of a state-of-the-art academy on the new plot, will be prioritized.

During his stint as the NCA chairman, Anil Kumble had submitted a report on the Academy and how its functioning could be enhanced. I had done likewise, as per the instructions of Mr Srinivasan. It will be great if Laxman looks into these reports. Another thing that he could do is initiate the writing of a coaching manual from an Indian perspective. A manual was first written in 2000, when Rodney Marsh was the director, and another version was written in 2010, when Dav Whatmore was in charge. However, the Indian coaches at the Academy were not involved in either of these ventures. This needs to change.

It will also be wonderful if Laxman resurrects a project that the NCA had initiated in collaboration with the BKS Iyengar Institute. The idea, which was Brijesh Patel's brainchild, was to publish a book on yoga for cricketers. The book was compiled but not published due to some technicality. I remember going through a rough copy at the Cricket Centre. I hope it is published.

The NCA started conducting courses for coaches and granted accreditations to the successful candidates, way back in 2001. In 2016, it was decided to hold refresher courses for all those who had passed the Level-3 and Level-2 courses at the NCA, so that they could be updated on the latest coaching methods and technology. Dr Sridhar sought the help of CA in this regard and all those who had passed Level 3 were asked to attend a refresher course, which would be conducted by experts nominated by CA, and then appear for an assessment. The catch was that there was no written agreement between the two Boards for this exercise. As a result, the COA refused to approve the payment due to CA, and CA, in turn, did not send us the results. I hope Laxman sorts this out.

The Board started specialist academies at Mumbai, Chennai and Mohali for batsmen, spinners and fast bowlers, respectively, in May 2010. Unlike the KSCA, which has never been compensated financially for lending its space to the NCA, the MCA, TNCA and PCA were sanctioned an annual sum of ₹1 crore for housing the specialist academies. However, these academies had to close down after it was discovered that they were not functional for more than three to four months in a year. A residential academy for umpires was also started in the premises of the Vidarbha Cricket Association at Nagpur in 2010, but it has sadly been non-functional since 2017.

The NCA can make optimal use of video footage and stills of Indian and overseas cricketers, both of which are available in abundance in the BCCI archives, in its coaching initiatives. This material can be shared with the state academies as well. If young hopefuls have to be taught how to play strokes such as the straight drive, cover drive or pull, for instance, why not show them footage of Sachin Tendulkar, Rahul Dravid, V.V.S. Laxman, Sourav Ganguly, Virender Sehwag, Virat Kohli and Rohit Sharma, playing those strokes, from different angles and in slow motion? There was a time when the NCA was branded the 'rehab centre' of the Board, with the treatment and recovery of injured players overshadowing cricket training. The rehab centre was shifted to the SRM Sports Medicine Centre in Chennai, undoubtedly the best facility in India for sportspersons, for a couple of years. However, some of our stars were reluctant to go to Chennai and felt more at home in Bengaluru. The rehab centre was shifted back to the NCA at their insistence. Despite limitations of space, the NCA continues to support Indian cricket solidly and competently, with its summer camps, pre-tour preparatory camps and educational initiatives for coaches, physiotherapists and trainers.

DOMESTIC CRICKET

Thanks to the timely advice and inputs provided by its Technical Committee over the years, the BCCI can proudly say today that it has the best domestic and junior cricket structure in the world. The Board organizes close to 2,100 matches for boys and girls at the under-16, under-19 and under-23 levels, as well as the senior men's and women's matches, every year. As many as 38 associations, which are affiliated to the BCCI, are involved in these junior- and senior-level matches.

I have recommended to the Board that with the addition of the newly affiliated states, we should go back to the tried-and-tested format of Elite and Plate groups in the Ranji Trophy. The top performers in the Plate group could be promoted to the Elite group, and the worst in the Elite group could be demoted to the Plate group. I also feel that guest players should not be allowed to participate in junior-level tournaments if the BCCI wants its new members to develop local talent. Only three guest players should be allowed per team at the senior level, and that too with proper scrutiny. Anil Kumble, while presenting the proposal for revised players' contracts in 2001, had suggested that incentives be offered to teams for winning Ranji Trophy matches outright. I feel the BCCI should consider implementing the same. The BCCI should also encourage the state units to institute annual retainerships for the Ranji Trophy players, from the funds they receive. Of late, a message going around, that selection in the Indian team for white-ball (limited-overs) cricket is done only on the basis of performances in the IPL, needs to be be corrected, so that the players who give their best in domestic tournaments year after year, are not disillusioned, and continue to give importance to domestic tournaments.

The Board, through its Anti-Corruption Unit, should keep an eye on agents who mislead parents and their children by promising to secure berths in teams and fleece them of money. The Delhi Police apprehended one such agent in 2019 and I am told that the Gurgaon police have also apprehended some individuals for the same offence, recently.

REVAMPING UNIVERSITY CRICKET

The BCCI needs to work out some plans to support University cricket, which until the 1970s, played a vital role in shaping India's cricketing journey. The Association of Indian Universities (ACU), an affiliate of the BCCI, which runs the Rohinton Baria Trophy, should accept changes in the format, which I believe will benefit University cricket in the long run. Currently, the AIU follows a four-zone structure for the tournament, but given the large number of universities participating in the tournament every year, it is invariably a struggle. The standard of cricket has fallen and the apathy of the organizers hasn't helped either. A few years ago, the final of the tournament was played on a matting wicket, which was laid out on a football ground, with the goalposts being a part of the playing arena.

I wish to recommend that the AIU adopts the BCCI's five-zone structure and calls for entries accordingly, for men and women. The tournament should be conducted with the help of the BCCI's state units. The Board could assign the responsibility of conducting the intra-zonal leg of the tournament on a knockout basis, to two of its members belonging to the zone in question, each year. The members units could provide the grounds, the BCCI could pay the match officials and the AIU could coordinate the accommodation of the teams. The top two teams from each zone will then qualify for the All-India Knockout to decide the winner. This is a workable solution and I think it will help University cricket bounce back.

WOMEN'S CRICKET

The BCCI took over women's cricket in India in 2006. We did our best to develop this vertical of Indian cricket, despite the ambivalent attitude of some members of the Board who initially saw it as a burden. A domestic cricket structure for senior and junior cricketers was designed, with inputs from former international cricketers such as Diana Edulji, Shanta Rangaswamy and Shubhangi Kulkarni. The tournaments for junior and senior cricketers have helped us unearth some outstanding talent. The top cricketers are eligible for annual contracts. Former international cricketers receive a monthly pension and are eligible for the Board's medical benevolent fund scheme. A Women's Challenger, which features three teams comprising top Indian and international cricketers, has been played during the men's IPL in 2018, 2019 and 2020. The BCCI took the landmark decision of permitting our top cricketers to play in the Big Bash League in Australia and T20 league in England as a special case, to give them additional exposure. The next big thing for women's Cricket would be a T20 league on the lines of the IPL, with six teams in the fray.

A lot more needs to be done at the grassroot level in most of the state units, especially those in the Northeast. Mithali Raj, Jhulan Goswami, Harmanpreet Kaur and Smriti Mandhana, to name just four cricketers, have become role models for girls across the country, and with the BCCI and the state units extending their support, many parents have been encouraging their daughters to take to cricket as a career. This is a good sign. Mithali has been to women's cricket what Sachin was to men's cricket.

One of the major problems is the lack of job opportunities for lady cricketers, with only the Railways being a prominent employer. The BCCI needs to plan more matches and series for the under-19 bunch level, as well as four-year programme for the India 'A' team, with at least one home series and tour every year, against top sides such as England, Australia and New Zealand. This exposure will make the girls more competitive and enhance their skills. There is no dearth of talent, but what is required is to nurture it effectively. The Board should appoint full-time coaches, preferably female, and qualified support staff for the India 'A' and under-19 squads, just like the senior team.

When I took charge of Women's Cricket in 2016, I met Mithali, Jhulan and Harmanpreet to understand from them the needs of the national team. They came up with a list of issues which needed the attention of the BCCI. I must state here that the COA, of which Diana, a former India captain, was a member, was very supportive. All the requests made by the lady cricketers, such as being treated on par with their male counterparts in terms of travel arrangements, hotel accommodation and the daily allowance, were accepted.

The ICC had called for a meeting of representatives of the Full Member countries along with its women's cricket committee, at Dubai in April 2017. Ways in which women's cricket could be further popularized, were discussed. Star Sports, ICC's broadcast partner, presented its plans to increase the visibility of women's cricket and announced that all the matches which the Indian team would play at the World Cup in the UK later that year, would be telecast live. When asked about how the BCCI was planning to promote women's cricket, I told the attendees that the solution was simple. All India had to do was win the World Cup and the fan following of women's cricket would grow manifold. My statement was laughed off by some.

I was in England, with the team, in the last phase of the World Cup and enjoyed the cricket played by the girls. Harmanpreet's innings in the semi-final against Australia was sensational. The final was played against England, in front of a capacity crowd at Lord's. I thought Mithali led the team well, but nervousness got the better of the players and we lost by a close margin. However, the fact was that the girls had made a mark. Vinod Rai called me to convey the COA's decision to give a cash incentive of ₹50 lakh to each of the players for reaching the final.

The prime minister of India had wished the team in a tweet on the day of the final. He later invited the players to his residence and felicitated them.

Having watched Women's Cricket closely since 2006, my advice to the Board would be to ensure that the appointment of selectors is done judiciously. Having witnessed some acrimonious selection meetings, I do hope that the selectors of the future are mature enough to forget their personal differences and egos whenever they meet to pick the team. May the best talent always be picked to represent the country!

THE AGE-FRAUD MENACE

One of the biggest problems in domestic cricket over the years has been that of overage players playing in age-group tournaments. I squarely blame some of the state units for willingly and knowingly looking the other way. I got a taste of this menace when I accompanied the Indian team for the Under-15 World Cup as its manager, in 2000. Roger Binny, the coach of the side, and I were embarrassed at the dinner hosted by the Indian High Commissioner for the team, when a cake was ordered for a player who was celebrating his 16th birthday.

While verifying the documents submitted by the boys who had been picked in the Indian team for the Under-19 World Cup in 2002, we discovered that the date of birth mentioned in the birth certificate of a player did not tally with the one mentioned in his passport. The player was then withdrawn from the team. A few years later, the captain of the team was dropped because information in his documents did not tally.

Thanks to the efforts of Dr Vece Paes and Dr Abhijit Salvi, who devised the Age Verification Programme, the Board was able to quell the problem to a significant extent. The courts supported the Board's endeavour to ensure a level playing field in age-group tournaments through the TW3 bone rating. Every player who registers with the BCCI has to undergo TW3 bone rating at the under-16 level. Birth or school documents which do not look authentic, are checked online with the issuing authorities. Players found to have provided fake information are sent notices and banned for a period of two years from BCCI tournaments. The BCCI has been wise enough to act on Rahul Dravid's suggestion that a boy will play only one Under-19 World Cup.

COURT CASES AND INVESTIGATIONS BY AGENCIES

Legal matters were undoubtedly my biggest challenge. They were time-consuming and tiring. I had to spend a lot of time reading and preparing myself for the numerous arbitrations where I appeared as the BCCI witness, including one in Dubai before the ICC DRF in the case filed by the PCB. Over the years, I appeared in different courts, including a district court in Pune, City Civil Courts, high courts and the SC. When the matter of the Lodha Committee's recommendations came up in the SC, I had to go through minutes of BCCI meetings from previous years and even decades, to gather pertinent information to be passed on to the legal team and the Counsel appearing on our behalf. One of the points that came to my notice was a directive from the central government that the BCCI follow a 'one state, one association' policy. The Board had argued well and assured the central government that it had been strictly following the principle since 1950. That is how associations that had been formed before Independence were able to continue functioning as separate entities. As we are aware, the state of Maharashtra is home to as many as three full members of the BCCI, namely the Mumbai CA, Maharashtra CA and Vidarbha CA. The state of Gujarat comprises the Gujarat CA, Saurashtra CA and Baroda CA.

I had to appear in the court on all the days when the matter related to the Lodha Committee's recommendations was being heard, and it was quite stressful.

From 2010 to 2017, I also appeared a number of times before the Enforcement Directorate on matters pertaining to the FEMA violations of IPL 2009 in South Africa and the investigations against Lalit Modi. In between, I had to appear before a team of investigators from the CBI, which was seeking information on the funds which were missing from the coffers of the JKCA, and also before a sports fraud wing which was investigating age-fraud cases. In 2011, I accompanied the office-bearers of the Board in an appearance before the Finance Committee of Parliament. It was quite an experience, with a panel of Parliamentarians grilling the office-bearers on issues relating to the IPL. I also figured in the ESPN-BCCI face-off in the Bombay High Court and later the Zee-BCCI bout in the SC in 2004. One of my responsibilities was also to prepare replies to the starred questions related to the BCCI and cricket, which were raised in Parliament.

EDUCATIONAL PROGRAMMES

I have already written about the many educational initiatives we launched in the Board, for umpires, match referees, scorers, curators and video analysts, among others, which helped in creating a pool of qualified personnel. It gave me great satisfaction to see S. Ravi being promoted to the ICC's Elite panel of umpires. Nitin Menon, another outstanding umpire, has also been inducted on the panel recently. We have some outstanding match referees, who are as good as any ICC match referee. Dr Paes and Dr Salvi created an educational video on anti-doping practices, in which some of our retired cricketers participated and provided soundbites. The start of every domestic season has been preceded by anti-doping and anti-corruption workshops for players and support staff members of the state units, attendance for which is compulsory.

The Lodha Committee recommended that the Board bring out a cricketers' handbook, along the lines of the athletes' handbook that had been published by the Bengaluru-based GoSports Foundation. This was an area of interest for me and I met Mr Nandan Kamath and his team at the Foundation in 2017, my last year in the Board, to discuss the same. GoSports then submitted a proposal comprising two aspects:

- Publishing a cricketers' handbook.
- Compiling video modules featuring our cricketing stalwarts, to educate young cricketers in key life-skills.

Fortunately, the CEO and COA backed this venture and the *Official BCCI Cricketer's Handbook* was published later that year.[41] It included everything that every professional cricketer must know. Copies of the same were distributed to the state units. The second part of the project—the compilation of videos—was yet to take off when I quit in 2018 and I hope that it has been completed.

We also sought the help of the GoSports Foundation in organizing sessions on media interactions and confidence-building for our lady and under-19 cricketers, just before they took off for the 2017 and 2018 World Cups, respectively. The cricketers enjoyed the sessions.

---

[41]'100 things every cricketer must know', http://relaunch-live.s3.amazonaws.com/cms/documents/59b2753661c86-The%20Official%20BCCI%20Cricketer's%20Handbook.pdf, Accessed on 13 November 2021.

MONKEYGATE

The calendar year of 2008 began on a controversial note. An event that occurred during the second Test of the 2007–08 series between India and Australia at Sydney, hit the headlines the world over. It led to a clash between the BCCI and CA and elicited extreme reactions by fans in both countries.

Andrew Symonds accused Harbhajan Singh of calling him a 'monkey' in an on-field altercation. Symonds's claim was backed by a couple of his teammates and a complaint of 'racial abuse' was lodged, first with the umpires and then the match referee. Harbhajan denied the charge, as did Sachin Tendulkar, who was batting with him at the time. The match had an acrimonious finish, with India being at the receiving end of several contentious umpiring decisions. The fury in the Indian camp was compounded when Mike Procter, the referee, deemed Harbhajan guilty and slapped him with a three-match ban. The Board stood behind the players and even threatened to call the tour off. The Indian team appealed against the ban and the ICC appointed Justice John Hansen as the appeals commissioner for the hearing, which was to take place during the fourth Test at Adelaide.

It helped that Anil Kumble was the captain. That made the job of the BCCI's office-bearers easier, as they could rely on him to handle the situation calmly and firmly. Anil was the bridge between the players and the Board. His presence also helped keep the 'breaking news' elements in the media and their 'sources' at bay.

The Board requested Mr V.R. Manohar, noted senior lawyer and father of Shashank, to appear for Harbhajan. He agreed to do so, but through a video conference and not in person. A video conference facility was set up at the Cricket Centre. The time difference between India and Australia meant that the proceedings began in the wee hours of the morning.

After hearing the arguments by both sides, Justice Hansen concluded that Harbhajan was not guilty of racial abuse. His three-match ban was overturned and he was handed a lighter penalty in the form of a fine of 50 per cent of his match fee. I must add here that Harbhajan was lucky because the ICC's legal team forgot to inform Justice Hansen that he had been penalized on two occasions in the past. They realized their mistake only after the judgement was delivered.

Attending a hearing on video conference was a unique experience. Harbhajan was exonerated of the charge of racial abuse and rightly so, but I must admit here that Mr Manohar was fuming when he saw the off-spinner on screen, standing with his hands in his pockets, when Justice Hansen was delivering his verdict. To Mr Manohar, it appeared as if Harbhajan was not showing any respect to the judge.

INCOME TAX EXEMPTION FOR ICC EVENTS

As mentioned earlier in the book, one of the conditions stipulated in the ICC's Host Nation Agreement, is the responsibility of the host board to ensure that the ICC's earnings from the tournament are exempted from income tax. The BCCI was fortunate to secure income tax exemption for the ICC's earnings from the Champions Trophy in 2006 and World Cup in 2011, both of which were played in India, thanks to the intervention of Dr Manmohan Singh, the then prime minister.

Mr Srinivasan, in his dual capacities as the BCCI president and ICC chairman, had got in touch with the finance ministry in 2014, to request that the ICC be exempted from income tax for the World T20 in 2016, the World T20 in 2020 (moved to 2021 because of the COVID pandemic) and the CWC 2023, all three of which were to be played in India. However, the finance ministry's response was negative. The ICC World T20

2016 was held as per schedule, but in the absence of income tax exemption, Star Sports, the ICC's broadcast partner, deducted withholding tax from the amount it was due to pay to the ICC, as per the law of the country. The ICC, in turn, deducted around ₹150 crore from the amount that it had to pay the BCCI as the latter's share of the surplus to be distributed among the Full members of the ICC.

The BCCI stands to lose a lot of money if the ICC is not granted income tax exemption for the World Cup in 2023. I recently read in media reports that the ICC will not insist on income tax exemption for the next cycle of ICC events (2024 to 2032) that have been allotted to (to be hosted by) India. I hope and pray that this is true.

The BCCI thus finds itself in a situation wherein it may have to weigh the pros and cons of hosting an ICC event. For a layman, it might appear as if the BCCI is paying the ICC to host its tournaments! I hope the government reconsiders its decision, as the country might lose out on hosting global cricketing tournaments otherwise. It will be ironic if India, the hub of the sport, stops hosting the ICC tournaments. The government should take into account the impact a tournament like the World Cup has on the economy. The gains for sectors such as hospitality and travel are substantial, with fans moving from centre to centre and several people flying to India from overseas and combining cricket-watching with tourism.

ACCREDITATION OF PLAYER MANAGEMENT COMPANIES

One of the points red-flagged by the Justice Mudgal Committee and later endorsed by the Justice Lodha Committee was the role of Player Management Companies. It was recommended that such companies get an accreditation from the BCCI under some norms, and every player representing the country declare the identity of their agent to the BCCI in writing. Surprisingly, the COA, during its two years in charge of the Board, did not bother to have this recommendation implemented. This allowed the rumour mills to cast aspersions on the agencies representing players such as M.S. Dhoni and Virat Kohli, among others. The only thing that the COA did was ask Mr Gavaskar to give up his stake in the player management company with which he was associated, if he wanted a commentary contract with the Board.

THE SCOURGE OF BETTING AND MATCH-FIXING

Whether we like to accept it or not, the fact is that one of the major challenges for the BCCI and other cricket boards in Asian countries is betting and match-fixing, especially in the limited-overs versions. Inspite of the BCCI taking a tough stand and punishing those involved, the menace is still rampant in the T20 Leagues, which are being conducted by the state units every year. Junior cricketers are most susceptible to this scourge as they can succumb to the temptation of making a quick buck. The Karnataka Premier League made the news for all the wrong reasons a couple of years ago, when team owners, support staff and players were found to be involved in malpractices.[42] The Anti-Corruption Unit of the BCCI has been raising this issue for a long time. However, it does not have the powers to investigate financial transactions and seek call records, and has to rely on the police. The Lodha Committee had recommended that the BCCI tie up with the police and provide financial support to the creation of an investigation

---

[42]Rasesh Mandani, 'KPL fixing: Plugging multiple gaps in state-run leagues', *Hindustan Times*, 19 January 2020, https://www.hindustantimes.com/cricket/kpl-investigation-plugging-multiple-gaps-in-state-run-leagues/story-6LBeyocbTwcNhw2u1fv2bL.html. Accessed on 6 December 2021.

wing to monitor cricket matches.

We did approach the Government of Maharashtra with a proposal to set up an operational wing under the jurisdiction of the Mumbai Police, assuring the financial backing of the Board to create infrastructure for the nodal agency. Although the government showed keenness, nothing materialized in terms of implementation.

The BCCI did frame the Anti Corruption Code on the lines of that of the ICC and appointed Ravi Savani as the Chief of Anti-Corruption Unit (ACU) of the BCCI in 2013. The ACU of the BCCI has been helpful in initiating measures not only in the IPL and bilateral international matches, but also at the domestic tournament matches. The ACU also educates the players before the start of the domestic season, every year. The Players Match Officials Area (PMOA) is monitored and access to it controlled, during all matches. The ACU on its own has been able to initiate proceedings with the help of the local police to prevent unauthorized tournaments and recommend action to the BCCI.

Hearteningly, the judge in the match-fixing case of 2013 at Delhi went on record to say that although the government has not done much since 2001, the BCCI has an anti-corruption code in place and is known to punish players who are found guilty. It needs to be understood that when S. Sreesanth challenged his life ban, the matter went upto the SC and the only relief he got was the reduction of his sentence from a life ban to seven years.

THE BCCI AND THE MEDIA

One of the biggest challenges for the BCCI is its handling of the media. Instead of sending out information to all the TV, print and digital media simultaneously, leaks still happen through so-called 'BCCI sources', which is extremely embarrassing. All announcements ought to first appear on the BCCI website, but what happens most of the times is that the official media release is sent out after select news channels have flashed 'breaking news' about BCCI. Lalit Modi appointed Adfactors PR to handle the IPL, in 2008. Adfactors PR was signed on again in 2017, when the COA took charge of the Board. However, the problem was that the agency ended up working in the interest of the BCCI bosses and not the BCCI itself, both times.

Some select journalists get the stories and the vast majority then runs around and frantically tries to contact 'BCCI sources' to get the official versions. As mentioned in an earlier chapter, Devendra Prabhudesai and I did our best to streamline the media management of the Board, during his stint at the Board. We tried to organize more media conferences and did our best to engage with the media on a regular basis. With greater support, we could have done even better. *Within the Boundary and Beyond*, the quarterly newsletter that we had launched in 2008, was abruptly terminated in 2014. The fact is that a lot of the good work done by the BCCI does not get published and cricket lovers do not know the facts.

BCCI MUSEUM AND HALL OF FAME

I will always regret my failure to make the BCCI museum a reality. I tried hard but did not succeed. Lalit got himself involved in the project in 2007, but his efforts to create a museum like those maintained by sporting teams in the US and Europe did not materialize. I then spoke to James Chadwick, the curator at the MCC Museum, and invited him to Mumbai with the permission of the office-bearers. We discussed the museum and he inspected the area on the first floor of the Cricket Centre, which had been set aside for the project. The museum was to be abutted by a viewing room, in which visitors would get to watch archival cricket footage. Chadwick designed a blueprint and the BCCI then invited interested parties to make presentations and even shortlisted a vendor. But post-2013, all projects took a back seat and the area earmarked for the museum started being used as a godown. I hope and pray that the BCCI pursues the museum project. It would also be great if the present office-bearers create a BCCI Hall of Fame.

CRICKET FOR THE DIFFERENTLY ABLED

The BCCI should lay down rules and regulations for the development and promotion of cricket for the differently abled in India.

19

ACE ADMINISTRATORS

I have written about Mr Jagmohan Dalmiya, Rajbhai, Dr Muthiah, Mr Bindra and Mr Lele in earlier chapters. The BCCI will always be indebted to them for their contribution to Indian cricket. In this chapter, I will focus on the Board's senior office-bearers of the twenty-first century, under whom I worked.

SHARAD PAWAR

I was a part of Mr Pawar's team not only at the MCA, but also the BCCI in later years. It was he who proposed that I become the chief administrative officer of the Board in 2006. I spent a lot of quality time with him, in the office and on official trips. I was greatly impressed by his memory, tactful handling of difficult situations and leadership qualities. Listening to him talk about his political career and the initiatives he undertook, was a memorable experience.

One of the country's senior-most politicians and a four-time chief minister of Maharashtra, Mr Pawar also served as the Union defence minister and had two full terms as the minister of agriculture in the Union Cabinet. He was by no means new to sports administration when he was elected president of the MCA in 2001. He had headed the Kabaddi and Wrestling Federations of Maharashtra earlier, as also the Maharashtra Olympic Association. He was not a stranger to cricket either. Sadashiv Shinde, his father-in-law and a leg-spinner, had represented India in seven Tests from 1946 to 1952.

Our first meeting in December 2000 was eventful. The MCA's elections were scheduled for early January in 2001 and Mr Pawar was to contest against Mr Ajit Wadekar, whose candidature had been backed by the Bal Mahaddalkar group, of which I was a part. I was in Pune for the prize-distribution ceremony of the Saamna Trophy Tournament initiated by Aditya Thackeray and I was to be felicitated at the hands of Kapil Dev, the chief guest. I received a phone call from Dnyaneshwar Agashe, who headed the Maharashtra Cricket Association and was a close friend of Mr Pawar. He told me that Mr Pawar wanted to meet me after the function and handed the phone to him. I spoke to Pawar and told him politely that I could not meet him in Pune, but would definitely meet him in Mumbai.

We met at the Oberoi Hotel in Mumbai the next day. I went along with Mahaddalkar, the leader of my group in the MCA. When I reiterated our group's decision to back Mr Wadekar in the upcoming election, Mr Pawar interrupted me and said that he only wanted an assurance from me that I would manage the administration of MCA to the best of my abilities after the election. He further said that it did not matter what our group thought, as he already had the numbers to win the election! I promised him that I would justify the faith he had in me and would not let him down. That marked the beginning of an association, which was based on trust, faith and mutual respect. He told me later that he appreciated my honesty with regard to the MCA election. When I joined the BCCI he cautioned me that some of his colleagues in the Board had viewed me with suspicion initially, as they felt that I was close to Mr Dalmiya.

It will by no means be incorrect to say that Mr Pawar's tenure as BCCI President from 2005 to 2008 was the most productive ever for the Board. A number of initiatives got a go-ahead during his tenure, primarily because of his decisive stand

and ability to convince the office-bearers and BCCI members to support the same. These included a permanent office for the Board, a pension scheme for retired cricketers, the takeover of women's cricket, the launch of the IPL and the raising of the infrastructure subsidy from ₹4 crore to ₹50 crore.

In 2008, Mr Pawar also convinced his colleagues in the Board to extend a helping hand to other sports. The BCCI donated a handsome ₹50 crore to the National Sports Development Fund (NSDF) of the Ministry of Youth Affairs and Sports. A corpus of ₹80 crore was created, with the Sports Ministry contributing ₹30 crore. The plan was to provide financial support to athletes who were associated with disciplines like archery, boxing, swimming, wrestling and gymnastics and preparing for events like the Olympics, Asian Games and Commonwealth Games.

The BCCI also gave cash prizes to the athletes who won medals at the Beijing Olympics in 2008. Ironically, the contribution of ₹50 crore to the NSDF boomeranged on the Board. We lost the income-tax exemption that had been granted to us, as the assessment officer in question contended that donating money to other sports was not among the objects of the BCCI. The BCCI had made the necessary amendment in its Memorandum of Association, but it did not take the permission of the Central Board of Direct Taxes before committing to the NSDF. This issue has not been resolved till date.

Some of us from the BCCI were also on the NSDF Committee, but stopped receiving updates on the NSDF after 2010. This was like adding insult to injury. I filed an RTI on behalf of the Board and discovered that only about ₹8 crore had been used in two years, most of it to finance the running of sports bodies and not the athletes. The moral of the story is that the Board tried to support a cause, only to end up with tax hassles.

Incidentally, the BCCI had decided to donate ₹50 lakh to the Prime Minister's Relief Fund during the Kargil War in

1999, but was advised against it as such donations were not part of its objects.

Mr Pawar was the second Indian after Mr Dalmiya to become the president of the ICC. He held the position from 2010 to 2012 and did a fine job, keeping the members together and initiating developmental activities in Associate Member nations, one of which was China. As ICC president, Mr Pawar had the honour of presenting the ICC CWC 2011 trophy to Dhoni, the victorious captain, at the Wankhede Stadium, on the evening of 2 April 2011. He wanted me to join the ICC in 2010, but I could not because of my commitment to the BCCI.

A project close to Mr Pawar's heart was a sports science centre for cricket, which was proposed by Dr Anant Joshi, the renowned Sports Medicine expert. Mr Pawar had even identified a plot in Mumbai for the same, but the project did not take off after his tenure as BCCI president ended.

The launch of the IPL was the highlight of Mr Pawar's stint as the BCCI president. The IPL would not have taken off had he not trusted and backed Lalit and prevailed upon his fellow office-bearers and members of the Board to do likewise. A decision he may well have regretted in hindsight was the one to permit India Cements to bid for the franchise rights of an IPL team. The BCCI amended its constitution to allow the same and was castigated by the courts subsequently for having done so. Some members of the Board felt that Lalit was being given too much freedom to take decisions, most of which were unilateral. This ultimately led to controversies and Lalit's expulsion from the Board.

SHASHANK MANOHAR

Shashank Manohar succeeded Mr Pawar as the BCCI president in 2008. A lawyer by profession and resident of Nagpur, Shashank had been involved in the promotion and development of cricket in Vidarbha for several years before he took over Indian cricket. He has his quirks. He does not wear a watch, but is always punctual. He does not use a mobile phone or a laptop and did not even have a passport till he had to travel to Dubai to attend an ICC meeting in 2008! He has always been forthright in his views on the sport and its administration.

As president and secretary, he and Mr Srinivasan made for an outstanding combination from 2008 to 2011. However, they fell out in 2013 following the allegations of betting against Mr Srinivasan's son-in-law. Shashank felt that Mr Srinivasan ought to resign and return after the matter had been resolved, but the latter disagreed.

The Vidarbha Cricket Association's new stadium and clubhouse at Jamtha on the outskirts of Nagpur and the cricket academy at the old stadium in the city bear testimony to Shashank's contribution to the game. These facilities were a turning point for cricket in the region. From being considered minnows for decades, Vidarbha won the Ranji Trophy twice in succession, in 2017–18 and 2018–19, respectively.

Shashank used to listen to others, but most of the times, he took his own decisions on matters concerning the Board. It was during his tenure as the president that the decision to extend amnesty to all the retired and contemporary cricketers who had joined the 'rebel' Indian Cricket League (ICL), was taken. This enabled the ICL players to return to the BCCI mainstream. He appointed Sandeep Patil as the chairman of NCA. Sandeep went on to become the chairman of the National Selection Committee, three years later. I don't think any other administrator would have taken the bold call of cancelling the bids for two additional IPL teams in 2010. Shashank was also instrumental in suspending Lalit Modi and initiating the ensuing enquiry by the BCCI disciplinary committee into alleged irregularities committed by Lalit as the chairman of IPL.

Shashank was a trusted lieutenant of Mr Pawar's till October

2015, when he acceded to Mr Jaitley's request to return as the BCCI president after Mr Dalmiya's demise, even as Mr Pawar was being favoured by many for the post. Shashank was thus at the helm of affairs when the Lodha Committee submitted its recommendations and the SC started hearing petitions, calling upon it to ensure that the recommendations of the committee were implemented. Shashank did implement some of the recommendations even before the Lodha Committee submitted the final part of its report to the SC. One of these was a third-party audit of the state units, which exposed the financial mismanagement in a number of state associations. However, the exercise was suspended after Shashank left the BCCI in May 2016 to join the ICC.

I feel Shashank as the Board president ought to have taken the initiative to meet the members of the Lodha Committee before they submitted their report, as some of the issues could have been resolved through discussions.

He went on to become the first independent chairman of the ICC and enjoyed two successful terms from 2016 to 2020. Mr Srinivasan, Shashank's predecessor at the ICC, had overseen the creation of a formula by the 'Big Three' (India, Australia and England). As per this formula, the BCCI was to get the lion's share of the ICC's revenue meant for the Full Members. Australia and England were also to get substantial shares. The revised governance rules gave the 'Big Three' a distinct advantage, as only their representatives could be elected to chair the ICC and its all important finance and accounts committee.

After taking over as chairman, Shashank allowed the ICC members to debate the decisions taken by the previous regime and change them. The BCCI was the worst affected by the reversal of the earlier decisions, as its share of the revenue went down by 15–20 per cent. Shashank, who till then had been revered by many in the BCCI, was branded a villain and accused of working against the interests of his own Board. To be fair to him, it was the BCCI members themselves who had agreed to reduce the Board's share by up to 15 per cent at a special general meeting, where only P.S. Raman (TNCA) and Brijesh Patel (KSCA) had voiced their concerns and reservations. The reversal of the decisions made Shashank very popular in the ICC, as the other members stood to benefit not only financially, but also due to the changes in the governance rules. Greg Barclay, who succeeded Shashank at the ICC, praised the outgoing chairman for his conduct and leadership.

N. SRINIVASAN

Mr Srinivasan, who succeeded Shashank as the BCCI president in 2011, had tackled many a challenge to build the India Cements empire. His contribution to cricket is not limited to what he did as president of the TNCA and later, office-bearer of the BCCI. Many a talented youngster had been identified and offered the opportunity to represent India Cements, the company he headed, in league tournaments in Chennai, one of them being Rahul Dravid, when he was in his teens. As the managing director of India Cements, Mr Srinivasan gave jobs to hundreds of youngsters and thus provided them financial security and the freedom to focus on their game.

In 2002, Mr Dalmiya acted against the advice of members of his group and appointed Mr Srinivasan as chairman of the Board's Finance Committee. Mr Srinivasan had, at that point, just joined the Board after winning the TNCA elections. However, their relationship soured in 2004, during the stand-off between Zee and ESPN over the telecast rights. Mr Srinivasan joined Mr Pawar's group when the latter decided to contest the presidential election against Ranbir Singh Mahendra, the Dalmiya group's candidate, later that year.

One of the best administrators the BCCI has ever seen, Mr

Srinivasan infused a 'corporate culture' and accountability in the corridors of the Cricket Centre. He was solely responsible for setting a proper pay structure for the employees of the Board, including retirement benefits. He was also mindful of the need to pay as much attention to domestic cricket as international cricket and backed our proposals to initiate educational programmes for umpires, scorers, video analysts, match referees and curators. Not only did he sanction the expenses for the same, but he would also keep track of the programmes and enquire about their progress.

Whenever he opposed Lalit Modi, it was only to safeguard the rights and interests of the Board. For instance, he ensured that the yearly fee which IMG was being paid to organize the league, which frankly was a bit much, was reduced.

The constitution of the Board was amended to enable India Cements to bid for an IPL team in 2008. India Cements won the bid for the Chennai Franchise and this was seen by many as the start of the conflict of interest issues in the Board. However, to be fair to Mr Srinivasan, he had taken the permission of the then BCCI president before participating in the bidding. However, it was never going to be easy to essay the dual roles of team owner and office-bearer. In later years, Lalit never missed an opportunity to hit out at him, even making allegations that umpire postings for matches featuring Chennai Super Kings were manipulated. This was totally incorrect, as the panel of umpires for the IPL was finalized by the umpire assessment committee and the postings were done by the operations team. Allegations were made against some of the Chennai Super Kings players too.

Mr Srinivasan came in for a lot of flak when his son-in-law, Gurunath Meiyappan, was accused of betting in 2013. He was the BCCI president then, but had little or no support from within the Board. The attacks on him were not limited to his position in BCCI, but also to India Cements, as the financial institutions that had invested in the company were instigated to act against the company. There is no doubt that there was a larger game plan to attack Mr Srinivasan. I spent a lot of time with him during this phase and observed the way he handled the situation. He refused to be cowed down. He was advised to resign in the interest of the BCCI, but he argued that he could not be held responsible for the allegations of betting against his son-in-law. He was willing to take on his detractors.

He was a tough character no doubt, but he too was human after all, and the incident was hurting him and his family, and yet he had to keep his emotions in check. The fact was that the secretary and treasurer had resigned and the five vice presidents and joint secretary were planning to resign, only to put pressure on him.

As president of the Board, Mr Srinivasan implemented the One-Time Benefit scheme for retired international and domestic cricketers in 2012. International cricketers apart, the scheme also covered those who had played at least 75 first-class matches. He is a very generous man and I know for a fact that he has helped a number of cricketers during medical emergencies. He cares for the 'unsung heroes' as well and wanted to introduce a benefit package for curators who had served state units for more than 20 years.

Mr Srinivasan was feared by the ICC Secretariat of the time. Like Mr Dalmiya, he was at loggerheads with the ICC over a number of issues, such as the 'whereabouts' clause in the anti-doping rules, the income-tax exemption requirement for ICC events, certain conditions in the Member Participation Agreement and the propensity of the ICC to interfere in bilateral series agreements between Full Members. He became the chairman of ICC in 2014 and introduced the 'Big Three' Formula for Governance review and financial distribution, with the England and Wales Cricket Board and Cricket Australia in tow.

Mr Srinivasan leveraged the Indian team's tours to get the support of the full members and got the formula approved. The formula was based on the logic that at least 75 per cent of the media rights revenue that the ICC earned from its broadcast partner, came from India. The BCCI was slated to get a larger share of the ICC's revenue, after taking care of the expenses.

That Mr Srinivasan took the ECB and CA along to frame the 'Big Three' formula was surprising, as it was the BCCI who, in 1997, had spearheaded the move to abolish the veto powers of the two Boards. The ECB and CA were happy with the turn of events as they were assured of the post of the ICC chairman, along with the BCCI's representatives, on a rotational basis, which they would have struggled to get otherwise. This was underscored when two successive candidates nominated by the ECB for the ICC chairmanship, failed to garner the requisite support, after Shashank dumped his predecessor's 'Big Three' formula.

Like Mr Dalmiya, Mr Srinivasan always wanted total control on the working of the BCCI. In 2013, he got the BCCI to amend a 50-year-old rule pertaining to the tenure of the president and got it increased from three years to six. In all probability, he would have contested for the president's post from the East Zone in 2014 as he had the support of the majority of the state units from that zone, but this did not happen as the SC did not allow him to contest. However, the amendment enabled Mr Dalmiya and Shashank to return later as president for a second term.

After Mr Dalmiya's death, Mr Srinivasan even offered to support Mr Pawar's candidature for the post of the BCCI president. However, Mr Jaitley won Shashank over to his side and ensured that the latter became the president. When this happened, it became obvious that Shashank would not allow Mr Srinivasan to continue as the chairman of the ICC. Sure enough, Shashank took over from him at the ICC in February 2016.

During my long and immensely satisfying association with Mr Srinivasan, there were times when I felt that he was ill-advised. The instructions to the Indian team touring England in 2014 to skip the annual ICC awards ceremony, ostensibly because there had been some friction between the office-bearers of the Board and the then CEO of the ICC, was one such instance. The Indian team, which comprised players who had been nominated for some of the awards, missed out on the ceremony as a result.

I also felt that we should not have taken on other full member boards on issues that were their prerogative, like suggesting who they should take on as a broadcast partner. The Board should have kept away from the internal matters of its counterparts.

Differences cropped up between the BCCI and CSA over India's proposed tour of the country in 2013–14. The president and CEO of CSA then flew to Mumbai to meet the office-bearers of the Board. I remember Mr Srinivasan telling me to attend the meeting, with him and Sanjay Patel, the secretary. The misunderstanding was ironed out and the Test series salvaged. We agreed to play three Tests instead of four, as had originally been scheduled.

NIRANJAN SHAH

Niranjan Shah was the secretary of the Board when I was appointed chief administrative officer. A former first-class cricketer, he was one of the senior-most members of the Board at the time, having attended meetings as the representative of the Saurashtra Cricket Association since the early 1980s. He was popular among the cricketers and the media. Niranjan's weak point was his mobile phone, which used to buzz all the time, even when he was in meetings.

His contribution to the development of the sport in Saurashtra is exemplary. He oversaw the construction of a splendid stadium and cricketing infrastructure. The recent successes of the Saurashtra cricket team are the outcome of the hard work put in by Niranjan and his team, over the years. They identified talent at the junior level and gave it plenty of scope and opportunities to flower. The Saurashtra Cricket Association, which gets the same amount of funds from the BCCI as any other member, can be proud of the way it has handled its finances. While most of the state units, which receive the same subsidy amount from the Board, are in the red more often than not, the Saurashtra Cricket Association has reserves of more than ₹200 crore at any given point of time and that too after creating good cricketing infrastructure.

I shared an excellent rapport with Niranjan during his stint as the secretary from 2005 to 2008. He used to spend a lot of time at the Cricket Centre and we used to discuss issues together. He was friendly with the staff and would get things done with his informal approach. He was a good administrator but stayed in the background in the presence of Mr Pawar, Shashank and Srinivasan. I remember Niranjan being very upset with me for not telling him about Rahul Dravid's resignation as the captain and keeping him in the dark about Gary Kirsten's trip to Delhi to be interviewed for the post of coach of the Indian team. After his stint as the secretary, Niranjan managed the Indian team on the tour of New Zealand in 2008–09 and was appointed vice chairman of the IPL under Lalit Modi. I must state here that he handled a tricky situation that arose during the 2009 season of the IPL in South Africa, very well. It could well have put some people in a spot had it been allowed to get out of hand, but Niranjan sorted things out.

ANURAG THAKUR

Anurag Thakur, who is today the Union Minister of Sports and Youth Affairs, and the Minister of Information and Broadcasting, was the joint secretary of the Board from 2011 to 2015, secretary from 2015 to 2016 and then president for a few months. He was among those who had to fight group politics at the local level, to first head his state association and then enter the BCCI. As president of the HPCA, he was involved in the creation of one of the most scenic cricketing stadia in the world, at Dharamshala. He also oversaw the creation of excellent facilities in the districts of the state. He set up the women's cricket academy in HPCA. He served the BCCI as a junior selector as well.

He took over as president from Shashank after the latter joined ICC as independent chairman. He was young and dynamic and I am sure he would have brought in several changes had he been allowed to serve his full term. As BCCI president, Anurag set his sights on the development of cricket in the north-eastern states and approved the creation of indoor cricket academies and cricket grounds in the region, with the help of the respective state governments. In fact, he sanctioned ₹5 crore each for academies at Shillong and Dimapur. Some of the important decisions taken by him were the direct transfer of match fees of players and match officials into their respective bank accounts, financial support to the registered bodies of differently-abled cricketers and annual retainerships for lady cricketers.

His term as the BCCI president came to a premature end when the SC held him and Ajay Shirke, the then secretary, responsible for the non-implementation of the Lodha Committee's recommendations and ordered them to relinquish their positions in January 2017.

Anurag had even initiated a discussion on renaming the

BCCI itself as he thought that 'Board of Control for Cricket in India' sounded far too bureaucratic.

SANJAY JAGDALE

Sanjay Jagdale served as the joint secretary of the Board from 2008 to 2011 and secretary from 2011 to 2013. He had earlier been a member of the junior and senior selection committees and had managed the Indian team during the ICC CWC 2007. He is a connoisseur of the sport and values its traditions. The BCCI museum may well have become a reality had he not resigned as secretary in 2013. Not wanting to get into any controversy, he stepped down when he was appointed on a committee, along with two judges, to delve into the allegations against Gurunath Meiyappan and Raj Kundra.

Sanjay was part of the MPCA for decades. M.M. Jagdale, his father, was a cricketing contemporary of Col. C.K. Nayudu's and that is how Sanjay knew icons such as the Colonel and Syed Mushtaq Ali, personally. A soft-spoken and reserved but approachable individual, he possesses a rich collection of cricket books, footage and anecdotes. It was at his suggestion that the Board started inviting Col. C.K. Nayudu's daughter, Chandra Nayudu, for the BCCI Awards ceremony every year.

I remember two incidents which he narrated to me, both related to selection committee meetings. The senior selection committee of which he was a member had assembled in the premises of the DDCA to pick the Indian team for a series. When the meeting started, Sanjay sensed that someone was standing outside the closed door and was trying to hear what was being discussed. He gestured to John Wright, the then coach and an attendee in the meeting, to tiptoe to the door and open it. When John did so, he and the other selectors were shocked to see a senior member of the DDCA sitting right outside with his ears to the door, not even realizing that he had been exposed. Years later, Sanjay walked out of a women's selection committee meeting, which he had convened as the secretary of the Board, because a couple of the selectors were getting into almost a physical fight over the selection of a player.

Sanjay took a keen interest in proposals to start tournaments for corporates particularly the public sector undertakings, banks, Income Tax and Customs and the CAG, all of whom have provided gainful employment opportunities to cricketers, over the years and decades. In 2009, he chaired a committee that oversaw the inception of a corporate tournament, which was played for the Raj Singh Dungarpur Trophy with a prize money of ₹1 crore. We later ventured into starting a limited-overs national tournament for schoolboys. However, we ran into cases of overage players being fielded, as well as instances of players being enrolled by schools just to play this tournament. Tragically, the BCCI discontinued both the Corporate Trophy and the Schools Tournament.

RANBIR SINGH MAHENDRA

Ranbir Singh served as the joint secretary, secretary, vice president and president of the BCCI. He was well versed with the working of the BCCI, but his one-year tenure as President was unfortunately affected by BCCI politics and the tussle between Sourav Ganguly and Greg Chappell, which threatened to destabilize Indian cricket. He played an important role in the organization of the 1987 World Cup in India. He has been the driving force behind the HCA.

ARUN JAITLEY

An eminent lawyer and highly respected politician, Mr Jaitley handled diverse ministerial portfolios in the governments headed by Shri Atal Behari Vajpayee and later Shri Narendra

Modi. He was also an excellent sports administrator and played a significant role in refurbishing the cricket stadium in Delhi. He served as the vice president of the BCCI and the Board depended a lot on his inputs on various issues. I accompanied him to a meeting of Sports Federations, which was convened by the Union Sports Ministry to disuss the proposed Sports Bill in June 2010. He had done his homework and he literally tore into the proposed bill, point-by-point.

I must mention some of the points he made in his presentation: (a) Sports is a state subject and the sports ministry can at best control the activities of the National Federations, which depend on government funds. (b) The BCCI is not registered with the Sports Ministry, but is the only body running cricket in India that is recognized by the ICC. (c) To say that only National Sports Federations can use the national flag is wrong, especially after the SC's verdict in favour of the Jindals, so far as the right to hoist the national flag is concerned. (d) The BCCI does not come under the ambit of RTI till such time that the Parliament does not amend the existing provisions, as the BCCI is an autonomous body and does not take any grants from the government.

I also had the pleasure of working with S.K. Nair, Kishore Rungta, Jyoti Bajpai, Anirudh Chaudhry and Sanjay Patel and Amitabh Choudhary, all of whom were office-bearers of BCCI at different times.

In conclusion, I would like to say that those who believe I discharged my responsibilities as an employee of the BCCI effectively and efficiently should know that the credit for my doing so was also due to the administrators I worked under. They had faith in me and encouraged me to do what was best for Indian cricket. They treated me as a colleague, never as an employee.

My role as an administrator gave me an opportunity to interact with some of the finest lot of cricketers who did the nation and the BCCI proud with their performances. The cricketers who led India during my tenure were great ambassadors for the game. The success of Indian cricket is due to the fact that the administrators and the cricketers complemented the efforts of each other.

ACKNOWLEDGEMENTS

I extend my sincere and heartfelt thanks to Kapish Mehra and Rudra Sharma of Rupa Publications for giving me the opportunity to write this book, and to Devendra Prabhudesai for motivating me to pen my memories down.

I am indebted to all those whom I have worked with at the MCA and the BCCI.

INDEX

#MeToo, 263

Aamby Valley City, 101, 102
Abbas, Zaheer, 73
Abdi, Mehmood, 199
Abdullah, Farooq, 111
Adfactors PR, 286
Adidas, 188
administration, 28, 47, 104, 136, 169, 225, 227, 235, 241, 251, 288, 289, 292
Advani, L.K., 109
Agashe, Dnyaneshwar, 57, 126, 127, 129, 131, 132, 133, 246, 289
Age Verification Programme, 278
Ahmed, Ghulam, 178
Ahmed, Subhan, 122
Airtel, 111
Akhtar, Shoaib, 80, 118, 121
All-India Inter University Championship, 33
Amarnath, Mohinder, 140, 239
Ambani, Dhirubhai, 56
Ambani, Mukesh, 245
Amin, Chirayu, 152, 199
Amin, Hemang, 170, 207, 217
Amin, Narhari, 147
Amladi, Vasant, 34
Amre, Pravin, 234, 250
Ananth, M., 127
Annual General Meeting (AGM), 1990, 1997, 1999, 2001, 2004, 2005, 2006, 2008, 2010, 2011, 2012, 2013, 2015, 2016, 29, 31, 54, 57, 87, 102, 124, 125, 126, 127, 128, 129, 130, 131, 132, 133, 135, 136, 137, 138, 148, 149, 153, 186, 187, 199, 216, 217, 219, 223, 225, 226, 233, 246, 248, 253
Ansari, Shahid, 34
anti-corruption code, 285
Anti-Corruption Officer, 147
Anti-Corruption Unit, 170, 210, 218, 259, 273, 284, 285
Anti-Doping, 170
Asia Cup, 64, 66, 68, 73, 89, 253
Asian Cricket Council (ACC), 80, 107, 173
Asian Games, 290
Assam Cricket Association, 131, 225
Association of Indian Universities (ACU), 274
Azad, Yashovardhan, 108
Azharuddin, Mohammed, 65, 66, 67, 74, 83, 96

Babu, Mohammed, Ali, Ahsan, 6
Bahutule, Sairaj, 236, 250
Balaji, Lakshmipathi, 119
Balwinder Sandhu, 236, 250
Bandra-Kurla Complex (BKC), 77, 242
Bangar, Sanjay, 184
Bangladesh Cricket Board (BCB), 3, 4
Bank of Baroda, 6

Baroda Cricket Association, 57, 126
Barve, Pravin, 43, 128, 129
Basu, Indranil, 118
BCA Tournament Committee, 233
BCCI Awards, 177, 178, 180, 183, 188, 217, 301
BCCI Cricket Rating sponsor, 188
BCCI Museum and Hall of Fame, 286
BCCI politics, 11, 49, 124, 149, 152, 302
Bedi, Bishan, 99
Beloff, Michael, 123
Bharat Arun, 184
Bharati, Prasar, 105, 189
Bharat Ratna, 223
Bharucha, E.P., 248
Bhatia, Vimal, 34
Bhogle, Harsha, 262
Bhosle, Vijay, 250
Bhowmick, Ashish, 175
Bhuvad, Devendra, 169, 198
Big Bash League, 208, 275
Bihar Cricket Association, 88, 89, 220
Bindra, Inderjit, 2, 13, 57
Binny, Roger, 89, 277
biobubbles, 212
Board of Control for Cricket in India (BCCI), 2–9, 11, 14, 19, 20, 21, 22, 28, 29, 30, 46, 47, 49, 50, 52–63, 67, 73–78, 80–84, 90, 93, 94, 95, 98, 99, 103–106, 108, 110, 111, 122–125, 127, 128, 130, 131, 133–139, 141–145, 147, 149–155, 158, 159, 160, 162, 165, 167, 169, 170, 171, 173, 174, 175, 177, 178, 180, 181, 183, 184, 185, 187, 188, 189, 190, 192–195, 198–202, 204–207, 209–214, 216–222, 224–231, 233–237, 239, 241, 242, 246–249, 251, 252, 254, 255, 257,
259, 260, 262, 264, 265, 267, 268, 269, 270, 272–276, 278–305
Bombay Cricket Association (BCA), viii, 27, 29, 30, 31, 32, 34, 36, 37, 39, 40, 41, 43, 44, 45, 46, 47, 48, 49, 56, 57, 75, 233, 234, 235
Bombay High Court, 19, 104, 132, 220, 236, 248, 279
Bombay Hockey Association, 31
Bombay Presidency Cricket Association, 38
Bombay Stock Exchange (BSE), 9
Bombay University Cricket Tournament Committee, 34, 37, 233
Borde, A.J., Prof., 22, 28
Borde, Chandrakant, 'Chandu', 161
Border–Gavaskar Trophy, 101, 140, 182
Border Security Force (BSF), 112
Brabourne Stadium, 27, 29, 30, 31, 82, 146, 147, 155, 168, 183, 191, 192
Bradman, Don, 240
Bucknor, Steve, 119
Bunt community, 23

Calcutta High Court, 135, 152, 153
catchment areas, 186
Central Bureau of Investigation (CBI), 63, 93, 94, 95, 96, 98, 225, 260, 261, 279
Central Industrial Security Force (CISF), 6, 15
Central Organising Committee (COC), 4, 5
Champions League, 183, 199, 207
Chandgadkar, Madhukar, Vinayak, (M.V.), Prof., 29, 50, 103
Chandrachud, Y.V., 66, 67, 91, 93
Chappell, Greg, 72, 82, 100, 140, 159, 302

INDEX

Charity Commissioner, 228
Chatterjee, Somnath, 98
Chatterjee, Taposh, 175
Chaudhari, Suryakant, 34
Chaudhary, Sudhir, Kumar, 19
Chavan, Prithviraj, 18
Chidambaram, M.A., 10, 52, 86, 177, 185, 215
Chidambaram, P., 145
chief administrative officer, 2, 149, 150, 251, 260, 288, 298
chief financial officer (CFO), 226, 227, 254
Chougule, Vijay, 130
Clarke, Giles, 199
Col. C.K. Nayudu Lifetime Achievement Award, 75, 177, 178, 263
Committee of Administrators (COA), 254, 255, 256, 257, 258, 259, 262, 263, 264, 265, 270, 271, 276, 277, 280, 284, 286
Commonwealth Games, 2010, 6
Communist Party of India, 98
Competition Commission of India, 188
Comptroller and Auditor General of India (CAG), 252, 254, 302
conflict of interest, 226, 229, 258, 295
Constitutional Review Committee, 78
Contractor, Nariman, 99, 179, 236
Cricket Advisory Committee (CAC), 154, 256, 257
Cricket Association of Bengal (CAB), 11, 78, 134, 152, 221
Cricket Australia (CA), 88, 171, 199, 202
Cricket Club of India (CCI), 29, 30, 31, 32, 82, 83, 84, 90, 143, 146, 148, 168, 237

Cricketers Benefit Fund Series (CBFS), 75, 95
Cricket Improvement Committee (CIC), 241
Cricket South Africa (CSA), 80, 172, 199, 202, 298
Cronje, Hansie, 92, 93, 239
Crowe, Jeff, 18

Dadar Union Sports Club, 40
Dalmiya, Jagmohan, 11, 261, 288
Dalvi, Hemu, 233
Dandeniya, Suraj, 6
Dara, Singh, Vindu, 218
Das, B.B., 129
Dasgupta, Gautam, 134
Das, R.K., 6
Dawoodbhoy, Hussain, 72
Deccan Chargers (Hyderabad), 204
Decision Review System (DRS), 173
defence minister, 288
Delhi Daredevils, 204, 208
Delhi Police, 92, 93, 210, 218, 274
Deloitte, 226
de Mello, Anthony, 29, 50, 84
Deora, Milind, 221
Desai, Bakul, 234
Desai, Chetan, 137
Desai, Morarji, 25
Desai, M.W., 31
Desai, Ramakant, 31, 44, 250
Deshmukh, Vilasrao, 243, 246
Deshpande, Mohini, 167
de Silva, Aravinda, 72
Devi, Rabri, 88
Dev, Kapil, 10, 47, 63, 90, 93, 158, 179, 289
Dhoni, M.S., 1, 12, 18, 19, 20, 164, 165, 177, 182, 198, 205, 206, 219, 221, 284, 291
Dhulap, Nilesh, 169, 198
Dhume, Pankaj, 33

Dighe, Sameer, 46, 250
DigiBeta tapes, 190
Directorate of Revenue Intelligence (DRI), 196, 197, 210, 260
Disciplinary Committee, 95, 152, 199, 218
District Cricket Association (DDCA), 118, 123, 132, 138, 301
Divan, Shyam, 33
Divecha, Ramesh, 29
Diwadkar, Sharad, 88, 94, 102, 103
Doordarshan, 58, 59, 103, 105, 189
Dotiwalla, Dara, 44
Dravid, Rahul, 71, 72, 86, 97, 100, 114, 119, 142, 154, 159, 180, 184, 204, 258, 270, 272, 278, 294, 299
Dr Muthiah, 86, 87, 88, 89, 90, 95, 96, 125, 128, 130, 131, 132, 149, 186, 261, 288
D'Souza, Marvine, 167
Dudhia, Macky, 145
Dudley, Colin, 240
Duleep Trophy, 60, 173
Dungarpur, Raj, Singh, 59, 68, 82, 246, 261, 302
Durani, Salim, 83
Dutta, Nilay, 220
Dutt, B.N., 56
D.Y. Patil Stadium, 10, 192, 198, 209, 243

East Stand, 27, 28
Eden Gardens, 10, 56, 61, 215
Edulji, Diana, 254, 275
Election Commissioner of India, 136, 139
Elite Force of the Punjab Province, 111
Emburey, John, 161
Emergency, 25
Enforcement Directorate, 193, 209, 210, 260, 261, 279

Engineer, Farokh, 180
England and Wales Cricket Board, 199, 296
English County Championship, 2000, 100
ESPN, 10, 103, 104, 185, 189, 279, 294
Essar group, 238

Fan Parks, 208
Finance and Legal issues, 168
finance committee, 104, 139, 230, 244
finance ministry, 282
Fleming, Stephen, 164
Ford, Graham, 160
Foreign Exchange Management Act (FEMA), 193, 209, 279
Fort Vijay, 40
Frazer, Ian, 141
Full Member, 51, 61, 62, 79, 81, 202, 207, 231, 251, 268, 269, 276, 293, 296

Gaddafi Stadium, 3
Gaekwad, Aunshuman, 69, 85
Gaekwad, Dattajirao, 176
Gambhir, Gautam, 18
Game Development, 168, 169, 216
Gandhi, Priyanka, 113
Gandhi, Rahul, 113
Gandhi, Rajiv, 56
Ganguly, Sourav, 69, 80, 82, 86, 92, 97, 98, 154, 180, 204, 230, 256, 263, 272, 302
Garware Club House, 18, 235, 236, 241, 246
Garware Pavilion, 17, 44
Gauhati University, 26
Gavaskar, Sunil, 26, 39, 44, 47, 77, 249
General Elections, 192, 211, 212

INDEX 311

general officer commanding (GOC), 115
Ghavri, Karsan, 250
Ghosh, Kunal, Kanti, 79
Giles Shield, 40
Gillani, Yousaf, Raza, 13
Gilligan, Arthur, 50
Girgaum Chowpatty, 25
Global Cricket Corporation (GCC), 81
Goa Cricket Association, 130, 225
Godbole, Vilas, 44, 46
Godrej, 151
Goel, Rajinder, 263
goods and services tax (GST), 208
GoSports Foundation, 280
Goswami, Jhulan, 275
Gothaskar, Madhav, 44
Government of India, 63, 123, 144, 223
Government of Maharashtra, 14, 30, 32, 285
Guha, Ramachandra, 254, 262
Gujarat Cricket Association, 138, 147, 215, 247
Gujarat Lions, 211
Gupte, Dinar, 174
Gupte, Kedar, 6
Gupte, M. Y., 44

Hadlee, Richard, 77
Halbe, Shripad, 17, 48, 244
Hansen, John, 281
Harris Shield, 40, 51, 71
Haryana Cricket Association (HCA), 47, 56, 125, 132, 259, 260, 302
Hasina, Sheikh, 10
Haslingden Cricket Club, 54
HDFC Bank, 211
High Court of Rajasthan, 259
Himachal Pradesh Cricket Association (HPCA), 129, 186,

300
Home Ministry, 7, 16, 109
host liaison manager, 9
host tournament director, 1, 9, 21
Hukku, Sudhanshu, 33
Husain, M.F., 49
Hyderabad Cricket Association (HCA), 47, 56, 125, 132, 259, 260, 302

ICC Champions Trophy 2002, 2006, 4, 81
ICC Cricket World Cup (CWC), 2003, 2011, 1999, 2003, 2007, 2, 4, 5, 9, 11, 20, 21, 63, 64, 81, 85, 92, 101, 156, 161, 162, 168, 182, 184, 195, 223, 243, 244, 245, 260, 261, 291, 301
ICC rankings, 160
ICC Under-15 World Cup, 277
ICC Under-19 World Cup, 205, 258, 277, 278
ICC Women's World Cup, 2017, 253
ICC World T20, 2007, 2, 201, 202, 261
Income Tax and Customs, 302
India Cements, 218, 291, 294, 295
Indian Army, 115
Indian Cricket League (ICL), 158, 164, 292
Indian High Commission, 72
Indian High Commissioner, 72, 277
Indian Premier League (IPL), 2018, 2019, 2020, 275
Indian Summers, 155
infrastructure committee, 244
Institute of Science Mumbai, 28
Insurance Shield Cricket Tournament, 43
International Cricket Council (ICC), 1, 2, 3, 4, 5, 6, 7, 8, 9, 10, 11, 14, 15, 16, 19, 20, 21, 51, 58, 61, 62,

63, 64, 70, 73, 78, 79, 80, 81, 82,
97, 101, 105, 107, 112, 123, 131,
138, 144, 145, 146, 147, 151, 156,
158, 160, 161, 162, 163, 164, 165,
166, 167, 168, 172, 173, 176, 182,
184, 190, 195, 196, 201, 202, 205,
207, 210, 223, 227, 242, 243, 244,
245, 247, 248, 251, 252, 253, 254,
255, 260, 261, 276, 278, 279, 280,
281, 282, 283, 285, 291, 292, 293,
294, 296, 297, 298, 300, 301, 303
International Management Group
 (IMG), 49, 58, 193, 195, 201, 202,
 205, 207, 211, 216, 295
International Olympic Association,
 187
Invitation Shield, 238
Inzamam-ul-Haq, 116
IPL Governing Council, 82, 191,
 198, 199
Irani, Ali, Dr, 65, 96
Irani, Z.R., 52
Islam, Shafiul, 11
Iyengar, B.K.S., 271

Jadeja, Ajay, 70, 96
Jadeja, Rajendrasinh, 99
Jadhav, Deepak, 34
Jaffer, Wasim, 250
Jagdale, M.M., 216, 301
Jagdale, Sanjay, 159, 175, 216, 218,
 219, 225, 301
Jai, L.P., 28, 34
Jaisimha, M.L., 178
Jaitley, Arun, 113, 132, 199, 219,
 225, 302
Jammu & Kashmir Cricket
 Association (JKCA), 132, 225,
 265, 279
Jawaharlal Nehru Cup, 56
Jayantilal, Kenia, 236
Jayawardene, Mahela, 18

Jhaveri, Jayant, 6, 257
Jinnah, Mohammed, Ali, 115
Johri, Rahul, 227, 251, 254, 263
joint secretary, 48, 64, 102, 134, 137,
 153, 155, 175, 191, 214, 233, 235,
 251, 253, 267, 296, 300, 301, 302
Joshi, Manohar, 46, 49, 57, 64, 126,
 128, 186, 225, 237, 246
Jukar, R.D., 234
Junior College Cricket Tournament,
 235
Junior College Sports Association
 (JCSA), 36, 37
Justice John Hansen, 281
Justice K.N. Singh, 135
Justice Lodha Committee, 211, 224,
 261, 283
Justice Madan Mohan Punchhi
 (Retd), 135

Kabaddi and Wrestling Federations
 of Maharashtra, 288
Kadri, Faisal, 34
Kaif, Mohammad, 114
Kamaluddin, Salim, 34
Kamath, Nandan, 280
Kanga, H.D., Dr, 29, 40
Kanga League, 26, 29, 40, 41, 42
Kapil's Devils, 20, 34, 178
Kargil War, 290
Karkera, Prakash, 34
Karmarkar, N.D., 103
Karnataka Cricket Club, 40
Karnataka Premier League, 284
Karnataka State Cricket Association
 (KSCA), 11, 98, 171, 265, 269,
 272, 294
Katju, Markandey, 252
Kaur, Harmanpreet, 275
Kelkar, Prakash, 45
Kennedy Sea Face (Marine Drive),
 26

INDEX

Kerala Cricket Association, 225
Khan, Imran, 10, 117, 119
Khan, Shaharyar, 108, 122
Khan, Shah Rukh, 205, 245
Khan, Shah, Rukh, 205, 245
Khan, Zaheer, 18, 97, 163
Khan, Zakir, 122
Kher, B.G., 25
King, Greg, 100, 116
Kings XI Punjab (Mohali), 204
Kirsten, Gary, 183, 299
Kohli, Virat, 11, 18, 205, 256, 272, 284
Kolkata Knight Riders, 204, 205, 210, 245
Korn Ferry, 227
Kosambia, Ramesh, 234
KPMG, 226
Krishnamoorthy, J., S., 136
Kudrolli, Rashid, 234, 240
Kulasekara, Nuwan, 1
Kulkarni, Nilesh, 65, 69, 236, 250
Kulkarni, Raju, 46
Kulkarni, Shubhangi, 181, 275
Kumar, Neeraj, 259
Kumat, Ashok, 131, 132
Kumble, Anil, 11, 41, 71, 72, 86, 87, 97, 119, 165, 179, 180, 182, 184, 255, 257, 262, 271, 273, 281
Kundra, Raj, 210, 218, 301
Kuruvilla, Abey, 48, 65, 236

Lahore University of Management Studies, 119
Lala Amarnath Awards, 178
Lala Lajpatrai College, 36
Lalchand Rajput, 44, 46, 250
Lal, Madan, 65, 67, 68, 69, 71, 74
Lara, Brian, 69, 148
Latif, Rashid, 67, 74, 114
Laureate Ernest Rutherford, 26
Laxman, B., 167, 257

Laxman, V.V.S., 47, 97, 118, 119, 154, 180, 256, 271, 272
Lele, Jaywant, 62, 64, 90, 132
Le Roux, Adrian, 100, 116
Liberation Tigers of Tamil Eelam (LTTE), 65
Lifetime Achievement Award, 75, 177, 178, 263
Limaye, Vikram, 254, 262
Limay, Vikram, 254
Lloyd, Clive, 10, 32
Lloyd's Reclamation ground, 31
Lodha Committee, 139, 211, 224, 225, 226, 227, 228, 229, 230, 231, 232, 242, 252, 253, 254, 255, 260, 261, 262, 263, 264, 266, 278, 279, 280, 283, 284, 293, 300
Lodha, R.M., 224
Loksatta, 33
Lorgat, Haroon, 4

M.A. Chidambaram Stadium, 10, 185, 215
Mackichan, Dugald, Dr, 29
Madhavan, K., 96
Madhya Pradesh Cricket Association (MPCA), 60, 61, 131, 301
Madugalle, Ranjan, 112, 118, 163
Mafatlal family, 236
Mahaddalkar, Bal, 45, 57, 234, 237, 289
Mahanta, Prafulla, Kumar, 131
Maharashtra Cricket Association, 57, 126, 127, 132, 133, 289
Maharashtra Cricket Association (West Zone), 126
Maharashtra Olympic Association, 288
Maharashtra Public Universities Act 1985, 64
Mahmood, Fazal, 120
Malinga, Lasith, 18

Mallapurkar, Sumeet, 169
Mallya, Vijay, 205
Managing Committee, 46, 126, 133, 150, 233
Mandela, Nelson, 57
Mandhana, Smriti, 275
Mandrekar, Ravi, 57
Mangaldas, Cyril, Amarchand, 226, 255
Mangeshkar, Lata, 86, 115, 126, 166, 179
Manipal University, 24
Manjrekar, Rekha, 181
Manjrekar, Sanjay, 46, 77, 250
Manjrekar, Vijay, 54, 178, 181
Mankad, Ashok, 250
Mankad, Vinoo, 39, 54, 150, 178
Manohar, Shashank, 11, 98, 125, 127, 130, 131, 137, 138, 149, 152, 153, 175, 209, 255, 261, 291
Manohar, V.R., 281
Man, Singh, P.R., 178
Mansoor Ali Khan Pataudi Memorial Lecture, 180
Mantri, Madhav, 31, 44, 46, 235, 237, 246
Marsh, Geoffrey, 100
Marsh, Rodney, 'Rod', 99, 271
Martyn, Damien, 148
Mascarenhas, Mark, 240
Mathew, T.C., 138
MCA Lounge, 17
MCA Sachin Tendulkar Gymkhana, 242
McCullum, Brendon, 205
McGrath, Glenn, 164
Media Relations and Corporate Affairs, 169, 198
Mega Vision Video Screen, 239
Mehta, Usha, 25
Meiyappan, Gurunath, 210, 218, 295, 301

Melbourne Cricket Ground, 240
Member Participation Agreement, 296
Memorandum of Association, 224, 290
memorandum of understanding (MOU), 236
Menon, Dinesh, 169
Menon, Nitin, 279
Menon, Shivshankar, 108, 121
Merchant, Vijay, 30, 32, 178
Merck Shield, 43
Mhambrey, Paras, 236, 250, 258
Miandad, Javed, 117
MIG Cricket Club, 40
minister of civil aviation, 7
Minister of Information and Broadcasting, 300
Ministry of Home Affairs, 15
Ministry of Youth Affairs and Sports, 45, 290
Modi Entertainment Networks (MEN), 185
Modi, Lalit, 63, 129, 135, 139, 145, 147, 165, 279, 286, 292, 295, 299
Modi, Narendra, 12, 138, 215, 251, 302
Modi, Rusi, 83
mohalla cricket tournament, 238
Mohan, S., 133
Mongia, Nayan, 66, 68
Monopolies and Restrictive Trade Practices Act, 60
Moody, Tom, 140
Morarka, Kamal, 96
More, Kiran, 143
Mukherjee, Manoj, 95
Mukherjee, Raju, 99
Mumbai Cricket Association (MCA), viii, 3
Mumbaikars, 22, 23, 38, 41, 166
Mumbai Police, 15, 16, 65, 153, 166,

183, 238, 285
Mumbai Schools Sports Association (MSSA), 36
Municipal Corporation of Greater Mumbai (MCGM), 23
Murkar, Deepak, 77
Murzello, Clayton, 155
Musharraf, Pervez, 108
Mustafa, Asad, 122
Muthiah, A.C., Dr, 84, 86
Muttahida Qaumi Movement (MQM), 109

Nadkarni, Bapu, 31, 44
Nagaraj, C., 78
Naidu, Ramesh, 239
Naik, C.S., 77, 132, 235, 240, 246
Naik, Sudhir, 44, 244
Nair, S.K., 102, 110, 134, 303
Narasimhan, P.S., 228
Narendra Modi stadium, 215
National Cricket Academy (NCA), 98, 99, 100, 154, 160, 174, 190, 253, 258, 261, 270, 271, 272, 292
National Cricket Club, 40, 134
National Democratic Alliance (NDA), 145
National Egg Co-Ordination Committee (NECC), 241
National Security Guard [NSG], 111, 183
National Sports Development Fund (NSDF), 290
National Sports Federation, 7, 303
National Stock Exchange, 262
Nayak, Suru, 6, 12, 44, 168, 223
Nayudu, C.K., 50, 54, 75, 177, 178, 263, 301
New Area Development Committee, 78
Nike, 188
Nirlon House, 145, 196

Nissar, Mohammad, 122, 123
Noora, Rani, 181
North Stand, 17, 30, 31, 48, 49, 103, 146, 155

Odisha Cricket Association, 225
O'Farrell, Barry, 246
Official BCCI Cricketer's Handbook, 280
Olympics, 290
One-Day International (ODI), 16, 58, 59, 64, 68, 69, 71, 72, 74, 92, 93, 96, 101, 108, 109, 110, 112, 113, 114, 115, 119, 121, 123, 141, 142, 143, 144, 156, 157, 160, 165, 181, 183, 190, 237, 239, 240, 243, 247, 261, 263
One-Time Benefit scheme, 296
Outlook, 67

Padmakar Talim Shield, 40
Paes, Vece, Dr, 170, 278
Pahlan Ratanji 'Polly' Umrigar (Polly kaka), 39, 75, 76, 77, 88, 103, 235, 241, 242
Pakistan Cricket Board (PCB), 3, 108, 109, 111, 122, 123, 278
Pakistan Rangers, 112
Palghar-Dahanu Taluka Sports Association, 242
Pandit, Chandrakant, 44, 46, 60
Pandit, Vikas, 167
Pandove, M.P., 13, 153, 175
Parab, Ramesh, 174
Paranjape, Jatin, 46
Paranjape, Vasudeo, 'Vasu', 99
Parekh, Deepak, 211
Parliament Hall, 26
Parsana, Dhiraj, 175
Parsi Cyclists, 40
Participating Nations Agreement (PNA), 1, 2, 63

Pataudi, Iftikhar, Ali, Khan, 33
Pataudi, Mansoor, Ali, Khan, 32, 108, 180
Patel, Brijesh, 78, 85, 98, 99, 271, 294
Patel, Munaf, 48
Patel, Parthiv, 120
Patel, Sanjay, 137, 219, 223, 298, 303
Patet, Ashok, 28
Patil, Bipin, 242
Patil, Pratibha, 14, 251
Patil, R.R., 166
Patil, Sandeep, 44, 292
Patil, Vijay, Dr, 192
Patnaik, Arup, 15
Patnaik, Naveen, 169
Pawar, Sharad, 3, 32, 45, 63, 225, 238, 242, 261, 288
PCA Stadium, 13, 146, 185
Pepsi, 60
Phadkar, Dattu, 54, 178
Phadkar, Dattu, 54, 178
Pietersen, Kevin, 180
PILCOM/INDCOM, 152
pioneer, 146, 208
Player Management Companies, 283
Players Match Officials Area (PMOA), 285
Ponting, Ricky, 148
Powar, Ramesh, 117
Prabhakar, Manoj, 63, 93, 96
Prabhudesai, Devendra, 6, 169, 176, 198, 217, 286, 305
Prabhudesai, V.B., 34, 234
Prabhu, K.N., 177
Prasad, K.M., Ram, 96
Prasad, Venkatesh, 160
Prasanna, Erapalli, 99
President's Box, 18, 19, 222
Prime Focus Technologies (PFT), 190
Prime Minister's Office (PMO), 56,
110, 222
Prime Minister's Relief Fund, 290
Prince Ghanshyamsinhji of Limbdi, 52
Procter, Mike, 281
Professional Management Group, 86, 169, 177
Purshottam Shield, 40
Puttaparthi, 73

Quit India movement, 25

racial abuse, 281, 282
Rahul Johri's, 251
railway minister, 125, 126
Railways Sports Promotion Board (RSPB), 125
Rai, Vinod, 254, 256, 263, 277
Rajapaksa, Mahinda, 6, 10
Raja, Ramiz, 108, 148
Rajasthan Cricket Association, 63, 147, 187, 259
Rajasthan Royals (Jaipur), 204
Raj Bhavan, 20
Raj, Mithali, 275
Rajput, Lalchand, 44, 46, 250
Raj Singh Dungarpur Trophy, 302
Ramakrishnan, S., 'Ramky', 110, 116, 172
Raman, P.S., 294
Raman, Sundar, 176, 207, 216, 224
Ramaswamy, V.K., 172
Rambagh Palace, 128, 129
Ramchand, Gulabrai, 39
Ramnarain Ruia College, 36
Ram Prasad, K.M., 96
Ranatunga, Arjuna, 10, 72
Rangaswamy, Shanta, 275
Rangnekar, Santosh, 227
Ranjan Madugalle, 112, 118, 163
Ranji Trophy, 29, 38, 39, 42, 44, 46, 47, 53, 60, 76, 77, 82, 83, 84, 95,

121, 122, 172, 174, 177, 178, 216, 234, 236, 241, 249, 250, 264, 268, 273, 292
Rao, L., 220
Rao, M.S., 77
Rao, Shriniwas, 259
R.A. Podar College of Commerce and Economics, 29
Rashid Kudrolli, 234, 240
Rashtriya Chemicals & Fertilizers Ltd, 238
Rayudu, Ambati, 89
Rege, Milind, 6, 12, 44, 250
Registrar of Societies, 153, 262
Rego, James, 192, 217
Reliance Industries, 56
Reliance World Cup 1987, 56
Rendezvous Sports World, 195, 209
Reporter, Piloo, 44
Richards, Barry, 72
Rising Pune Supergiant, 211
Rohinton Baria Trophy, 274
Roshanara Club Grant Govan, 50
Royal Challengers Bangalore, 204, 205
Roy, Subrata, 101
R. Premadasa Stadium, 66, 69
Rungta, Kishore, 187, 303
Rungta, P.M., 57, 59, 78, 129, 265

Saamna Trophy Tournament, 289
SAARC Summit, 2003, 108
Saba, Karim, Syed, Saba, 66
Sahara, 61, 80, 81, 101, 195, 209
Sahara 'Friendship' Cup, 61
Sahara Pariwar, 101
Saldanha, Stanley, 169, 173
Salve, Harish, 95, 104
Salve, N.K.P., 56, 104
Salvi, Abhijit, Dr, 170
Sammy, Daren, 221
Samsung, 111

Sandhu, Balwinder, 236, 250
Sangakkara, Kumara, 18
Sanzgiri, Shailesh, 34
Saraiya, Suresh, 29
Sardar Patel (Motera) Stadium, 146
Sardar Patel Stadium, 12, 147
Sardesai, Dilip, 27, 29, 39, 44, 77, 178, 250
Sardesai, Rajdeep, 34
Sarwate, Chandu, 60
Saurashtra CA, 229, 279
Savani, Ravi, 170, 285
Sawai Mansingh Stadium, 146, 190
Sawani, Ravi, 218, 259
Saxena, Gaurav, 170, 217
Scindia, Madhavrao, 56, 76, 125, 130, 131, 132, 178, 225
Secondary School Certificate (SSC), 25, 69
Section 25, 228
security bubble, 65
Sehwag, Virender, 'Viru', 11, 12, 18, 114, 116, 118, 120, 121, 180, 204, 255, 256, 257, 272
Sen, Vikramjit, 135
Shah, Jay, 230
Shah, Niranjan, 132, 134, 153, 158, 184, 227, 298
Shah, R.P., 252
Shardashram High School, 71
Sharjah, 75, 94, 95, 211
Sharma, Rohit, 39, 272
Shastri, Ravi, 39, 72, 151, 160, 184, 222, 240, 270
Sher-e-Bangla Stadium, 13
Sheth, J. K., 167
Shetty, Sharada, 22
Shetty, Shivaram, 22
Shinde, Sadashiv, 289
Shinde, Sushilkumar, 151
Shipping Shield Cricket Tournament, 43

Shivaji Park Gymkhana, 40
Shivaji Park Youngsters, 40
Shivalkar, Padmakar, 263
Shiv Sena, 8, 20, 49, 168, 236, 243
Shriyan, Dev, 173, 192
Shukla, Rajeev, 110, 113, 131, 134, 137
Sibal, Kapil, 221
Siddharth College, 26
Sidhu, Navjot, 66
Simpson, Bob, 85
Simpson, Catherine, 49
Singh, Daljit, 174, 175
Singh, Dara, 218
Singh, Hanumant, 99
Singh, Harbhajan, 97, 208, 281, 282
Singh, K.N., 135
Singh, Maharaja, 50, 51, 52
Singh, Manmohan, Dr, 13, 144, 222, 251, 282
Singh, M.N., 133
Singh, Ranbir, 78, 128, 132, 135, 142, 187, 294, 302
Singh, Robin, 160
Singh, Yuvraj, 12, 97, 117, 119, 165, 204
smoke money, 55
Solomon, P.T., Dr, 36
Sony, 194, 204, 205, 209
SOS Children's Village, 118
South African Airways, 81
South African Broadcasting Corporation (SABC), 58
Special General Meeting (SGM), 138, 152, 153, 199
Speed, Malcolm, 145, 149, 151, 248
Sports Advisory Board, 34
Sports Journalists' Federation of India (SJFI), 155
Sports Ministry, 7, 290, 303
Sreesanth, S., 163, 208, 285
Sridhar, M.V., Dr, 223

Srikkanth, K., 108
Sri Lanka Cricket (SLC), 3, 4
Srinath, Javagal, 11, 97
Srinivasan, N., 45, 104, 125, 137, 175, 261, 294
Sri Sathya Sai Baba, 73
SRM Sports Medicine Centre, 272
St Andrew's House, 28
Star Sports, 10, 276, 283
Star TV network, 58
St Joseph's High School, 24
Stumpy, 20
St Xavier's College, 26
Subramanium, Gopal, 228
Sugwekar, Shantanu, 34
Sule, Avi, 239
Sundar Raman, 176, 207, 216, 224
Sunderam, Venkat, 175
SunRisers Hyderabad, 211
Supreme Court (SC), 59
Sutherland, James, 248
Swamy, Subramanian, 220
Syed Mushtaq Ali Trophy, 162

Talent Officers, 99
Talent Resource Development Officer (TRDO), 99, 236
Talim, Sandeep, 34
Tambe, Sitaram, 167, 257
Tamhane, Naren, 44, 57
Tamil Nadu Cricket Association (TNCA), 45, 86, 128, 171, 272, 294
Tata Consultancy Services (TCS), 167, 168, 169, 216
Taufel, Simon, 171
Taylor, H.J., Dr, 26
Team India, 54, 121, 188
Team India 'A', 215
Technical Committee, 82, 263, 273
Telgi, Sunil, 167
Temkar, Kiran, 34

INDEX

Tendulkar, Sachin, 12, 18, 39, 45, 48, 65, 86, 92, 97, 154, 180, 204, 242, 249, 250, 255, 256, 272, 281
Ten Sports, 111
Test Mace, 261
Test specialist, 71
Tetley, Chris, 9
Thackeray, Balasaheb, 31
Thackeray, Uddhav, 20
Thakur, Anurag, 131, 137, 138, 188, 225, 226, 227, 300
Thakur, Shardul, 250
Tharoor, Shashi, 195
Thawani, Harish, 129, 192
the Brihanmumbai Municipal Corporation (BMC), 242
Theckedath, K.K., Prof., 25
The Hindu, 68, 69
The Sportstar, 87
The Times of India, 177, 259
Thorve, Balasaheb, 132
Times of India Cricket Challenge Shield, 40, 42
Titan Cup, 59, 60, 239
Tournament Directorate, 3
TransWorld International (TWI), 58, 59, 103
TV production team, 173
Twenty20 (T20), 2
Tyson, Frank, 236

Ul, Hasan, Sami, 122
umpires' assessment project, 172, 173
umpiring examinations, 171
Union Cabinet, 195, 288
United Cricket Board of South Africa (UCBSA), 58, 80
United Progressive Alliance (UPA), 145
Uttarakhand Cricket Association, 259

Uttar Pradesh Cricket Association (UPCA), 60, 123

Vadolikar, Dalpat, 167
Vaidya, Sudhir, 44, 174
Vajpayee, Atal, Behari, 107, 259, 302
Valthaty, Paul, 100
Vasudeo, Vinod, 41
Vaughan, Michael, 163
Vengsarkar, Dilip, 39, 43, 44, 48, 99, 162, 164, 179, 239, 249, 250
Venkataraghavan, S., 27, 172
Venugopal, K.K., 104
Versace, Gianni, 70
Vidarbha Cricket Association, 126, 129, 180, 272, 292
Vidarbha Cricket Association (Central Zone), 126
Vinod, G., 145
Viswanath, Gundappa, 26, 179
Vithal Divecha Pavilion, 1
Vizzy Trophy, 34, 78

Wadia, Dina, 115
Wadia, Ness, 211
Wagah Border, 111, 119
Wagle, Kaustubh, 34
Waingankar, Makarand, 99, 236
Wankhede, S.K., 30, 43, 225, 237
Wankhede Stadium, 1, 3, 10, 14, 15, 16, 17, 21, 32, 35, 43, 44, 45, 46, 48, 49, 60, 76, 77, 84, 89, 103, 144, 146, 150, 151, 165, 179, 180, 182, 185, 210, 211, 215, 221, 222, 235, 238, 239, 240, 243, 244, 245, 255, 291
Warne, Shane, 79, 206
Waugh, Mark, 49, 79
West Indies Cricket Board (WICB), 157
Whatmore, Dav, 160, 271
Wheelchair Sports Organisation, 240

white-ball (limited-overs) cricket, 273
Wilson College, 22, 25, 28, 29, 33, 34, 47, 64, 66, 103, 233, 236, 264
Wilson College Gymkhana, 29
Within the Boundary and Beyond, 176, 286
Women's Challenger, 263, 275
Women's Cricket Association of India (WCAI), 181
Woolmer, Bob, 148
Working Committee, 2, 55, 78, 87, 143, 219, 247
World Championship of Cricket, 1985, 156

World Cup Enclave, 102
World Sport Group (WSG), 194
WorldTel, 240
World War II, 29
Wright, John, 100, 116, 120, 140, 155, 301

Yadav, Lalu, Prasad, 88, 89
Yadav, Shivlal, 88, 137, 210, 220, 223

Zee, 103, 104, 105, 158, 189, 190, 279, 294
Zinta, Preity, 211